Redefining the Muslim Community

Redefining the Muslim Community

Ethnicity, Religion, and Politics
in the Thought of Alfarabi

Alexander Orwin

PENN

UNIVERSITY OF PENNSYLVANIA PRESS

PHILADELPHIA

Copyright © 2017 University of Pennsylvania Press

All rights reserved. Except for brief quotations used for
purposes of review or scholarly citation, none of this book
may be reproduced in any form by any means without
written permission from the publisher.

Published by
University of Pennsylvania Press
Philadelphia, Pennsylvania 19104-4112
www.upenn.edu/pennpress

Printed in the United States of America on acid-free paper

1 3 5 7 9 10 8 6 4 2

Library of Congress Cataloging-in-Publication Data
ISBN 978-0-8122-4904-0

Contents

A Note on Citations
and Abbreviations

I have cited every work in both Arabic and, if available, English, or in one case French. In some cases, a dual English-Arabic edition or conscious decision by the translator to follow the numbers of the original Arabic means that the same citation applies to both languages. When this is not the case, I have cited the English followed by the Arabic, with the latter marked "Ar." I decided not to cite Alfarabi's works according to the accidental date of the publication of an edition, since that would not help the reader immediately identify the work. Instead, I have included abbreviated titles of the works, as follows.

AH	*Attainment of Happiness*
BD	*Book of Demonstration*
BDi	*Book of Dialectic*
BL	*Book of Letters*
BM	*Great Book of Music*
BO	*Book of One and Unity*
BR	*Book of Religion*
BRh	*Book of Rhetoric*
CA	*Commentary and Short Treatise on Aristotle's "De interpretatione"*
DA	*Didascalia in Rethoricam Aristotelis ex glosa Alpharabi*
EH	*Epistle Indicating the Way to Happiness*
EI	*Epistle on the Intellect*
EP	*Epistle on the Canons of Poetry*
ES	*Enumeration of the Sciences*
FL	*Alfarabi on Logic*
HS	*Harmonization of the Two Opinions of the Divine Sages*
PA	*Philosophy of Aristotle*

PP   *Philosophy of Plato*
SA   *Selected Aphorisms*
SL   *Summary of Plato's "Laws"*
SP   *Short Commentary on the "Poetics"*
SS   *Short Book on the Syllogism*
VC   *Opinions of the Inhabitants of the Virtuous City*

Redefining the Muslim Community

Introduction. Alfarabi and the Question of the Umma (Nation)

The overarching theme of this book is Alfarabi's understanding of the Umma, an Arabic term most frequently translated as "nation." The subject of the nation is, in most respects, a highly familiar one. The rise of nationalism has created a modern international community composed of nation-states, in which membership through national self-determination has come to be regarded as an almost sacred right. The terms "nation" and "nationalism" occur daily on the news, and have been the subject of a vast amount of scholarly research.

Yet when we turn to the history of political thought, the significance of the nation becomes somewhat harder to discern. It does not appear to have been a primary subject of concern for most of the major political philosophers. In ancient political thought, exemplified by Aristotle, the nation appears subordinate to the city, while in modern political thought, exemplified by Hobbes, it appears subordinate to the state. This sweeping formulation nevertheless helps capture the relative obscurity of the nation throughout much of the history of political philosophy. The marginalization of the nation changed only with Rousseau, who lived at the threshold of modern nationalism. I will eventually have occasion to discuss both the interest of Rousseau in the nation and the disinterest of some of his predecessors, along with the striking exception presented by Alfarabi. But I wish to begin with a more general question: why do we need to discuss the pre-nationalist nation at all? It might be argued that an examination of nationalism, through which the nation became an important political entity, is sufficient.

Nationalism and the Pre-Nationalist Nation

An extensive discussion of modern nationalism and the massive body of scholarship devoted to it lies far beyond the scope of this book. However, a brief consideration of three of the most influential scholarly studies of this subject will help to frame, and justify, the ensuing discussion. All three studies trace the origin of the phenomenon to the turn of the nineteenth century. Elie Kedourie ascribes the triumph of nationalism to a new kind of political and intellectual propaganda, which he describes in rather derogatory terms (Kedourie, 20 ff.). Ernest Gellner traces the growth of nationalism to the same epoch, but attributes it to the more general social phenomena of industrialization and literacy (Gellner 1997, 25 ff.; 2006, 38 ff.). Benedict Anderson focuses heavily on print capitalism, and its ability to create a new kind of communal consciousness (Anderson, 37 ff.). These three accounts of the formation of nationalism all emphasize the transformative power of intellectual or historical forces that were completely unknown in premodern times. Yet such transformations might remake existing communities, rather than constitute entirely new ones from scratch. The founders of nationalism were undoubtedly shrewd politicians and propagandists, but did they have the power of magicians, managing to pull a strong national identity out of a completely empty hat? It seems more plausible to assert that they based their new movement on human ties and institutions that had been present for centuries without ever being fully exploited for political ends. One could pose similar questions about industrialization and print capitalism: did they give birth to entirely new communities, or simply reconfigure old ones?

The answers given by each of these three authors to these questions are intelligent, and therefore somewhat ambiguous. As much as Kedourie likes to bring out the sheer fantasy, bordering on madness, that lay behind the spread of nationalist doctrines, he quietly admits that these doctrines "annexed . . . universally held sentiments" such as patriotism, group loyalty, and xenophobia (Kedourie, 73–74). Kedourie acknowledges the existence of different ethnic groups prior to nationalism, while arguing that nationalism makes their relations worse: empires that granted cultural autonomy to the various ethnic groups subject to them actually provided greater political stability than the nationalist agitators who eventually dissolved these empires (115–17). Gellner, who argues for the modernity of nationalism, nonetheless admits that nations had "navels" on which nationalism was based, some of which were stronger than others (Gellner 1997, 90 ff.). Pre-unification Germany was a stronger nation than pre-independence Czechoslovakia, while pre-nationalist Estonia barely existed at all. Yet even in this extreme case the people who became Estonians had some kind of pre-national name for themselves, thus distinguishing themselves from the Russians and Swedes who also inhabited their territory (96–97). They also, I may add, spoke their own distinct language. Gellner states elsewhere that pre-nationalist peoples are "richly endowed with cultural and hence (potentially and actually) ethnic differences" (Gellner 1994, 35). Anderson notes that the power of print capitalism to create nations is a result of "the primordial fatality of particular languages and their association with particular territorial units" (Anderson, 43). In short, none of these authors go so far as to completely dissociate nationalism from certain pre-nationalist nations that rendered it possible.

While these authors do not reject the existence of pre-nationalist nations, none provide a very compelling account of them. From the point of view of nationalism this approach is understandable: very few of these pre-nationalist nations had the power or cohesion needed to form independent political units of their own. Yet from a cultural point of view neglect of these early nations appears harder to justify. Most nations that have left a strong imprint on human civilization existed as recognizable entities well before the nationalist era, understood as beginning in the late eighteenth century. This statement applies not merely to the major nations of Western Europe, such as England, France, Spain, Germany, and Italy, but even less ambiguously to the great peoples of antiquity and the Orient, such as the Greeks, Israelites, Arabs, Persians, Indians, and Chinese.

It may seem natural for a scholar seeking to understand the pre-nationalist nation to turn to the most famous names in the history of political thought. But as I have already indicated, the leading political philosophers tend to discuss this theme rather sparingly. I contend that the most obvious exception to this generalization is Alfarabi. The Umma appears in almost all his major political works, often in a very prominent role. Alfarabi argues for the broad cultural, political, and religious significance of the Umma in an era in which nationalism did not yet have any meaning. This is not to say that Alfarabi's interest in the Umma lacks any specific historical cause. The Umma, which appears dozens of times in the Qur'ān, had long since become the term of choice for Muslims in defining their own religious community. This religious meaning of Umma may be all too easily forgotten when reading Alfarabi, who appears to employ the term mainly in the ethnic sense. However, I will show that Alfarabi's understanding of the Umma has an Islamic as well as an ethnic component. His treatment of the Umma sheds light both on a religious problem particular to Muslims, and on a broader issue strangely neglected by the history of political philosophy: what is the ethnic nation, and how does it influence other human institutions and activities, such as philosophy, religion, and politics? My goal in this book is to provide a comprehensive account of Alfarabi's response to these questions.

Alfarabi: Some Introductory Remarks

Alfarabi was born somewhere in Turkestan around A.D. 870, spent many decades in Baghdad, and died around 950, probably in Damascus. Most of the details of his life are veiled in obscurity, and seem destined to remain so due to lack of reliable historical sources.[1] For the purposes of my argument I have assumed, safely I think, that he was a non-Arab who wrote entirely in Arabic, and an immigrant of remote Central Asian origins who spent most of his intellectual career in Baghdad.

Alfarabi enjoyed an extraordinary reputation in the medieval philosophical community. His three most famous successors, Avicenna, Maimonides, and Averroes, all esteemed him as their teacher. Their testimonies of admiration have frequently been cited, but there is no harm in citing them briefly again here. Avicenna recounts in his autobiography how fruitlessly he toiled over Aristotle's *Metaphysics*, until a chance encounter with Alfarabi's short commentary on the work unlocked its secrets for him (Gutas 1988, 28). Maimonides, in a letter to Ibn Tibbon, extols "the wise Abu Nasr Alfarabi" for his writings on logic, as well as his treatise "The Principles of the Beings," otherwise known as the *Political Regime*; he even goes so far as to contrast Alfarabi favorably to Avicenna (Maimonides 1987, 552–54). Averroes freely incorporates paraphrases of Alfarabi's *Attainment of Happiness* and *Political Regime* into his commentary on Plato's *Republic*, implying that Alfarabi may be no less an authority on political matters than Plato (Averroes 1974, 29.31 ff., 80.17 ff.). These citations are by no means comprehensive, but they suffice to show how highly regarded Alfarabi was among medieval philosophers in fields as diverse as metaphysics, logic, and political science.

By the nineteenth century, however, Alfarabi had fallen into relative obscurity, to the point where most of his writings seemed lost. This was the culmination of a long process of neglect. Alfarabi was less widely translated into Latin during the European Middle Ages than Averroes and Avicenna (Fakhry, 148–50). Many of the Latin translations of Alfarabi cited by medieval authors such as Roger Bacon and Albert the Great never seem to have been printed, a clear sign of diminishing European interest in them (Salmon, 245–61). None of the modern European philosophers, from Machiavelli to Nietzsche, seem to have had any access to Alfarabi, even in translation. Meanwhile, the leading intellectual authorities in the Islamic world also appear to have gradually lost interest in Alfarabi, failing to preserve many of his works. The important late nineteenth-century Muslim reformers, such as Jamāl al-Dīn al-Afghānī, would have been able to read only the small selection of Alfarabi's works that were still available. These included the *Virtuous City*, *Political Regime*, and *Harmonization of the Opinions of the Two Sages*, but not the *Book of Religion* or *Book of Letters*, which will play so crucial a role in this book.

Owing to the diligence of leading philologists such as Franz Rosenthal, Richard Walzer, and Muhsin Mahdi, several additional works have been unearthed in the past century, and edited in competent critical editions. Translations into major European languages have gradually followed. Muhsin Mahdi has observed that although we still have less than half the works attributed to Alfarabi in medieval catalogues, we already have enough to appreciate the power of his thought (Mahdi 2001, 51–52).[2] I would add that some caveats still apply: most importantly, whenever one says that "Alfarabi never treats a subject," one must continue, implicitly if not explicitly, "in the works that have come down to us." We should continue to look forward to the discovery of new works by Alfarabi with the greatest anticipation, but we may already proceed to interpret him on the basis of extant works.

The increased availability of new editions and translations of Alfarabi has spawned further scholarly research. Several books and articles written on Alfarabi in recent years are of very high quality, but they have hardly covered all the bases.[3] The topic of this book is a case in point. There is remarkably little scholarship on Alfarabi's treatment of the Umma, despite its intrinsic interest. While themes related to the Umma have been examined, the Umma itself has somehow slipped between the cracks. Muhsin Mahdi has treated Alfarabi's views of politics and religion in great depth, but he has left only some preliminary reflections on the Umma (Mahdi 2001, 142–43). The same can be said of Joshua Parens, although he does discuss the subject at somewhat greater length than Mahdi (Parens 2006a, 88–90,

1995, 51–52, 166 n. 4). Miriam Galston provides a useful but inconclusive discussion, where she openly confesses that the subject "needs to be studied further" (Galston 1990, 153). All three scholars focus on the treatment in the *Political Regime* without examining the more thorough account of the development of the Umma in the *Book of Letters*. Ilai Alon, coauthor with Shukri Abed of a lexicon of Alfarabi's philosophical vocabulary, gives a cursory definition of the term, which observes that Alfarabi never seems to speak of the Umma in the traditional Muslim fashion (Alon, 12; cf. Vajda, 250). The most comprehensive treatment of the subject exists in Arabic: Nāṣīf Naṣṣār has devoted an entire chapter to Alfarabi's concept of the Umma in his book on the meaning of Umma in classical Islamic thought (Naṣṣār 1978, 31–53). This chapter contains many interesting insights, but it too fails to give adequate consideration to Alfarabi's most fundamental discussion of the Umma in the *Book of Letters* (BL 39, 41–42, 46–47), and accepts the prevailing view that Alfarabi "does not use the term Umma in a religious sense" (40).

The study of the *Book of Letters* has developed rather slowly since Muhsin Mahdi published the first critical edition in 1969, but has recently picked up pace. Georges Vajda responded to that publication with an excellent summary of the second chapter, in which he observes the importance of the Umma several times, but does not really elaborate on it (Vajda, 250–51, 256–58). The section is discussed in greater detail by Jacques Langhade, who provides a very thorough summary of Alfarabi's account of the development of language, as well as some illuminating background to it (Langhade, 190–311). Deborah Black explains Alfarabi's inclusion of poetics and rhetoric in the *Organon* (Black, 63–71). Shukri Abed provides some good insight into the linguistic and philosophical teachings of the *Book of Letters* (Abed, 59 ff.), while Stephen Menn conducts an intelligent inquiry into its metaphysical teachings (Menn, 59–97). Emma Gannagé, Thérèse-Anne Druart, and Luis Xavier López-Farjeat have also written useful articles on its middle section (Gannagé, 229 ff.; Druart 2012, 51–56; López-Farjeat, 193–215).

These scholarly contributions all contain some helpful suggestions, but never anything resembling a detailed analysis of the term Umma, or an exploration of its broader role within Alfarabi's philosophy. In short, there is an evident lacuna in scholarship that the present work aims to address. Before addressing it, however, I need to say a few words about reading Alfarabi in general, and briefly discuss his use of Greek and Hellenistic sources in light of the new political and intellectual challenges posed by the rise of Islam.

How Should One Read Alfarabi?

This question is fundamental for approaching most major philosophers, and Alfarabi is no exception. While I do not expect to resolve this question here, I do hope to justify my own interpretative procedure. The works of Alfarabi that have come down to us contain no direct cross-references or comments on Alfarabi's own manner of writing. They do include, however, several comments on the manner of writing employed by Plato and Aristotle, which should provide at least some indications about Alfarabi's own (Galston 1990, 35 ff.). Yet these references do not provide a single, unified account of how a philosopher should write. Although Plato and Aristotle both wrote obscurely in order to conceal their teaching, each did so in his own particular manner: in the *Harmonization of the Opinions of the Divine Sages*, Alfarabi suggests that Plato proclaimed his use of riddles more openly than Aristotle (HS 131–32, #12–13, Ar. 84–85).[4] In keeping with his own suggestion, Alfarabi's clearest exposition of the use of riddles comes in his *Summary of Plato's "Laws"* (SL 130–31, Intro. 2, Ar. 125), while there is no comparable passage in any of his summaries of Aristotle. If Alfarabi's two most revered philosophic predecessors each employed his own distinctive manner of writing, it is plausible to infer that Alfarabi may have developed his own as well.

Some scholars of Alfarabi, such as E. I. J. Rosenthal, decry much of his writing for being "diffuse, repetitive, and lacking in clarity and precision" (E. I. J. Rosenthal, 158). Yet such criticisms tend to ignore what Alfarabi says about the riddling ways of his philosophic predecessors, and the possibility that he followed in their footsteps. I hope to cast doubt on such charges by carefully and profitably analyzing Alfarabi word by word, showing that many of his apparent repetitions and imprecisions in fact have a deliberate meaning. In so doing I build on two noteworthy attempts by Leo Strauss and Miriam Galston to elucidate Alfarabi's obscure writing style.

Leo Strauss, in a seminal 1945 article titled "Farabi's Plato," presents a very detailed interpretation of one of Alfarabi's most important texts, which had just recently become available to scholars. The interpretative techniques developed by Strauss, which pay careful attention to contradictions (Strauss

1945, 369), repetitions (382), and the density of important terms such as "city" (*madīna*, 379 n. 53) and "human" (*insān*, 392 n. 99), all while weaving these minute details into a compelling interpretation of the whole, make this article a cornerstone of scholarship on Alfarabi. The same can be said of Strauss's equally brilliant article on Alfarabi's *Summary of Plato's "Laws"*, written about a decade later, which among other things profitably explores the relationship between Alfarabi's two most explicitly Platonic writings (Strauss 1959, 138–39, 152–54). Yet Strauss sheds less light on the question of the relationship between Alfarabi's two presentations of Plato and his various other works. Strauss makes the astonishing claim that Alfarabi's truest and most candid teaching, insofar as it can be expressed in writing, is found in the *Philosophy of Plato*, and never in other works (Strauss 1945, 375). We must not forget that in 1945 the vast majority of Alfarabi's works were still unavailable, a fact that was hardly unknown to Strauss (357–60). It might therefore be best to interpret Strauss's bold proclamation as applying to themes discussed so brilliantly in his article, such as the afterlife and the relationship between philosophy and politics, whose fullest expression indeed occurs in the *Philosophy of Plato*. But how could it apply to the sundry themes that are barely touched upon in the twenty-odd pages of this short treatise? It may be Alfarabi's most revealing work, but it is certainly not his most comprehensive.

Miriam Galston has made a more recent attempt to describe Alfarabi's manner of writing, and in particular the relationship between his works. Galston suggests that something about the subject can be learned from Alfarabi's logical works, with a special emphasis on his treatment of dialectic (Galston 1990, 39–43, 48). Galston cites a number of memorable passages about the role of dialectic in fostering philosophical inquiry. By exposing the initiate to a wide variety of different and often contradictory arguments, dialectic prepares him for the pursuit of demonstrative philosophy (40–41). Galston concludes that "both rhetorical and dialectical modes are present in Alfarabi's treatises, and that the former are subordinated to the latter" (54).

Galston's conclusion is valuable in encouraging the study and comparison of Alfarabi's numerous works, each of which is distinct in its own way. But it may be somewhat overstated. For one thing, Galston herself calls it only an "assumption," and acknowledges that Alfarabi employed rhetorical as well as dialectical modes of writing (Galston 1990, 54). It should be added that Alfarabi may have employed demonstrative, poetic, or even sophistic modes as well. In the *Enumeration of the Sciences*, all five methods are presented as perfectly respectable uses of the logical art under certain circumstances (ES 103–13). That same work contains an introduction that indicates, if not the manner in which it is written, at least its intended audience (51–53). That audience, which includes both genuine men of science and crude impostors (Mahdi 2001, 66–67), is diverse enough to encourage the view that the work must be written in various ways for various readers.

What Galston does show is that if Alfarabi's works can all be construed as an introduction to philosophy, then they must proceed dialectically, since dialectical training is indeed the best way to approach philosophy. Yet Alfarabi never proclaims that all his works serve only that function: as we just saw in the introduction to the *Enumeration of the Sciences*, he regards his varied readership as comprising more than just potential philosophers. In the absence of any indication from Alfarabi that all his works are written dialectically, we cannot corroborate Galston's assumption. However, Galston's idea of determining Alfarabi's manner of writing by means of his logical works should not be discarded. On the contrary, further research in that direction is required. The challenge of integrating Alfarabi's logical and political works, which together constitute the lion's share of the writings that have come down to us, may ultimately prove as daunting as the challenge of integrating all the works of Aristotle into a single whole. As worthy as this project may be, it far exceeds anything that I can undertake here. In the absence of such an effort, how can we even begin to interpret Alfarabi's works?

The lack of any comprehensive account of how to read Alfarabi does not make it impossible to approach my particular topic. Alfarabi's writings are divided into a large number of treatises, and his treatment of any given theme varies from work to work. These variations might have something to do with the peculiar context and purpose of each work. Indeed, the unique aim and character of any major treatise of Alfarabi could become the subject of a valuable scholarly monograph. Yet in the undeveloped state of scholarship on Alfarabi, such works are generally not at our disposal: apart from Joshua Parens's thorough interpretation of Alfarabi's *Summary of Plato's "Laws"* (Parens 1995) and Strauss's lengthy article on the *Philosophy of Plato* (Strauss 1945), I cannot name a single one. In the absence of such works and the assistance they might afford, the project of interpreting every single treatise comprehensively within the confines of a single volume appears extraordinarily ambitious.

Three other recently published books on Alfarabi, by Galston (1990), Colmo (2005), and Parens himself (Parens 2006a), have taken a more thematic approach, exploring specific themes throughout Alfarabi's writings. I follow up on that approach, offering a thematic interpretation of the Umma as it appears across many works. I strive to read each account with the care recommended by Strauss, assessing its depth and completeness while keeping in mind the general argument of the book to which it belongs. I will show that some accounts treat the Umma more thoroughly and satisfactorily than others. Most notably, the discussion in the *Book of Letters*, which focuses on language, is more revealing about the character of the Umma than the discussion in the *Political Regime*, which focuses on climate and nutrition. But no one account in any work is complete, so that each needs to be supplemented by others. The *Book of Letters* gives the fullest account of the Umma. However, with regard to the role of the stories of the Umma in the development of philosophy, it needs to be supplemented by the *Philosophy of Aristotle*; with regard to the precise relationship between philosophical language and the governance of the Ummas, by the *Attainment of Happiness*; with regard to the relationship between the Umma and religion, by the *Book of Religion*; and with regard to the nutrition of the Umma and its relationship to politics, by the *Political Regime*, *Virtuous City*, and *Selected Aphorisms*. By proceeding thus from work to work, weaving together the various strands of Alfarabi's thought on the Umma into a single whole, I hope to provide a comprehensive account of the Umma's significance for Alfarabi.

Having described the advantages of this approach, let me point out its most obvious limitation: while I cannot interpret the discussion of the Umma in each work without also considering that work's general purpose, I am never able to fully elucidate that purpose. At most, I provide some observations that should facilitate the future study of each work. Finally, in dealing with an author of Alfarabi's profundity and obscurity, some passages will inevitably remain quite dark. Peculiarities that I have not been able to explain have been left to the reader to puzzle over. Is it not encouraging that there may always be new things to say about, and learn from, Alfarabi?

One other feature of Alfarabi's writing style that merits our attention is its apparent abstraction. The lack of references to specific people, countries, and events may indeed appear daunting. It should become less so if we are able through our own initiative to apply Alfarabi's general arguments to particular things, from both Alfarabi's epoch and our own. Indeed, many of Alfarabi's terms would have evoked strong particular associations among his early readers. To state only the most obvious examples, "religion" would have meant, at least to most of his readers, Islam, while "prophecy" would have immediately recalled Muhammad, as well as the whole gamut of prophets who came before him. In order to grasp many of these allusions, I have tried to familiarize myself with Alfarabi's historical milieu. Finally, Alfarabi does occasionally introduce particular references of his own. I have always paid special attention to these references, as the most solid indicators of Alfarabi's concrete meaning. In approaching Alfarabi in this way, I hope to show that he is much more attuned to worldly affairs than many people think.

Alfarabi as a Philosopher Among Muslims

The past century of Alfarabi scholarship has often focused on his role as a transmitter of Greek thought. This applies not only to the work of such scholars as Franz Rosenthal, Richard Walzer, and Samuel Stern, but also to the philosophic interpreter Leo Strauss, whose two most mature works on Alfarabi examine his treatment of Plato (Strauss 1945; 1959, 134–54). These extremely fruitful efforts have laid the groundwork for further research on Alfarabi. I do not wish to deny or even downplay the link between Alfarabi and the ancients, which I will discuss at some length in Chapter 1 and return to throughout the book. However, I do hope to make the case for a more Muslim-oriented approach to Alfarabi, as especially suited to both Alfarabi's concerns and our own.

While Alfarabi learned from the Greeks, he wrote primarily for Muslims and minorities living under Islamic rule.[5] An excessive emphasis on Alfarabi's Greek and Hellenistic sources risks losing sight of this simple and banal fact. It might have been easy enough to gloss over Alfarabi's contribution to the understanding of Islam while the religion seemed dormant, and its adherents were still reeling under the yoke of various kinds of colonial rule. Yet with the resurgence of Islam as a religious and political force in the world, and the sharpening of the debate, among both Muslims and non-Muslims, over the interpretation of its doctrines, Alfarabi's stature as the first great philosophic interpreter of Islam cannot be overemphasized.[6]

The futility of much Hellenistic source-hunting is already apparent in Franz Rosenthal and Richard Walzer's pioneering edition of the *Philosophy of Plato*. Rosenthal and Walzer assume a Hellenistic source for almost everything in this work and attempt to uncover it, but often reach the riveting conclusion that "nothing can be determined" (Rosenthal and Walzer 1943, xii–xvi). Residues of this preoccupation can still be found in Walzer's landmark 1985 edition of the *Virtuous City*, where he attempts to track Hellenistic sources for every doctrine in the work, without any "certain results" (VC, trans. Walzer, 9). Muhsin Mahdi's review of this edition includes a thorough critique of Walzer's "source-hunting" (Mahdi 1990, 696–705). With regard to our topic, the Umma, Walzer readily admits that "our evidence of the Hellenistic theory of language is very scanty" (VC, trans. Walzer, 431), but nonetheless concludes that Alfarabi's manifest political interest in the Umma can be traced to Hellenistic sources, "pieced together by scraps of miscellaneous information" (487). Walzer assembles an impressive array of sources, but most of them are fragmentary. Furthermore, they demonstrate little, as long as Alfarabi's access to them, and interest in their contents, remain unproven. As Mahdi points out, Alfarabi seems much more concerned with acknowledging his debt to Plato and Aristotle, whom he mentions regularly, than to later Hellenistic authors whom he seldom mentions at all (Mahdi 1990, 696, 703–5). The meager results of Walzer's quest for sources might rather point to the conclusion that Alfarabi was an original thinker in his own right, who did far more than merely transmit the ideas of the earlier authors to whom he happened to have access.

Walzer is hardly oblivious to historical change, admitting that "the political structure of the territories which make up the Islamic world has basically changed" since Hellenistic times (VC, trans. Walzer, 433). He also observes that Alfarabi "assumed his readers to be familiar with the religious, political, and local situation" (13). But he does not appear to draw the obvious conclusion from these premises: the meaning and significance of the Umma changed drastically with the coming of Islam, and this change is reflected in the thought of Alfarabi. The new empire, despite being just as multiethnic as its Hellenistic predecessors, was grounded in a religion that called itself an Umma and sought to spread its faith to all humankind. The term Umma thus came to acquire a double meaning: the old, ethnic Ummas of blood and language coexisted with the new, Islamic Umma of religion and faith. This dual meaning of Umma had no precedent in pre-Islamic times, and therefore could not have appeared in any Hellenistic source.[7] It fell to Alfarabi, the great heir to the Greek tradition within Islam, to grapple with the new historical situation on his own. Alfarabi succeeded in applying what he learned from the Greeks to a world that was in so many respects alien to them. In Chapters 4 and 5, I analyze Alfarabi's view of the new Umma in considerable detail.

I cannot conclude this introduction without raising an important objection: if Alfarabi's teachings are in fact intended for Muslims, why have they found relatively few Muslim readers? Alfarabi's influence in the Islamic world has for centuries been eclipsed by any number of later philosophers and theologians. He does not hold a central place in the curriculum of most Islamic countries today, as indicated by the paucity of studies in Arabic cited in the bibliography. And yet many Muslims seem to think that there is nothing more to study: a prominent Egyptian academic once told me that Alfarabi was *maʿrūf*, that is to say, already well understood. Such an attitude is sure to discourage any deeper exploration of Alfarabi.

A full answer to this question would require a far more thorough examination of Islamic intellectual history than I can possibly provide. I will therefore limit myself to repeating a useful suggestion made by Joshua Parens. The audacity of Alfarabi's praise of philosophy, along with his disregard of the particularities of Islamic doctrine and law, might have won him many admirers among the medieval philosophers, but few within the broader Islamic community (Parens 2006b, 45–46). As a non-Muslim, I am in no position to justify Alfarabi before the court of Islamic law. But I will argue, on many different occasions, that his subtle, sober teachings about the Umma could foster greater intellectual freedom, religious tolerance, and political stability, among both Muslims and non-Muslims. I am therefore inclined to agree with the claim of Muhsin Mahdi, that Alfarabi always had the best interests of his community at heart (Mahdi 2001, 62). Alfarabi may still represent, to most Muslims, the road not taken, but to a religious community whose recent history has been plagued by tyranny and tumult, precisely the road not taken may begin to warrant a second look.

Chapter 1

The Nation in Plato
and Aristotle: An Obstacle
to Virtuous Rule

I have suggested that most political philosophers apart from Alfarabi did not take the nation very seriously. This does not mean that they ignored it completely, or that it would not be worth our while to examine the reasons for their relative neglect. Since Alfarabi presents himself above all as a disciple of Plato and Aristotle, and frequently comments, directly or indirectly, on their works, an examination of the significance of the nation for these two Greek philosophers may serve as a useful segue into Alfarabi. We will begin by discussing Plato's *Republic*, followed by Alfarabi's interpretation of this dialogue, and then do the same with Aristotle's *Politics*. It will become clear that neither Plato nor Aristotle was as indifferent to the significance of nations as is sometimes believed, but that Alfarabi's interest in the Umma extends farther.

A comparison of Alfarabi and Plato ought to begin with a surprisingly difficult question: did Alfarabi in fact have knowledge of Plato's works? Since Alfarabi mentions most of the Platonic dialogues in the *Philosophy of Plato*, it is tempting to take his knowledge of Plato for granted. But an examination of the existing scholarship on the question reveals how little we know for certain about Alfarabi's actual exposure to Greek texts and Arabic translations of them. However dry and scholarly the issue of Alfarabi's access to Plato may appear to outsiders, it has spawned a number of polemics, especially with regard to Plato's *Laws*, on which Alfarabi wrote a commentary.

Since I am not considering the *Laws* in any detail here, I wish to take the liberty of consigning this particular debate to the footnotes.[1] Yet I can hardly evade the question of Alfarabi's knowledge of the *Republic*, and of Plato in general.

The biggest obstacle to demonstrating Alfarabi's knowledge of Plato is that we do not know of any extant medieval Arabic translations of the dialogues, as Franz Rosenthal and other scholars had long noted (F. Rosenthal 1940, 390–93, 410–11). Yet the late David Reisman made a careful review of the available material in light of his recent discovery of a tenth-century Arabic translation of an important passage of the *Republic*, and came to the conclusion that "there was more of Plato's *Republic* circulating among medieval Arabic authors than the synopsis of Galen" (Reisman, 270–71). I have not undertaken the thorough study of the manuscripts that would be necessary to settle this debate: on that score I defer to the source that I have just mentioned. Yet I wish to take issue with the suggestion that the true source might be a lost summary by Galen. This claim ignores a manifest feature of Alfarabi's own writings, namely, his repeated expressions of contempt for Galen (Mahdi 1961, 6). In the *Book of Rhetoric* and the *Didascalia*, Alfarabi flatly accuses Galen of abusing rhetorical methods in allegedly scientific studies, making particular reference to a book on the "opinions of Hippocrates and Plato" (BRh 71.8–73.2; DA 193). In the *Great Book of Music*, Alfarabi describes Galen as a "physician," often used as a term of dismissal among the medieval philosophers (BM 63.8; cf. Maimonides 1987, 552.5–8). Averroes, in his *Commentary on the "Republic,"* also criticizes Galen for his misunderstanding of Plato and ignorance of logic (Averroes 1974, 36.8, 46.7, 56.23–26, 105.1–2), making it highly unlikely that Averroes based his commentary on a summary by Galen.

I also wish to question the common assumption among scholars that Alfarabi did not know Greek (F. Rosenthal 1940, 410; Menn, 69). Many of Alfarabi's references to Greek words and titles, especially in the *Philosophy of Plato*, may seem strange, but not all are completely erroneous: for example, he correctly understands the meaning of the verb *menein* (PP 5.13). Unlike his successors Avicenna and Averroes, Alfarabi lived in a city whose Christian inhabitants often still knew Greek.[2] This fact alone should mean that the question of Alfarabi's knowledge of Greek is far from settled. His project of recovering the genuine thought of Plato and Aristotle, which he believed to have been blurred over time (AH 47.4–9, Ar. 97.65), would have given him every incentive to learn at least some Greek. If he had studied

Greek with certain heterodox Christian friends and associates, especially in the enemy kingdom of Byzantium,[3] he might have wished to conceal the company he kept, and therefore his linguistic knowledge, from his predominantly Muslim audience. Errors in the interpretation of Greek words, well attested in modern scholarship (Rudolph, 372–73), might indeed have been due to ignorance, but an alternative explanation would be that they were meant to hide his knowledge. On one occasion, however, Alfarabi appears to let down his guard. A frequently overlooked passage in the *Great Book of Music* reads as follows: "It is possible to learn about the circumstances [of Greece and Byzantium] because they are neighbors, and because of the abundance of immigrants from the lands of Greece and Byzantium to the lands of the kingdom of the Arabs, who bring us reports about them, as well as from the books that the ancient Greeks wrote on the subject of musical theory" (BM 110). To be sure, musical theory cannot be equated with language, but this statement should demonstrate beyond all reasonable doubt that Alfarabi attempted to learn as much as he could from ancient Greek works and Byzantine migrants on a wide variety of subjects. Unfortunately, just how much he was able to learn from them may always remain in doubt.

The simple fact is that as long as we have not discovered any tenth-century Arabic translations of Plato, or proof of Alfarabi's knowledge of Greek, we will never be able to determine with any exactitude what texts of Plato Alfarabi actually read. Due caution is therefore required. And yet I find myself strongly inclined to the view that Alfarabi must have had access to something closely resembling the original texts of the *Republic*, and probably several other Platonic dialogues. Alfarabi's summary of the *Republic* in the *Philosophy of Plato*, although extremely terse, contains most of the essential elements of the dialogue: the investigation of justice, the foundation of the city, the rule of the philosophers, and the description of other kinds of city (PP 19.14–20.14). But the strongest evidence in favor of this supposition is simply Alfarabi's own claim: why would he pretend to know Plato's *Republic*, as well as the thirty-odd other dialogues summarized in the *Philosophy of Plato*, if he in fact had no access to them? The same question applies to Averroes and his knowledge of the *Republic*, on which he wrote a full-blown commentary. But some might reply that these philosophers either lied or were deceived about their access to the original Plato. Let me examine each of these possibilities in turn.

Alfarabi and Averroes might have considered lying on certain occasions, but they would need to have a plausible reason for doing so. Feigning knowledge of Plato while writing purported commentaries on him would simply have exposed them to the ridicule of future generations, and risked discrediting their own philosophic project of reviving certain aspects of Plato's thought. If they really had so little access to Plato, and were fully aware of this fact, then why couldn't they simply have relied more heavily on Aristotle? Now Alfarabi and Averroes, like everyone else, were also capable of error. Yet there is plenty of evidence, especially in the *Book of Letters*,[4] that Alfarabi was sensitive to problems of translation, which makes it highly implausible that he would have reproduced, or even relied on, any Arabic translations or summaries without due reflection. Such reflection would presumably have cautioned him against mistaking the summaries of Galen the doctor and rhetorician for the dialogues of the philosopher Plato. Indeed, Alfarabi and Averroes would not have regarded Plato as a philosopher equal to Aristotle unless they themselves had read a version of Plato's writings that was complete enough to convey a convincingly philosophic teaching. It is hard to identify any Hellenistic or Roman commentator who could have produced such a work. In the absence of any reason for thinking that these philosophers lied or were deceived about their knowledge of Plato, we ought to take them at their word. The texts that they possessed may not have been identical to our texts, but they must have been adequate enough to convince them that Plato was a philosopher of the highest rank on whose works they could compose reliable commentaries.

I hope to strengthen my supposition by showing that the comments on Plato contained in Alfarabi's own writings display profound insight into him, especially with regard to the theme of this book. Proving that Alfarabi understood what Plato had to say about the nation does not establish that Alfarabi had access to every word that Plato wrote, but it does suggest, as we will soon see, that he must have had a considerable portion of the *Republic* at his disposal.

Is the City of the *Republic* Greek?

The most famous Platonic dialogue focuses on the founding of a new city, as Alfarabi clearly recognizes (PP 19.13–20.14, 21.1–2).[5] But Plato says nothing in the *Republic* about the founding of a new nation. This does not mean that he avoids the nation entirely. Plato needs to consider whether the new city will assume any existing ethnic identity, and if not, he must explain how it will define itself vis-à-vis the nations of the earth.

Any attempt to understand the significance of the nation for Plato must take into account the fact that Greek lacks a single, definite term that can be translated as "nation." Plato uses the terms *ethnos* and *genos* in a surprising variety of contexts.[6] In the absence of any distinct term for "nation," the issues surrounding ethnic identity are often raised in the more concrete form of the Greek-barbarian distinction, which occurs frequently enough in the *Republic* to serve as the starting point of our investigation. An obvious question emerges: is the city founded in the dialogue Greek, barbarian, both, or neither? I wish to analyze the *Republic* with this question in mind.

The ethnic character of the city in *Republic* appears at first glance to be established in Book V, where the city is declared Greek (470e4–6). But upon closer examination this declaration belongs entirely to Glaucon. Socrates does no more than ask the question, "Won't the city that you are founding be Greek?" (470e4–6), while it is Glaucon who replies in the affirmative. One may wonder why Socrates needs to raise this question at all. Isn't the Greek identity of the city self-evident from the start? Who could imagine Glaucon, Adeimantus, or even Socrates founding a city that wasn't Greek? The very fact that Socrates poses the question implies that something unusual may be afoot. Let us review the earlier portions of the dialogue for evidence that the city is indeed Greek.

The opening discussions about justice in the first book contain no reference to any particular people: a satisfactory definition of justice as such must be universal. But one would expect Socrates to address the question of ethnic identity when he undertakes the founding of a city, which must come into being in some particular place and among some particular people if it is to exist at all. Although Socrates may encourage his interlocutors to think that the city is Greek, several aspects of his presentation seem to evade the question. Most notably, Socrates never calls the city Greek. The scene in which the city first comes into being describes the general human needs that give rise to cities, but says little about the circumstances surrounding this particular city's founding. Socrates gives the impression that the first inhabitants are aboriginals who form a settlement of their own accord for the sake of mutual help (369c1–4). But are they Greek aboriginals? Socrates acknowledges that the city will be founded "in a place of some sort" (*toiouton topon*; 370e5–7), but since the qualities of this place remain completely indefinite, so does the stock of its first inhabitants. The vagueness with which the location of the city is described in the *Republic* stands in contrast to the precision with which it is described in the *Laws* (704c ff.).

The material description of the luxurious city, which includes couches, rhapsodes, actors, and choruses (*Republic* 372e ff.), is indeed evocative of Greece. Given the cultural background of the interlocutors in the dialogue, it would make no sense for Socrates to fill the city with unknown Persian delicacies. Thus the question remains: in assuming that the city is Greek, does Socrates speak with a view to his still-inexperienced interlocutors, or to his own understanding of the character of the city?

The same uncertainty prevails in the account of the guardians' education. It is based on the reform of Greek music and poetry (376d ff.), but neither Glaucon nor even Socrates could be expected to hold a discussion on any other kind of song or rhyme. Moreover, many of the traditional Greek models are introduced only to be roundly rejected. One counts some instances where Homer, considered by many to be the "teacher of Greece" (606e1–3), is cited as a model (389e4, 390d1–5, 404b11–c9), but others where he is presented as a potential corrupter of the young guardians (377d5, 383a7, 387b1, 393b1). Socrates continues to cite Greek sources, although hardly as models, in highly unconventional accounts of music, gymnastic, and medicine (398d ff.). But Socrates identifies the noble lie, a centerpiece of the city's education, with the Phoenicians, a barbarian people (414c4); the interlocutors probably refer this designation to the Greek myth of Cadmus, the Phoenician founder of Thebes, but Socrates's intention remains murky. Neither the word "Greek" nor any of its cognates appears in the first three books.

The discussion of the city's stance toward foreign relations and war in Book IV yields similarly inconclusive results. Socrates proposes to Adeimantus that the city take an equally suspicious view of all foreign cities and encourage faction among them, noting that this policy should be applied to cities inhabited by both Greeks and barbarians alike (423a8–b1). The very first mention of the Greek-barbarian distinction in the dialogue suggests that the city should ignore it, at least with regard to fateful questions of war and peace.

The next reference to ethnic differences comes in the well-known passage on the spiritedness of the Thracians and Scythians who live in the north, the greed of the Egyptians and Phoenicians, and the love of learning of the people who live in the "place around us" (435e3–436a3). Yet Socrates refrains both from mentioning Greece by name and from classifying non-Greek peoples as barbarian. Love of learning is not ascribed explicitly to Greece, but rather to the highly equivocal "place around us" (*ton par' hēmin . . . topon*; 435e6–436a1). Assuming that "us" refers to the participants in the dialogue, one could define the land surrounding them in various ways, from the Piraeus to the entire Mediterranean region. It would be hasty to assume, as many interpreters as well as the interlocutors probably do,[7] that this phrase refers to Greece, as it could easily signify a region either much larger or much smaller than it. We may also ask whether the city, whose location at this point in the dialogue remains indeterminate, is founded in the "place around us." If not, then this passage reveals nothing about the city's ethnic identity.

It is not until the discussion of women and the family that the Greeks are even mentioned for the second time. Although Socrates praises them for allowing men to exercise naked, a practice still deemed shameful among the barbarians, he admits that they would still be unable to tolerate naked women performing the same activities, as ought to occur in the new city (452a7 ff.).[8] The subsequent proposals for the equality of women and men, not to mention the dissolution of the family, remove the city still farther from prevailing Greek custom and precedent. The current institutions of the family are "against nature," but at present they prevail everywhere (456c1–3), that is to say, among both Greeks and barbarians.

The discussion of the ethnicity of the city thus far has been largely inconclusive. Socrates probably expects his interlocutors to consider the city Greek, despite its evident eccentricities. But Socrates never calls it Greek, and its frequent divergence from most Greek norms ought to give the reader of the dialogue pause. Until the discussion of war in Book V, the potentially explosive issue of the city's ethnic identity is effectively avoided. In this discussion, however, it comes to the fore. Let us take a closer look.

Socrates begins by asking whether Greeks should reduce Greek cities to slavery (469b8–c4). This question is posed well before anyone has confirmed that the city is Greek (cf. 470e4), which at this point is simply presumed. Moreover, the broader relevance of this issue for the city is difficult to discern, owing to the relative lack of evidence for the presence of slaves of any ethnicity in the city.[9] But Socrates' purpose soon becomes clear enough: he aims to put Glaucon into a philhellenic mood. He argues that Greeks should spare Greeks from enslavement precisely in order to avoid enslavement of the entire Greek *genos* at the hands of barbarians. Glaucon promptly agrees (469c5–6): he is clearly delighted to listen to any opinion (*doxa*) asserting the solidarity of Greeks against barbarians (470a8). Socrates takes advantage of Glaucon's eagerness to introduce a more sweeping argument on the natural affinity of Greeks and their natural hostility to barbarians (470b4 ff.). This allows him to present warfare between Greek cities as a kind of civil strife. Glaucon does not show the slightest sign of opposition. Glaucon's answer to the question "Won't the city that you are founding be Greek?" is thus entirely predictable.

The question about the Greek identity of the city turns out to be part of a sequence of queries specifically designed to induce an affirmative answer. However, the use of the singular pronoun "you" in posing the question allows Socrates to evade full responsibility for this answer. The shift from "we" to "you" had already begun to take place earlier, with Socrates surrendering possession of the city's soldiers just before he imposes on them the task of ending faction in Greece, replacing *hēmin* in 469b5 with *soi* in 470a6. The switch to "you" gives the impression that Glaucon's answers might apply only to a city founded of his own accord, without the careful guidance of Socrates. Glaucon's city may be Greek, but Socrates's is never identified as such.

The change in pronoun is linked to a strong disagreement between Socrates and Glaucon, which gradually emerges in the course of the discussion. While the questions posed by Socrates tend to encourage Glaucon's strong philhellenic sentiments, and corresponding dislike of barbarians, some of Socrates's own statements and demurrals point in a different direction. While Socrates argues that Greeks should spare other Greeks in order to defend themselves collectively against the barbarians, Glaucon responds by proclaiming that Greeks should launch an offensive against barbarians (469c6–7). Rather than sanction so aggressive a policy, which was in no way implied in his question, Socrates promptly changes the subject to smaller matters of battlefield conduct (469c8 ff.). One might retort that Socrates's subsequent argument on the kinship of Greeks and the foreignness of barbarians, in which he resumes using the pronoun "we" in calling warring barbarians and Greeks "enemies by nature" (470c5–7), does justify a war against barbarians.[10] Yet whether we ought to go to war with our enemies by nature, or merely stay away from them, remains unclear. Furthermore, it is remarkable how quickly Socrates loses interest in barbarians after this point. He stops mentioning them altogether after 470c5, and turns once again to the evils of certain types of warfare, such as the burning of land and destruction of houses, when practiced among fellow Greeks (470d5–8). He proceeds to redirect the energies of the city away from attacking barbarians and toward reprimanding quarrelsome Greeks (471a6–7). Glaucon makes one more effort to reintroduce barbarians into the discussion, wishing that the cruel acts frequently perpetrated by Greeks against Greeks could somehow be directed against the barbarians (471b7–8).[11] But Socrates again refuses to take the bait, calmly concluding that the guardians of the city shouldn't engage in ravaging the property of any enemy under any circumstance, thus dropping the distinction between Greeks and barbarians altogether (471c1–2; cf. 469c8 ff.).[12] Impatient to learn about the possibility of the city, and perhaps dissatisfied by his failure to instigate a war against the barbarians, Glaucon promptly changes the subject (471c3 ff.).[13]

The disagreement between Socrates and Glaucon about the urgency of fighting barbarians strengthens our suspicion that they may disagree about the Greek identity of the city as well. Socrates will later announce that the city is most likely to come into being among remote barbarians (499c7–d1). If this constitutes Socrates's definitive statement on the matter, then why does he deceive Glaucon into believing that the city is Greek? To answer this question, we need to integrate the argument into Socrates's overarching aims.

Panhellenism, Kinship, and the City's Gentler Foreign Policy

Socrates's success in persuading Glaucon that the city is Greek, along with his invocation of Greek unity, may not represent his last word on these subjects, but it serves an important function in the dialogue. It both restates the foreign policy of the city and deepens Glaucon's understanding of kinship.

The earlier discussion of foreign affairs between Socrates and Adeimantus in Book IV presented every other city, Greek and barbarian, as a potential enemy (423a8–b1). According to that account, all such enemies are to be dealt with in the same way: the city must foment faction within them by inciting the poor against the rich and promising them their property (422e6–423a5). This extremely dour account of international politics assumes that the only thing that matters for the city is its own self-defense, and the only thing that matters for factions in foreign cities is power and material gain. By adopting a policy of bribe, divide, and conquer, the city would not even offer its guardians much of an opportunity to display their vaunted courage and valor (cf. 422a8–c9 with 422e4–423b7).[14] The new depiction of international politics, on the other hand, does not attempt to reduce them to money or power, but appeals to the broader and loftier sentiment of Greek kinship.[15]

Faced with the aggressive, anti-barbarian statements of Glaucon, which expose the dangerous side of this sentiment, Socrates takes care to endow the Greeks with unqualified goodness and gentleness (470e7, 471c1–2).[16] He ceases to speak about the allegedly "hostile" barbarians, but encourages the city to put its energy into chastising errant and fractious Greeks (471a6–7). The formerly isolated, self-absorbed city has managed to appoint itself the arbiter of Greece.[17] It might be worth asking whether the other Greeks would allow so peculiar a city, whose customs on matters as diverse as poetry and the role of women share so little in common with their own, to become the policeman of Greek unity. But what exactly do the Greeks share in common? Does Socrates present a satisfactory definition of Greek identity in the discussion?

Alfarabi will begin his account of the Umma with a positive definition of it, but it is much harder to find such a definition in Plato. Socrates's appeal to Greek identity in the *Republic* is deliberately vague, and unaccompanied by a satisfactory definition of it. Language is cited as a cause of the distinctiveness of the Greeks in the *Menexenus* (242a1–2), but not necessarily in the *Republic*.[18] The same Socrates who told the Phoenician "noble lie" makes no attempt to argue for the common ancestry of the Greeks.[19] The sharpest distinction made by Socrates between Greeks and barbarians concerns the sacred things, which the Greeks are supposed to share in common (470e10). But does the city of the *Republic* share in the Greek deities? Its most important god ranks as "the ancestral interpreter of such [sacred] things for all humankind" (427c2–4). Although this god is linked to the famous oracle of Apollo at Delphi (427b2–3), his broad audience does not suggest any particular interest in, or concern for, Greece. If the god were to enjoin the guardians to disregard Panhellenic sentiment and present captured Greek weapons as offerings at temples, they would be required to obey (469e7–470a3). Meanwhile, the Homeric description of the gods has been mostly rejected by the city (377d3 ff.). Although the poets and gods certainly help define Greek identity in the *Republic*, they do not seem to suit the city established in it. We shall soon see that the clearest definition of Greek identity in the *Republic* occurs only in Book X, after Socrates has ceased to talk of the city.

Despite these difficulties, Socrates argues that by nature the Greeks are akin and friendly with one another, while the barbarians are foreign and hostile to Greeks (470c1–d1). The meaning of all these terms is somewhat vague, but Glaucon accepts them without asking for any clarification (470c4, 470d2): he seems deeply wedded to the notion of Greek unity and kinship without being able to articulate why. The significance of the words *oikeios* and *allotrios*[20] can be traced back to an earlier part of the dialogue, since they have already appeared in the description of the philosopher-dogs who were adduced as a model for the guardians. These marvelous creatures "define the *oikeios* by their acquaintance with it and the *allotrios* by their ignorance of it" (376b5–6): it follows that they are gentle toward the former and harsh toward the latter. Could these terms thus understood really apply to relations among Greeks? Spartan ways were often familiar to other Greeks only insofar as they were detested, while Cretans regarded even Homer as "foreign poetry" (see *Laws* 680c1–5). Massalia and Miletus were separated by hundreds of miles of ocean, and each might have had closer ties and familiarity with neighboring barbarian peoples than with one another. While Plato displays great awareness of such difficulties in the *Laws*, Socrates in the *Republic* does not even try to grapple with any intra-Hellenic distinctions. He barely touches upon the important division between Dorian and Ionian Greeks, and only in his discussion of musical modes (398e10–399a4).

It would nevertheless be wrong to assume that Socrates is deluded by a romantic brand of Panhellenism that bears no relation to fact. His invocations of Greek unity represent a deliberate attempt to broaden Glaucon's horizons. The notion that knowledge, philosophy, and sound political sense among humans can be equated with the instinctive awareness of dogs is, of course, a joke.[21] Its naïveté is corrected to some extent by the appeal to Panhellenism, the effectiveness of which shows that humans in general, and Glaucon in particular, have attachments that extend beyond the crudely familiar. Socrates never even mentions Athens, which would have been truly *oikeios* to Glaucon. In this respect, the Panhellenic argument in the *Republic* differs dramatically from its counterpart in the *Menexenus*, which places Athens unabashedly at the head of Greece (*Menexenus* 245c6–d7). In the discussion of dogs, guardians, and philosophers, Socrates employs several different terms corresponding to different kinds of knowing, each broader and deeper than its predecessor. He begins with the word *gnorimos*, a basic term for "acquaintance," but substitutes *philomathos*, or "love of learning," and, finally, *philosophos* (375e3, 376b5–c2). In the final, "bold" statement, philosophers and lovers of learning are again said to be gentle toward those whom they know, but harshness toward strangers is omitted (376b11–c2). This same pattern is repeated in the discussion of Panhellenism leading up to the introduction of philosophy. Glaucon's horizons are expanded by the successive introduction of three words, each connoting a wider attachment than its predecessor:

philopolis, *philellēn*, and, finally, *philosophos* (470d7, 470e9, 473c11 ff.).[22] Socrates manages to equate love of the city with love of civilized (*hēmeros*) Greece (470e7–9), before finally proceeding to philosophy, or love of all wisdom as such. This expansion of the sphere of Glaucon's interest and the attempt to soften his martial inclinations open the way for the introduction of philosophy, whose love of knowledge of all things transcends, and ultimately breaks down, the distinction between familiar and unfamiliar (475c6–8).[23] If the people of the "place around us" who love learning can be identified with the philosophers (435e7; cf. 376b9–c2), they might not belong to any particular geographical community.

Socrates's creation of the smoke screen of the city's Greek identity is admittedly risky and double-edged. He hopes that the city's newfound sense of community with its immediate neighbors can be used to broaden Glaucon's attachments and forestall disruptive wars without resorting to the cunning machinations required by his earlier discussion with Adeimantus. Yet Glaucon, not one to be satisfied by a city that eschews war (372b9 ff.), is inclined to view Greek unity as a pretext to initiate a still larger war against the barbarians. Socrates hopes that he can counteract this tendency by joining the city to a Greek nation deemed gentle rather than savage. But does Socrates ever fully purge Glaucon of his aggressive, Panhellenic longings? I do not think that the dialogue ever provides any conclusive proof. When Socrates announces that the rule of the philosophers is most likely to come into being "in some barbarian place, far outside our range of vision" (499c9–d1), it is Adeimantus who consents, but at least Glaucon does not interrupt.[24]

The Untraceable Origin of the City

The introduction of the theme of Greek kinship serves several distinct purposes. It softens the attitudes of the city, reconciles its citizens to their fractious neighbors, and helps prepare Glaucon for the introduction of philosophy. Yet it does not succeed in integrating the city into any ethnic community, or in shedding light on its origins.

Socrates's attribution of the city to a remote barbarian place (499c9) dislocates the city from Greece, without locating it in Phoenicia, Egypt, Thrace, or any other known barbarian region. The basic problem inherent in the founding scene is never resolved: where is the city located, and who are its first inhabitants? To the best of my knowledge, there is but one passage in the

Republic that gives an account of their origins. It is, of course, the notorious "noble lie" (414d ff., cf. 369c1–4, 470d8–9). This tale is literally no more true than it purports to be, but its shameless mendacity points to the heart of the problem: we know nothing whatsoever about the origins of this city and its people. They might just as well have sprung from the earth.

Socrates's refusal to elucidate the origins of the city's first inhabitants serves the convenient purpose of avoiding all the thorny problems associated with settling actual cities. The location of the city and the origins of the first inhabitants become from the very beginning a major obstacle to the legislative project of the *Laws* (704c ff.), but there is no comparable discussion in the *Republic*. The appearance of the philosopher-kings, who are ostensibly introduced to render the city possible (471c6 ff.), reorients the discussion away from the founding of a new city, and toward explaining how philosophers might emerge and come to power in existing cities. The new-found emphasis on existing cities pushes the question of the new city and its origins into the background.

Adeimantus senses that the prolonged discussion of philosophy and its travails in existing cities has somehow shifted the terrain. He asks Socrates whether any of the current regimes is worthy of philosophy (497a9–10). Socrates replies that none are, but that the best regime would be (497b1–c3). However, Socrates no longer identifies the best regime with the one that has been elaborated in the dialogue, since he anticipates the question of "what this [best] regime is" (497c4). Somewhat confused, Adeimantus responds by asking Socrates whether the best regime and the city founded by the interlocutors in the dialogue are indeed the same (497c5–6). Socrates seems to answer in the affirmative, but with a major qualification: the philosophers could rule in any city possessing the same *logos* that was embodied in Adeimantus's lawgiving (497c7–d2). Socrates also substitutes the second person singular "you" for Adeimantus's "we" (cf. 497c6, 497d2), as if to suggest that he has again ceased to take part in this lawgiving. Furthermore, the use of the imperfect tense of the verb *tithēmi* to signify Adeimantus's lawgiving seems to relegate it to the past. Whatever one might make of this surprising exchange,[25] this much is clear: in the ensuing discussion the city that dominated the first half of the dialogue plays a diminished role. Socrates drops the phrases "this city" and "our city" in explaining how an indefinite "city" can take up philosophy without being destroyed (497d8). The word "city" without an article recurs multiple times as Socrates explores the possibility of the rule of philosophers (499b2, 499c7, 501a2, 502b4). Socrates's attention has shifted away from the city founded in the first half of dialogue toward whatever existing city might be amenable to the rule of philosophers. He now speaks of the sons of kings or other current rulers acquiring a passion for philosophy, which would indeed seem a much quicker and less risky route to philosopher-kings than establishing a new city from scratch (499b7–c1, 502a5–6). It allows Socrates to evade the unresolved question of the city's ethnic identity. And yet this new proposal will soon meet opposition from the *ethnos* as well.

In the subsequent discussion, Socrates does reintroduce "the laws and practices that we have gone through" in the first half of the dialogue (502b6–7). But the absence of the city for which these laws were initially intended means that they have been detached from their original context and integrated into a program of legislative reform for a preexisting city that has been rendered obedient to philosopher rulers (502b4–5). The old approach was based on "beholding a city coming to be in speech" (369a5–6), while the new approach is based on philosophers designing a divine model and striving to implement it in existing cities (500e1–3). It now seems that the city was never meant to be founded in deed, but rather elaborated in speech, so that it may serve as a model for the drastic reforms that philosophers will impose once they have taken over existing cities. When Socrates and Glaucon return as founders, their primary task is no longer to design legislation for a new city, but rather to compel the philosophers to concern themselves with government in general (519c8ff.).

The philosopher kings, once they have been compelled to rule, would not be content with existing norms. They would have to purify the city and the ways of its inhabitants, like a tablet that an eraser has returned to a state of pristine blankness. Only then can they initiate the desired reforms (501a2–c2). The precise meaning of this purification appears in graphic terms at the end of Book VII, with its ludicrous proposal for the expulsion of all the inhabitants over ten years of age, once "the true philosophers, either one or many, come to power in *a* city" (540d3–4, italics mine). The sweeping expulsion of the parents followed by the sound education of the children along the lines elaborated in the first half of the dialogue is the only way a city in any nation (*ethnos*) could become truly happy (541a5–6). Socrates's rare mention of the *ethnos* here is highly significant. By noting that such an expulsion would be equally necessary in any *ethnos*, Socrates indicates how completely the customs of every nation are likely to resist the establishment of his city. The notion that a city rooted in parricide and the destruction of ancestral customs could somehow "profit the nation in which it arises" (541a6–7) is absurd: it recalls and generalizes Socrates's earlier assertion that the city that had just abolished the family and introduced women into the army could reconcile warring Greeks (471a6–7). The broadening of the dialogue's concern from a city to the nation to which the city belongs serves to reiterate the practical impossibility of the city. Glaucon was induced to call the city Greek; Socrates eventually consigned it to some remote barbarian place; now it has become equally anathema to the ways of every nation on earth. Socrates eventually confirms that this city is a model existing only in heaven and in the minds of the humans who contemplate it (592a10–b4). Since no founder of an earthly city would have the luxury of flouting the ways of the nation in which the city comes to be (cf. 541a6–7), it is only as a founder of a heavenly city that Socrates can afford to abstract from merely "ethnic" considerations.[26]

Back to the Nation: Poetry and the Myth of Er

The conclusion that the city of the *Republic* does not bear any ethnic stamp seems to have brought our discussion of ethnicity in the *Republic* to an end. But the dialogue does not end with an elaboration of the city. In Book X, Socrates once again discusses poetry, a subject more closely linked to Greek national character than the city that has dominated much of the dialogue.

Socrates's purpose is ostensibly to justify his earlier policy of restricting poetry within the city (595a3–6). Yet if the city, as Glaucon has proclaimed, does not exist anywhere on earth, how can poetry be censored in it? Socrates later implies that the real question might be the relationship between poetry and soul, or else between poetry and the regime within the soul (595a7–b1, 605b7–8, 608b1). The issue is no longer whether poetry is good for the city, but whether it is good for the individual soul. In treating this question, Socrates attempts to steer Glaucon and the other interlocutors away from their attachment to traditional Greek poetry. We recall our earlier uncertainty about whether Socrates has managed to dissuade Glaucon from his excessive attachment to Greece, and consequent desire to wage a war against barbarians. Perhaps the gentle Greek city, which eventually turns out to be a remote barbarian city and finally a city in heaven, is insufficient for attaining that goal. In addition to the city, a more direct and personal confrontation with Greek poetry and civilization is required.

This discussion contains what appears to be the clearest statement about Greek identity in the *Republic*. Socrates remarks that many people call Homer "the educator of Greece" (606e2–3), and wish to lead their life according to his precepts. The implication is that Greece might be defined as a civilization that learned its way of life from Homer and his poetry (606e1–607a1). In linking national Greek identity to the poetry of Homer, Plato gestures toward a theme that will become the basis of Alfarabi's presentation of the Umma as a civilization rooted in language, national legends, and poetry. Socrates, however, does not appear entirely convinced by this view. He admits that he himself has been fond of Homer since childhood and is therefore ashamed to criticize him (595b9–10), but manages to overcome this shame. Homer, he insists, did not educate anybody, in either medicine, generalship, governance, artisanship, or way of life (599b9–600e2). Yet as many commentators have noted, there is a certain amount of irony in this passage (Rosen, 370; *Republic*, trans. Bloom, 429–30). The eccentric, pre-Socratic philosopher Pythagoras, not to mention the sophists Protagoras and Prodicus, are adduced as genuine educators, while the criticisms cast upon Homer for his lack of political, military, and artisanal success might easily apply to Socrates himself. Furthermore, Socrates's acknowledgment that many of the best and brightest Greeks strive to model their life after Homer's poems (606e1–607a2) appears to contradict his claim that Homer was truly ineffectual as an educator. One could say that while Homer was hardly the sole educator of Greece, he ranks along with Solon, Lycurgus, and Thales as one of its major educators. Civilized human beings are a complex and variable composite of what generations of poets, legislators, scientists, and philosophers have made them. What Homer may lack in specific, direct impact on a particular place or art, he makes up for by his broad appeal. While Lycurgus gave laws only to the Spartans, and Thales inspired a small group of philosophers, Homer alone produced poems that influenced almost all the Greeks.[27] Only Homer, therefore, ever received the title "educator of Greece." It is also possible that Homer's influence was deeper. Even when speaking to sophisticated young Athenians, Socrates displays far more interest in Homer than in Solon or other great Athenians, as if the former is a greater rival for his interlocutor's souls.[28] The regime in the soul is more likely to be disturbed by the pleasure of poetry than by the severity of the law (607a6–8, 608b1–2).

Socrates's final response to the challenge of Homer is to construct a story on his own, namely, the myth of Er. Yet even Socratic mythmaking fails to escape entirely from Homer's shadow. Rather than invent his own characters from scratch, Socrates chooses to rewrite the Alcinous section of the *Odyssey*, which chronicles Odysseus's ascent into Hades (614b2–3; Rosen 382). The new version of the myth recasts many of the greatest Homeric heroes in an unflattering way. Basing his account of these heroes on characteristics given to them by Homer himself, Socrates shows how their love of glory eventually leads to pain and misanthropy; most suffer so greatly as men that they choose to assume an animal form in the next life (619e6 ff.). Ajax, who remembers his humiliating failure to attain Achilles' arms, prefers the form of a lion (620b1–3; *Odyssey* 11.620 ff.), while Agamemnon, who hates humankind because of his untimely death at the hands of his wife, prefers to become an eagle (620b3–5; *Odyssey* 11.460 ff.). The implication is that these mighty Homeric heroes, if properly understood, are more reminiscent of spirited, predatory beasts than human beings. It is perhaps only here that Socrates finally succeeds in calming Glaucon's own passions for Greek heroism and war. Myth, or the recasting thereof, steps in where philosophy fails (Rosen, 387–88). But the recasting of myth must begin with the poetry of a particular nation: it follows that grappling with the stories of the nation emerges as a necessary complement, even in speech, to the project of founding a city shorn of all ethnic qualities. At the end of the great, otherworldly adventure of the *Republic*, the philosopher Socrates has not entirely ceased to be a Greek speaking to Greeks.

The nation in the *Republic* does indeed form one of the many obstacles to the imposition of the rule of the philosophers and the establishment of the heavenly city on earth, but it also plays a crucial role in both political and cultural education. It introduces a political attachment that stretches beyond the interlocutors' immediate clan, city, and surroundings, and tells stories about human beings and the cosmos that continue to form the basis of their understanding of the world, even after the tale of the heavenly city has run its course. These are matters to keep in mind when we turn to Alfarabi. While his account of the Umma is more elaborate than Plato's, it never strays far from these essential themes.

The Elusive Other Umma of Alfarabi's Plato

I have suggested that a useful way to approach the question of Alfarabi's knowledge of Plato would be to examine Alfarabi's interpretation of him,

and see how it compares to our own. Alfarabi sets down much of this interpretation in a work titled *Philosophy of Plato*, which purports to describe the
parts of Plato's philosophy from beginning to end (PP 3.1). This memorable
treatise gives a summary of most of the extant dialogues. Both the summary of the *Republic* and the subject of the Umma play an important role in
it. By interpreting this work with these two themes in mind, I hope to shed
light on Alfarabi's view of Plato, as well as foreshadow some of his own investigations.[29]

Plato begins his search for knowledge by investigating a number of generally accepted arts and ways of life in existing human communities. These
investigations take place in both the Ummas[30] and the cities (PP 6.9, 16.12).
However, there are certain important passages in which Alfarabi has Plato
speak of one kind of community but not the other. The first such passage
occurs during Plato's investigation of language, whose meanings are ascribed
to the multitude of a given Umma. Plato thus recognizes the connection between the Umma and language (7.1–8). The investigations of poetry and
rhetoric that follow (7.9–8.5) are not ascribed explicitly to the Umma or the
city. However, Alfarabi indicates in the *Book of Letters* that these arts are
closely linked to a particular language and Umma (BL 142.6 ff., #129 ff.).[31]
Alfarabi's Plato also acknowledges that both poetry and rhetoric have something to contribute to his quest for wisdom and virtue (7.18–19, 8.4–5). While
failing to provide the certain knowledge that Plato seeks, they are clearly
worthy subjects of investigation. Poetry in particular has a great influence
on human character and way of life (7.14–17). Insofar as the Umma is linked
to language and poetry, it plays an important part in the philosopher's investigations.

While the section of the *Philosophy of Plato* that treats the linguistic arts
mentions only the Umma, certain other sections mention only the city (PP
3.7, 13.12–20). These passages relate to politics: the first speaks of ruling "over
a city or group," while the second treats moderation and courage, both political virtues defined in Book IV of the *Republic*. Alfarabi recognizes that
in the domain of politics, Plato gives strong priority to cities. The city and
Umma are further distinguished near the end of the *Philosophy of Plato*, where
the Umma is associated with ways of life, and the city is associated with laws
(22.18–23.1). Alfarabi's Plato perceives a strong link between language, poetry, ways of life, and the Umma on the one hand, and political virtues, ruling, and cities on the other.[32]

There are also prominent passages that ignore both the city and the Umma. When Alfarabi's Plato turns from moderation and courage to friendship and love, he drops the city without reintroducing the Umma (PP 14.1–3). Friendship and love lead in turn to a discussion of reveling, seduction, and related qualities, both human and divine, and how they must be practiced by the philosopher (14.4–15.17). This section, too, is notable for its omission of both the city and the Umma, as well as any other particular human community. By making Plato speak anachronistically of the praiseworthy, divine madness that is cultivated in both "mosques and temples" (14.18), Alfarabi implies that his discussion of these themes pertains equally to civilizations as disparate as classical Greece and medieval Islam. Not only philosophy, but also a set of private human qualities that lead up to it, seem to transcend all particular communities. Particular Ummas may establish human language and literary tradition, while particular cities bind their inhabitants with laws. Yet the power of love (14.1 ff.; cf. 22.5), along with the various qualities associated with it, cannot be so easily tamed. With regard to friendship, this point is not difficult to understand: friendships based on love, piety, and philosophy have all been known to survive the most savage wars and political disputes. Most perplexing, however, is the inclusion of statesmanship and royal authority among these same, transnational qualities, since they too occur in passages that contain no reference to either Ummas or cities (13.4–11, 14.5, 15.16).[33] It is only a very peculiar kind of statesman or king[34] who does not deal with particular communities: he is far removed from the ordinary ruler examined at the beginning of Plato's investigation, who governs a well-defined city or group (3.7). Since this figure is identified repeatedly with the philosopher (13.7, 14.5, 15.15–16), one may infer that his aversion to particular communities and their norms follows from his uncompromising devotion to wisdom and virtue. Alfarabi soon reintroduces Ummas and cities, but only in order to emphasize that the philosopher-king is too busy reveling in his acts and own peculiar craft to pay much attention to the generally accepted opinions of Ummas and cities, so that he cannot make use of his abilities in any of the Ummas and cities existing in Plato's time (16.11–16).

Alfarabi's Plato eventually concludes that the existing cities and Ummas are woefully inadequate: "another city and another Umma," where the best humans can attain their perfection, will have to be considered (PP 19.12–13). This new, particular community might succeed in persuading the philosopher-kings to participate in it, by elevating them to the highest rank within the city

(20.9–10, 22.9–14).[35] In the subsequent summary of the *Republic*, Plato immediately sets out to describe the other city, but seems to forget about the other Umma (19.13 ff.).[36] The ensuing investigation concerns only the city (19.14 ff.), and the next several sections mention the city repeatedly, but never the Umma. The Umma therefore appears to be absent from the *Republic* and the several other Platonic dialogues that deal with the other city (19.14–21.14).[37] While Alfarabi's Plato investigates the possibility of a legislator founding a new city in speech and then in deed (20.15, 21.12–13), he never speaks of any legislator or founder of a new Umma. His silence on this point is echoed by Alfarabi himself, who never refers to the founders of Ummas in the works that have come down to us.

The Umma's status in the *Republic*, however, remains ambiguous. Alfarabi normally concludes each section by naming the dialogue to which it belongs. In the passage situated between the naming of the *Phaedo* (PP 18.2–3) and the naming of the *Republic* (20.14), no other dialogue is cited. It therefore seems that Alfarabi ascribes this entire passage to the *Republic*, even though his summary of what is conventionally known as the *Republic* begins only with the investigation of justice in 19.15. The implication is that the various subjects discussed between 18.3 and 19.15 were very much on Plato's mind when he wrote the *Republic*, even if they do not find direct expression in Alfarabi's summary of the dialogue proper. The need for another Umma occurs last among these subjects, and its connection with the investigation of the other city is indicated by the the use of the word "therefore" (19.13–14). The shadow of the "other Umma" hangs over the *Republic*, with lingering effects on the argument of the dialogue. This hint of Alfarabi's is borne out, I believe, in my analysis of the *Republic*. Socrates neither founds a new nation nor succeeds in integrating his city into any of the nations of the earth. The problem as Alfarabi sees it is that even if a new Umma is as dearly needed as a new city for attaining human happiness, it cannot be implemented in deed or even expounded in speech. The language and ways of life on which the Umma is based grew up over many generations, and cannot be produced anew by a mere legislator. The absence of a new Umma may well hinder the establishment of a new city. What is this city's relationship to the existing Ummas? Alfarabi passes over the matter in silence, which might well indicate a quiet agreement with Plato: the new city in speech would not be accepted by any of the Ummas of the earth. When Alfarabi finally turns to the legislator who establishes the city in deed, he investigates him but does not explain how or whether he accomplishes his aim

(21.11–14). At this juncture, Alfarabi's Plato drops the new city entirely, and returns again to "the education of the inhabitants of cities and Ummas," that is to say, the existing communities whose unjust opinions and ways of life his philosophic reveling had once so roundly rejected (21.15–17; cf. 16.11–17.1, 19.6–14).

Alfarabi's *Philosophy of Plato* follows the structure of the *Republic* in one crucial respect: the elaboration of the perfect city in speech precedes the conclusion of the work. The supplement in the *Republic* is the discussion of Greek poetry and the myth of Er, which appears to be omitted from Alfarabi's summary of the *Republic* (PP 20.13–14). But Alfarabi does hint at some awareness of the contents of Book X. He mentions Plato's concern with the power of poetry to shape human ways of life (7.14–16; cf. *Republic* 606e1–607a2), as well as his dissatisfaction with the conventional poetic method (7.19–20). In Alfarabi's prelude to the *Republic*, he describes Plato's interest in the metamorphosis of humans into animals (18.3–19.3), a prominent theme of the myth of Er (*Republic* 619e6–620d5). Furthermore, Alfarabi's successor Averroes refuses to treat Book X in his much longer summary of the *Republic*, even while admitting that he had access to it (Averroes 1974, 105.13–26). For reasons that I will examine in Chapter 5, the Muslim successors to Plato did not invent poetic myths in the manner of their Greek teachers. These considerations lead me to suspect that Alfarabi did have access to the final book, but was loath to discuss its subject matter. If Alfarabi's Plato avoided any direct confrontation with poetic notions of virtue and the afterlife, what alternative course did he pursue?

Alfarabi's Plato concludes by turning away from the establishment of the other city and back toward proposals for instruction and gradual reform among existing peoples. Since philosopher-kingship as such is impossible, not the least because it ignores particular communities, the philosopher eventually realizes that he needs to act within the conventional framework of cities and Ummas. He tries to reform the laws and ways of life of his own people, the Athenians (PP 23.4). Although we might expect Alfarabi's Plato to call Athens a city, he prefers to designate his native country a *qawm*, a more generic term for "group." By suggesting that both its laws and ways of life need to be reformed (23.4–5), Alfarabi's Plato implies that the Athenian *qawm* contains elements of both a city and an Umma (22.18–23.1), such as the laws of Athens and the language and ways of life of the Greeks. The term *qawm* is employed quite sparingly by Alfarabi, and on only one other occasion in the *Philosophy of Plato*: Socrates tried to establish scientific investigation within his *qawm* and impress upon them the ignorance in which they were plunged (22.1–2). But while Plato's teacher, Socrates, had so vehemently and publicly protested against Athens, and as a result died by its hand (18.2, 19.5), Plato employs all the discretion entailed by private letters, presumably written to prominent individuals (22.18).[38] The philosopher can thereby incrementally improve the customs of his people, without exposing himself to any public backlash (see Strauss 1945, 383–84).

This approach seems similar in spirit, if not in substance, to Book X of the *Republic*. Alfarabi's Plato, no less than Socrates in the *Republic*, supplements the account of the other city with education, an alternative to direct political action. Gradual, discrete reform of the existing peoples by means of instruction of their elite emerges as a more practicable project than trying to found a city anew, just as the reform of existing Greek poetry among a few interlocutors emerges in the *Republic* as an easier alternative to the construction of a city in speech.

The foregoing discussion has uncovered some intriguing parallels between the role of the nation in Plato's *Republic* and Alfarabi's account of it. In both cases, the deeply ingrained customs of the nation emerge not only as an incontrovertible obstacle to the establishment of the good city, but also as a stimulus for education. Alfarabi was not the first political philosopher to investigate the nation, and does not claim that distinction for himself, but takes the investigation many steps farther. The various hints about the nation already present in Plato's *Republic*, and picked up by Alfarabi's *Philosophy of Plato*, are developed in great detail in Alfarabi's own work. The Umma constituted a more formidable presence in medieval Islam than the *ethnos* or *genos* ever did in classical Greece, and thus requires a firmer, more comprehensive treatment. Yet its basic contours remain the same: a community staunchly devoted to ancestral languages and ways of life that have established themselves inexorably over many generations, whose authority the philosopher can ill afford to ignore.

Nation and City in Aristotle and Alfarabi

The political thought of Aristotle is perhaps even more closely associated than the thought of Plato with the *polis*. This follows from the title of Aristotle's most important political work, as well as its manifest focus on Greek cities. And yet this focus is not exclusive, since Aristotle also treats the *eth-*

nos on several occasions. In addition, some of the passages that deal with the *ethnos* seem to have had some influence on Alfarabi. The same old question inevitably arises: did Alfarabi have knowledge of Aristotle's *Politics*? This issue has not engendered as much controversy as that of Alfarabi's knowledge of Plato, but it may be no less enigmatic.

It has been universally accepted since the nineteenth century that most of Aristotle's works, including the *Organon, Physics, Metaphysics,* and *Ethics,* along with a number of shorter works, were translated into medieval Arabic.[39] Alfarabi and Averroes both wrote numerous commentaries on them. The same cannot be said, however, of Aristotle's *Politics.* No medieval translation of this work is known to have circulated, and Alfarabi never clearly refers to it.

I am aware of three important scholarly treatments of this subject. Taken together, they succeed admirably in bringing the principal questions surrounding it into focus. In 1975, Shlomo Pines examined the works of Alfarabi along with those of his less famous contemporary al-ʿĀmirī, finding a number of quotations reminiscent of Aristotle's *Politics*; in one of them Alfarabi even mentions an Aristotelian "book on political science" (Pines, 154; BL 91.13–15). Yet these citations are highly imprecise, and all appear to come from Book I of the *Politics.* Another author from the same period, Miskawayh, states that either one or two books of the *Politics* are listed in the catalogue of Aristotle's writings with which he was familiar (Pines, 153, 155). Pines suggests that only the first two books were available, and perhaps not in the form known to us, but rather in a Hellenistic or Roman paraphrase (155, 160). Pines also raises the possibility that Alfarabi could have altered Aristotle for his own purposes, especially in the *Political Regime* (156–59).

In an article written in 1993, Rémi Brague comes to a conclusion similar to that of Pines, although he adopts a somewhat more strident tone. Brague also calls our attention to some new pieces of evidence, most notably a couple of quotations from Averroes (Brague 1993, 428–30). According to the first, Aristotle's *Politics* "did not fall into our hands" (Averroes 1974, 22.4–6). Whomever "our" may refer to, it evidently does not include Alfarabi, since a second passage, cited by Brague in Latin, suggests that in Averroes's view Alfarabi did possess this work (Brague 1993, 429). But how could Averroes in twelfth-century Andalūs know what books Alfarabi would have possessed in tenth-century Baghdad? Averroes's claim appears especially problematic given that Alfarabi has left us no explicit references to the *Politics,* even in his treatise titled the *Philosophy of Aristotle.*[40] Brague shows, with painstaking philological analysis, that the passage in which Alfarabi invokes an Aristotelian work on political science in fact refers to the *Ethics* (430–32). He concludes by echoing and even citing Pines: the medieval Muslims had at best unreliable quotations and summaries of the *Politics* (432).

None of this circumstantial evidence ever convinced Muhsin Mahdi that Alfarabi was unfamiliar with the *Politics* (Mahdi 2001, 34–36). Mahdi observes that Alfarabi does not explicitly declare his unfamiliarity with the work, and silence does not prove ignorance (35). Yet doesn't Averroes declare his unfamiliarity? True, but he never declares Alfarabi's (cf. Brague 1993, 429). Furthermore, the context of Averroes's claim is suspicious. He states that the presence of Plato's *Republic* compensates for the absence of the *Politics*, since both contain the practical part of political science. But if Averroes was truly unfamiliar with the contents of the *Politics*, on what grounds could he claim that it contains the practical part of political science, or that Plato's *Republic* represents an adequate substitute for it (Mahdi 2001, 35)? Finally, Mahdi doubts that a book which had simply been absent from the Muslim world could resurface so quickly and easily in medieval Europe (34). Mahdi accounts for the absence of the *Politics* by supposing that the philosophers concealed it deliberately, because they regarded the political philosophy of Plato as more suitable for their project of reviving philosophy in the Islamic world. In particular, Aristotle's arguments for the self-sufficiency of practical wisdom would have seemed preposterous in a world dominated by divine law (35–36). Mahdi's conjecture about Alfarabi pretending not to know the *Politics* resembles my earlier conjecture about Alfarabi pretending not to know Greek: he wished to conceal from his contemporaries his familiarity with something many of them would have viewed with suspicion. Such guesses are plausible and intriguing in both cases, but they hardly amount to certainty.

I regard Alfarabi's knowledge of Aristotle's *Politics* as more doubtful than his knowledge of Plato. As far as Plato is concerned, we should be inclined to take Alfarabi at this word, but in the case of Aristotle's *Politics*, there is no such word, since Alfarabi neither betrays nor claims thorough knowledge of the work. Alfarabi certainly could have appreciated Aristotle's stature as a philosopher, and even as a political philosopher, on the basis of his other works, including the *Ethics* (cf. Mahdi 2001, 35). I therefore remain somewhat skeptical about Alfarabi's knowledge of the *Politics*, and do not attempt to show that he interprets its teachings in any detail. Nevertheless, the passages of Alfarabi that seem most reminiscent of Aristotle, leading both

Pines and Brague to think that he must have had access to some summary of Book I (Brague 1993, 432; Pines, 157), can still be profitably compared and contrasted with Aristotle. This will at the very least shed light on the substantial difference between the politics and political philosophy of ancient Greece and medieval Islam, thus helping to explain why the *Politics* never gained much currency in the medieval Islamic world in the first place.

One of the passages adduced by Pines as having left some echoes in medieval Islam occurs in the very first chapter of the *Politics*. Pines makes a useful and sensible comparison between this passage and some parallel passages in Alfarabi (Pines 156–59), and I wish to build on his example. Aristotle famously claims that "man is a political animal" (*Politics* 1253b7–8), and a version of this statement recurs in Alfarabi, in both the *Virtuous City* and *Political Regime* (VC 228.1–8; PR 60.64, Ar. 69.16–17). Yet the terms used by each philosopher diverge already at this point. Aristotle speaks of humans as *politikon*, an adjective whose root is linked to the Greek *polis*, and takes care to distinguish the *ethnē* unfavorably from the developed *polis* (*Politics* 1252b19–20). Alfarabi speaks of humans as attaining perfection only in an *ijtimāʿ*, or association, which in Arabic signifies a cooperative political community of undefined size: it could describe a household, city, nation, many nations, or even the entire inhabited world (PR 60.64, Ar. 69.17–19, VC 228.10–230.2). This points to a possible difference between the two philosophers: while Aristotle privileges the *polis*, in this chapter in particular and throughout the *Politics* in general, it is by no means clear that Alfarabi follows him on this point. Scholarly discussion of this question has been largely inconclusive. Let us take a closer look.

The passages most often cited in favor of the city occur in the *Political Regime* and the *Virtuous City*. In the former, Alfarabi says that "The city is the first in the rankings of perfections" (PR 60.64, Ar. 69.20). In the latter, Alfarabi says that "The noblest good and the furthest perfection are obtained first of all in a city, not in any association that is more deficient than it" (VC 230.3–4).[41] Fauzi Najjar links this statement to the recently cited passage in Aristotle's *Politics* that praises the city (Najjar 1954, 108–9). But Najjar's assumption seems somewhat hasty. Given how unsure we are about Alfarabi's knowledge of the *Politics*, we can hardly suppose that he agreed with it on all points. Besides, Alfarabi distinguishes between the city, Umma, and the multinational association in two major ways: size and capacity for perfection (cf. Naṣṣār 1978, 36–37). The meaning of Alfarabi's statements therefore depends on the interpretation of "first." Does it mean first in perfection, as

Najjar assumes, or simply smallest in size, among the communities that are
equally capable of perfection? The context seems to suggest the latter, since
in both passages the city, Umma, and multinational association are listed
according to size rather than virtue. These three types of association are all
defined as "perfect," in contrast to households, streets, neighborhoods, and
villages, deficient associations that ought to be subordinate to the city (PR
60.64, Ar. 69.19–70.1; VC 228.10–230.1). Thus "first" is more plausibly taken
to signify the city's superiority to these deficient, subpolitical associations,
rather than its relation to the Umma. Alfarabi defines the city as the smallest of the associations that are capable of human perfection: on this point
he agrees with Aristotle (*Politics* 1252a27–30). But Alfarabi does not follow
Aristotle in proclaiming its superiority to larger associations, as some scholars
have already noted (Mahdi 2001, 140; *Cité vertueuse*, trans. Cherni, 218 n. 4).
The smallest might actually mean the weakest, as Naṣṣār assumes, arguing that
"the perfection realized in each of these associations differs from the other in
degree: the association arising in a city is beneath the association arising in an
Umma, and the latter is beneath the association comprising all of humanity"
(Naṣṣār 1978, 37). Alfarabi also states that "the unqualifiedly perfect human
community is divided into Ummas" (PR 60.64, Ar. 70.5), which Pines plausibly interprets to mean that "bigger communities are more perfect" (Pines, 156).

A further proof that Alfarabi does not regard small size as inherently
good is that he makes no attempt, even in his commentaries on Greek works,
to limit either the territory or population of the political community to any
numerical size. Plato's restriction of the city of the *Laws* to 5,040 households
(*Laws* 737e ff.) is still deemed too large by Aristotle (*Politics* 1265a15–18), but
it is omitted entirely from Alfarabi's *Summary of Plato's "Laws"*, which focuses on the equalization of property without any reference to the number
of inhabitants (SL 157, 5.14, Ar. 141; see Parens 1995, 62–67). Averroes's approach to Plato's *Republic* is even more explicit. One passage in the dialogue
appears to limit the city to a thousand guardians (*Republic* 423a9). Averroes
praises the view that a community should have a limited size, but adds that
its proper bounds vary considerably across space and time, and can be fixed
in each case only by political deliberation (Averroes 1974, 46.1–5). Plato's choice
of only one thousand guardians was appropriate for Greece, but in Averroes's
own time the required number would be somewhat larger (46.5–15).

Nevertheless, Mahdi takes a statement that occurs in the *Virtuous City*
to imply a certain preference for the city. "The city whose association in-
tends cooperation concerning the things through which true happiness is

attained, is the virtuous city . . . .The Umma, all of whose cities cooperate to attain happiness, is the virtuous Umma" (VC 230.9–10). In Mahdi's view, the second phrase indicates that "The virtuous nation [Umma] . . . presupposes virtuous cities" (Mahdi 2001, 143). This reading would be convincing if the cities of the virtuous Umma were themselves qualified as virtuous. But since they are not so qualified, it remains unclear whether cooperation entails virtue filtering up from the cities to the Umma or down from the Umma to the cities.[42] Perhaps both are possible, in which case the view of the equal receptivity of cities and Ummas to virtue and happiness still holds. The obscurity of these passages does not end here. Galston has observed that while mere "happiness" is attained in the Umma, "true happiness" is attained only in the city (Galston 1990, 152; VC 230.7–9). It is hard to grasp the meaning of this distinction. Alfarabi sometimes sets "true happiness" in opposition to "what is supposed to be happiness without being such" (BR 101.20–22, Ar. 52.10–12), but does not do so here. As tempting as it may be to regard the mere "happiness" of the Umma as inferior to the "true happiness" of the city, we lack any clear point of reference for interpreting this distinction.[43]

The ambiguity of these passages remains frustrating. As Galston concludes, "The relationship between cities and nations in Alfarabi's political thought is ambiguous and needs to be studied further" (Galston 1990, 153). We will have many occasions to study this issue further throughout the rest of this book. Even at this stage of the discussion, it already seems clear that Alfarabi's ambiguity about the superiority of the city to other political forms contrasts starkly with Aristotle's forthright declaration of it.

It must be emphasized, however, that Aristotle's focus on the *polis* and its uniqueness does not betray any innocence about the significance of the *ethnos*. It is discussed at some length in the opening chapter of the *Politics*. According to Aristotle, both the city and the *ethnos* emerge gradually from the household. But only the former is based on partnership, first of households into villages, then of villages into cities (*Politics* 1252b15–31). In both cases, the partnership implies a degree of political cooperation that transforms the character of the original community, permitting it to live a full and independent political life for the sake of living well (1252b28–31, 1280b33–35). This seems to involve, among other things, ruling and being ruled in turn (1277a30–33, b8–16). But with regard to the *ethnos*, Aristotle says nothing about partnership or shared rulership. Instead, the *ethnē* are ruled by kings, just as households are ruled by patriarchs. The original community of the household becomes bigger in size, first to a village and then to an *ethnos*, but does not change its patriarchal structure (1252b16–20). There is no clear limit to how large this community can become: kings may equally rule a *polis*, an *ethnos*, or many *ethnē* (1285b33–34). The *politeia*, however, can flourish only in a small community such as the *polis*, where everybody knows one another and the assembly or army is not so large as to be unable to hear the voice of orators (1326b2–7). For Alfarabi, political cooperation in its highest sense is possible in a community of any size (VC 230.7–11), while for Aristotle political partnership is limited to the *polis*. It is important to note the difference in meaning between the Greek *koinōneia* and its imperfect Arabic translation *taʿāwan*: while the former implies a measure of equality and political participation, the latter, usually rendered into English as "cooperation," could easily describe a strictly hierarchical society where everybody performs his particular function well. This is indeed how Alfarabi proceeds to describe the virtuous city (230.12 ff.).

Despite these differences between Aristotle and Alfarabi on the relative stature of nations and cities, both emphasize the actual prevalence of nations. Aristotle implies that the *ethnos* ruled by a king, far from being an outlier, is the kind of government and society that initially prevails everywhere. He observes that all humans speak of the gods as being ruled by a king, thus assimilating the gods to themselves (*Politics* 1252b24–27). "All humans" surely includes the Greeks, since they too were ruled by kings when they first fancied Zeus to be king of the gods. By quoting Homer in this context (1252b22–23), Aristotle indicates that the *polis* as he knew it was yet to exist in Homeric times. Even among the Greeks of Aristotle's own time, the *polis* had not established itself universally. Aristotle speaks explicitly of Greek *ethnē*, such as the Arcadians, who have never managed to organize themselves into a *polis* (1261a29–31). He later suggests that the Greeks are divided into *ethnē* of various qualities, some as wild as the people of Europe and others as docile as the people of Asia (1327b33–36). Among the non-Greeks, the *polis* hardly seems to exist at all: even nominal cities such as Babylon are large enough to be called *ethnē* (1276a28–30).

The foregoing analysis suggests that in Aristotle's view the *ethnē* comprise the vast majority of humankind, and even a significant portion of the Greeks. The bulk of Aristotle's work on politics treats a political form that by his own acknowledgment is quite rare. Aristotle evidently thinks that there is something unique and noble about the vibrant, self-sufficient political life of the *polis*. The *ethnos* does have a distinct meaning, but a rather negative one: it is a loosely defined community that cannot be governed in the free, political manner of a city (1326b5). The Greek-barbarian distinction becomes less important than the distinction between potentially free cities and unfree *ethnē*.[44] Aristotle's exclusion of the *ethnē* from the blessings of political life attained only in a few cities could even be said to foreshadow a certain Judaeo-Christian usage of the term, according to which a few faithful believers live surrounded by many, almost anonymous, gentiles.

The elevation of the city vis-à-vis the nation constitutes a central theme of Aristotle's *Politics*, but it is absent in Alfarabi. And why would Alfarabi have wanted to elevate the city? While the city was rare enough in Aristotle's time, and limited mainly to Greece, in Alfarabi's Babylon and neighboring Byzantium its last vestiges had long been engulfed by a series of vast empires and sweeping claims to revelation. The only kind of government known to Alfarabi and his contemporaries was kingly and imperial: this remained true in the Islamic world well into the twentieth century. Praising or even discussing a political form that no longer existed might have appeared hopelessly anachronistic. The absence of independent cities or popular governments in the thought and practice of the medieval Islamic world might be another major reason why the *Politics* never gained much currency within it. Unfamiliarity with the contents of the *Politics* would have discouraged translations, and even if translations were made, philosophers might have been leery of publicizing something that would have seemed so preposterous to much of their audience. The political situation in thirteenth-century Europe, in which the *Politics* publicly resurfaced, was already quite different: republics had emerged in northern Italy, so that thinkers like Marsilius and even Thomas Aquinas felt free to ask the Aristotelian question of whether kings, aristocracies, or popular assemblies should rule.[45] The rediscovery of the *Politics* helped stimulate a centuries-long European debate over which class of people should govern: no comparable debate occurred in the Islamic world until the twentieth century.[46] I propose this as a plausible answer to the query with which Brague concludes his article: how do we explain the relative lack of interest in the *Politics* in the Hellenistic, Roman, Byzantine, and Muslim worlds (Brague 1993, 432)?

Our analysis of Plato and Aristotle has shown that their treatment of nations does not display simple indifference or contempt. On the contrary, they acknowledge the prevalence and importance of nations for much of humankind. These nations constitute a major obstacle to the realization of the best city and regime, and, in the case of Plato, a useful tool for education. Yet neither philosopher attempts to define them in any strict way. We have seen how loosely Plato employs terms such as *ethnos* and *genos*, and how neg-atively Aristotle defines the *ethnos*. This means that their discussions of nations are often inconclusive and vague. I contend that Alfarabi goes beyond his classical predecessors in providing a working definition of the Umma. Reflecting on this definition and its various applications will distinguish Alfarabi decisively from Plato and Aristotle and help to clarify some of the problems that have emerged in determining the significance of the nation thus far. It is by establishing this definition that we will commence our analysis of Alfarabi and his concept of the Umma.

Chapter 2

From Speechlessness to Civilization: The Evolution of the Umma

What are nations? Why is humankind divided into them, and what are the consequences, cultural, religious, and political, of this division? These are basic questions that ought to inform any comprehensive discussion of the topic. Yet Alfarabi does not frequently engage in such a discussion. Although the term Umma appears in almost all Alfarabi's political works, it is often unaccompanied by any obvious explanation of its meaning. Such is the case in the *Book of Religion* and the *Attainment of Happiness*, which will be discussed in Chapters 4 through 6. Only two works, the *Book of Letters* and the *Political Regime*, give a thematic account of the Umma, its causes, and its character. They therefore constitute the focal point of Alfarabi's treatment of the Umma. Any attempt to determine the significance of the concept, and apply it to Alfarabi's oeuvre as a whole, must begin with these two works. In this chapter, I will analyze Alfarabi's thematic definition of the Umma and contrast it with the presentation of the same theme by some of his most illustrious contemporaries.

The Natural Causes of the Umma, and Its Conventional Character

The starting point of Alfarabi's account of the Umma is nature. The emphasis on nature is strongest in the *Political Regime*, where Alfarabi states that "One Umma is distinguished from another by two natural things:

natural temperaments and natural states of character" (PR 61.65, Ar. 70.5–
6).[1] Alfarabi proceeds to elaborate in some detail the natural causes that give
rise to the differences among the Ummas. His emphasis on these differences is so acute that he employs the verb "to differ" (*ikhtalaf*) and its cognates over thirty times in less than two pages. The different climates
produced by the uneven motions of the heavenly bodies and their varying
positions vis-à-vis the earth's surface affect the air, earth, and water in each
region, which in turn allow different kinds of animals and plants to thrive
in each region. The plants and animals become the nutriments of each Umma,
and their effects on the bodies of the people nourished by them are con-
solidated through breeding and procreation. The result is a habitable world
divided into Ummas, each of which occupies a particular spot on the earth's
surface and possesses a fixed and inalienable character (61.65–62.67, Ar.
70.5–71.7).

As Joshua Parens has already detected (Parens 2006a, 88–90), Alfarabi's rather naive description of the Umma in the *Political Regime* is not
entirely revealing. It suffers from some noteworthy omissions. While the
largely physical meaning of "natural temperaments" is clear enough from
the emphasis on nutrition and procreation, the meaning of "natural states
of character" remains mysterious. Does it point beyond the body toward
the soul? Alfarabi also admits that he has not mentioned all the ways in
which the heavenly bodies and air influence the character of humans,
without elaborating further (PR 62.66, Ar. 71.5–7). This puzzling statement
might hint at the passage's plainly inadequate account of language. Alfarabi mentions language as a distinguishing mark of each Umma: "a third,
conventional, thing having some basis in natural things, namely, the
tongue—I mean, the language through which expression comes about"
(61.65, Ar. 70.6–7).[2] Yet this single, terse sentence constitutes the sum total
of Alfarabi's treatment of language in the *Political Regime*. In the *Book of
Letters*, by contrast, Alfarabi's thorough account of language and its evolution covers many pages.

Conversely, the account of the evolution of the Umma in the *Book of
Letters* is prefaced by a remark that seems to compress the entire discussion
of the Umma in the *Political Regime* into a single sentence. Alfarabi describes
the first humans, who have not yet undergone any linguistic development
and therefore cannot even speak, as follows: "They are in a specific dwelling
place and country, and endowed by nature with a form and constitution in

their specific bodies, and their bodies will have specific qualities and mixtures" (BL 134.20–135.1, #114).[3] The causes of this condition, such as the heavenly bodies, climate, and nutrition, are not explicitly mentioned here but seem to be presupposed. The *Book of Letters* thus confirms the assumption of the *Political Regime* concerning humankind's primordial dispersal over the surface of the earth. The varied natural features on the surface of the earth create marked bodily differences among humans in different regions even before language begins to evolve within their souls.

In the next clause Alfarabi introduces the soul and its inclination toward knowledge (BL 135.1–2, #114), a theme that was noticeably absent from the comparable discussion in the *Political Regime*, thus opening the way for a full-blown treatment of language. Language gradually establishes itself in the soul and emerges as the driving force behind the growth and particularity of the Umma in ways largely unaccounted for by the limited scope of the discussion in the *Political Regime*. In the *Book of Letters*, language replaces climate as the primary cause of the difference (*ikhtilāf*) between Ummas (BL 137.1, #118). While language extends beyond physical causes, it also remains rooted in them, as Alfarabi observes in the *Political Regime* (PR 61.65, Ar. 70.6–7). Yet Alfarabi does not explain the relation between language and physical causes in that work, whose description of the effects of external physical causes on the human body remains so general that it does not mention specific bodily organs. In the *Book of Letters*, Alfarabi leaves no doubt that the most important of these organs is the tongue. The tongue represents the crucial link between physical nature and language. It is remarkable for the variety of movements and sounds of which it is capable by means of its diverse interactions with adjoining organs, which are described by Alfarabi in unusual detail (BL 136.5–13, #117).[4] Alfarabi suggests that the movements and sounds first adopted by each Umma are likely to be determined by the natural temperament of the tongues and surrounding organs of its members, who will adopt whichever articulations happen to be easiest for them to make. These articulations vary from one dwelling place to another. As a result, the first consonants of each language differ. This is the "first cause of the difference between the languages of the Ummas" (136.13–137.2, #118).

Alfarabi's account of the beginnings of Ummas and languages stands in contrast with the view of the Qur'ān, which declares, "What was humankind but one Umma, that later came to differ" (Qur'ān 10.19).[5] Alfarabi says absolutely nothing about the time of human unity that is supposed to have preceded the subsequent human dispersion. He does not look back beyond what can be posited through our knowledge of our present dispersion and observation of palpable, natural causes. For similar reasons, Alfarabi can ignore the Qur'ānic passage in which God teaches Adam the "the names of all things" (2.31). To the Islamic traditions that speculate freely about Adam's linguistic skills, one of which attributes seven hundred languages to him (Pedersen 1, 78), Alfarabi might have replied that the first humans in each and every Umma were speechless.[6]

The purely natural causes emphasized in the *Political Regime* are sufficient to ensure that the primary sounds of the languages, and by extension the languages themselves, will differ from Umma to Umma. But it is the conventional aspect of language that determines the subsequent course of the Umma's development.[7] In the *Book of Letters*, Alfarabi distinguishes between nature and custom by ascribing the actions performed by our original instincts to the former, and the actions established through repetition to the latter (BL 135.11–14, #115). It is hardly surprising that while nature should prevail at the beginning, when humankind does not yet bear the burden of experience, custom should come to dominate subsequently. Indeed, the very act of learning and memorizing a word involves repetition, and therefore custom. The statement that the evolving Umma displays a pronounced movement from nature toward custom will later require some qualification, but for the moment we may accept it as generally true.

Language develops further through an important intermediary, namely, chance agreement (*ittifāq*).[8] Alfarabi argues that particular words are fixed by chance agreement, as humans, making use of the sounds that their tongues have formed, begin to speak to one another in a fairly haphazard manner. Whenever two people happen to agree (*ittafaq*) to use a word in order to designate a certain meaning, they establish a linguistic convention (*iṣṭilāḥ*), which eventually spreads across a larger community (BL 137.17–21, 138.3–4, #120). Although the words established through these agreements eventually spread far beyond their originators, Alfarabi does not believe that even a long series of such agreements would be sufficient to create all the necessary words, so that a language-giver must arise at some point (138.4–8, #120). It is this language-giver who endows language with its conventional character (cf. PR 61.65, Ar. 70.6).[9] Convention creates and standardizes what fails to come into being instinctively through nature or haphazardly through chance.

Language could never emerge as an effective tool of communication among large groups, even for necessary things (BL 138.7–8, #120), until it becomes standardized and therefore conventional.[10]

Alfarabi explains the conventionality of language even more bluntly in his *Commentary and Short Treatise on Aristotle's "De interpretatione."* The primary sensibles and intelligibles are identical for all humans, experienced in the same way by Arabs and Indians. However, the words used to signify these terms, in writing and in speech, are already entirely conventional. The manifest proof of their conventionality is that they vary from Umma to Umma. Alfarabi goes so far as to compare the giver of utterances (*wāḍiʿ al-alfāẓ*) to the giver of laws (*wāḍiʿ ash-sharīʿa*): both are governors who establish pure conventions (CA 12.11–20, Ar. 27.9–18). To return from convention to nature seems quite impossible, at least with regard to language. If the simplest nouns are already conventional, then the thorough development of convention is the only way for language to evolve. Without it all humans would be equally natural, but equally ignorant: our natural faculties for observing the sensible and grasping the intelligible things (BL 135.6–14, #115) would simply remain uncultivated.

The *Book of Letters* confirms, and develops, this general point about the inherent conventionality of language. As the Umma and its language continue to evolve, they move farther and farther away from their natural origins. The more complex the language becomes, the more its speakers entrench themselves in the linguistic customs that have been standardized by earlier generations and passed down to their descendants (BL 141.16–142.4, #128). The gifts of beauty and refinement that are conferred upon the language by a class of language experts and storytellers serve to enhance its customary character (143.1 ff., 144.6–11, #130). The culmination of the process occurs with the development of linguistic science. Alfarabi explains how the dialect on which this science rests should be taken from the most remote and savage members of the Umma, whose life in the wilderness has protected them from contact with foreigners and left them least inclined to speak or understand utterances different from those to which they have been long accustomed (145.8–146.20, #143–44). Linguistic science, the last of the syllogistic arts developed by the Umma and peculiar to it (cf. 148.14–20, #138),[11] is the most inextricably rooted in the arbitrary customs of the Umma to which it belongs. Every Umma is formed by nature, but consummated only by custom, so that by the end of its development the natural elements seem

almost to have disappeared. Although the triumph of custom is not the end
of this ongoing story, it is certainly an important part of it.

Alfarabi's Definition of the Umma

I have shown that in Alfarabi's view the Umma and its language emerge out
of nature, but are perfected only through custom and convention. The link
between convention and the Umma is not unique to Alfarabi, but implicit
in the traditional Arabic meaning of the term. One of the rarer Qur'ānic
meanings of Umma is "custom" or "way of life" (Qur'ān 43.22). Alfarabi echoes
this Qur'ānic meaning in the *Philosophy of Plato*, by associating the Umma
with a certain way of life (PP 22.18).[12] Yet in the absence of any description
of the conventions and ways of life characteristic of the Umma, our discussion is bound to remain vague. What kind of customary institution is the
Umma, and how does it come to embody a specific way of life?

We may begin with a process of elimination. Many political matters that
are elsewhere of the deepest significance to Alfarabi are not even mentioned
in the long account of the evolution of the Umma in the *Book of Letters*,
or in the shorter account of its physical traits in the *Political Regime*.[13] The
words for "regime" (*siyāsa*), "city" (*madīna*), "ruler" (*ra'īs*), "king" (*malik*), and
"association" (*ijtimā'*), which occur frequently in Alfarabi's political works, do
not appear at all.[14] The only discernible allusion to political power comes in
the sections describing the establishment of the language, which cannot take
place without some kind of binding authority (BL 138.4–8, #120), and the influence of the Umma's linguistic elite (143.5, #130). In these passages the word
"governor" (*mudabbar*) and its cognates are indeed used. But Alfarabi restricts
the governor's authority to linguistic matters (143.5–6, #130). It seems unlikely that purely linguistic authority could be upheld without the help of
some kind of external force, such as a king or a warlord. By saying nothing
about political authority, Alfarabi may imply that it does not help or hinder
the linguistic development of the Umma as much as one might think. The
Greek Umma flourished under a large variety of mixed regimes, mostly in
cities, while the Arab Umma flourished under tribalism followed by multinational empire.

While there are some vague references to politics in Alfarabi's account
of the origin of languages and Ummas, there are no references to religion at
all. Alfarabi invokes the Arabs once, as a model of the proper method of col-

lecting the words and phrases on which linguistic science is based (BL 145–47), but says nothing about the more famous exploits of their prophet Muhammad and his followers. In Alfarabi's two thematic accounts of the Umma in the *Book of Letters* and the *Political Regime*, no connection between religion and Umma is established. This omission may have helped convince some scholars that Alfarabi ignores the religious Umma (cf. Vajda, 250), an impression that can and will be corrected by considering other passages.

The Umma is therefore reduced to two things: natural, physical traits caused by climate and nutrition, and the mainly conventional trait of language. Of the two sets of qualities, those arising from language are in every way the more dynamic. Although language is passed down from generation to generation, it is not merely a static, inherited trait. In an earlier passage in the *Book of Letters*, Alfarabi quotes the anonymous opinions of people who designate an Umma according to natural qualities inherited from parents, and moral qualities inculcated by them. These opinions employ the Arabic terms *sha'b* and *qabīla*, frequently translated as "tribe" or "clan," as synonyms of Umma (BL 98.11–12). The implication is that these people fail to properly distinguish between clan and Umma. By occupying themselves merely with ancestry and the moral upbringing afforded by parents, they are left unable to properly define the Umma (98.9–14, 100.5–7).[15] Alfarabi points out an error that must have been endemic in his genealogy-obsessed age.[16] He reminds his contemporaries that even if parents and ancestry determine the material constituents of the child, they do not fix its form, or moral and intellectual character, any more than strong wood fixes the shape of a bed (99.21–100.5). While education within the home has an undeniable effect on character, it is wrong to assume[17] that all education takes place there (98.17–99.4). Language is learned from elders, but not solely from parents (142.1–2, #128, 143.8–9, #130). The broad, public dissemination of language lends the evolution of the Umma a vitality that could not be sustained within individual families or even small tribes. It allows some members of the Umma to enjoy a much richer education than could ever be provided by their immediate clans.[18]

The significance of the link between the Umma and language for Alfarabi is sharpened by comparing his teaching with the views set forth by David Hume in the essay "Of National Characters." Hume distinguishes between "moral" and "physical causes" of the differences among nations, attributing far greater significance to the former than to the latter (Hume, 198 ff.). Physical causes include "those qualities of air and climate, which are supposed to work insensibly on the temper, by altering the tone and habit of the body and giving a particular complexion." Moral causes include "the nature of the government, the revolutions of public affairs, the plenty or penury in which the people live" (198). Hume's understanding of physical causes, and rejection of their importance, resemble Alfarabi's. Both philosophers agree that air and climate have minimal influence on manners and culture. Hume gives a number of persuasive historical and empirical arguments against reducing any differences in manners and culture to physical causes (204 ff.). But he speaks of moral causes rather than language as the defining feature of the nation. He traces the moral causes of the nation above all to legislation and politics (198, 204). Hume's political understanding of the nation is ultimately closer to Rousseau's than Alfarabi's. We will have occasion to consider this question at greater length in Chapter 7.

For the present discussion, it is most crucial to note that Hume minimizes the connection between linguistic eloquence and cultural sophistication, since language depends less on manners than on the power of the original stock of sounds. Moreover, the perfection of manners tends to fix the language and dull its power. Thus the modern English are more civilized than the Homeric Greeks, even though the Homeric Greeks had a more expressive language (Hume, 209). Alfarabi, in contrast, understands manners as secondary or corollary to language in determining the development of the Umma. It is the eventual perfection of the language and stories told in it that establish the manners (*adāb*) of a given nation (BL 144.11, #130). *Ādāb* is the plural of *adab,* a wide-ranging term that means "literature" and "culture" as well. It also occurs in 98.19–20 of the *Book of Letters,* in the context of education within families. Both families and Ummas cultivate *adab,* but Ummas do so on a broader scale. Translated as "upbringing" by Charles Butterworth and "formation of character" by Muhsin Mahdi, *adab* plays an important role in the political education of both rulers and citizens (see AH 39.12–18, Ar. 78.43–44, SL 146.7–147.8, Ar. 134.7–8). The presence of this term in Alfarabi's account of the Umma serves as a hint of the Umma's broader political and religious significance, which will be explored in the ensuing chapters. For now, we restrict ourselves to the claim that the emphasis on language, its advance toward rhetoric, poetry, and linguistic science, and its enduring effects on the cultural sphere are characteristic of Alfarabi and his understanding of the Umma.

If this definition of the Umma is correct, then strict equality among all Ummas can hardly be expected: some Ummas will be linguistically, and therefore culturally, more sophisticated than others. Alfarabi begins to employ the term Umma immediately after the first sounds of a language have been formulated (BL 137.1, #118), indicating that any group possessing a language of its own qualifies in some sense as an Umma. Although Alfarabi describes a gradual progression toward the more sophisticated linguistic arts, such as poetry, rhetoric, and linguistic science, he never presents this progression as natural or inevitable. It appears particularly unpredictable when compared to other phases of intellectual development discussed in the *Book of Letters*: while the onset of dialectic inevitably leads toward philosophy, and the founding of religion eventually produces jurisprudence and *kalām* (132.5–8, #110),[19] no comparable necessity determines the development of language. This is indicated by a subtle shift in vocabulary. While the movements from dialectic toward philosophy and from religion toward *kalām* are described by the verbs *taqaddam* and *ta'ākhar*, which signify an ordered progression in time (129.12–13, 130.1–3, 132.5–11, #110),[20] the sequence that characterizes the development of the Umma and its language is described only with the words *sabaq* and *ba'd*, which signify anteriority and posteriority in time without any clear reference to causality (134.18, #114; 141.6, #127; 145.1, #132; 150.2, #140). The choice of terms implies a large measure of unpredictability in the evolution of the Umma, and therefore a considerable degree of variation among Ummas with regard to their level of linguistic development. The movement of the Umma toward the full perfection of its linguistic arts is hardly a foregone conclusion.

Nevertheless, it would be fair to say that Alfarabi himself is most interested in the more sophisticated Ummas, as is revealed by a quick glance at the Ummas mentioned in the *Book of Letters*. Alfarabi cites the Ethiopians, Indians, Persians, Assyrians,[21] Syrians, and Egyptians as neighbors of the Arabs (BL 147.9–10, #135). He gives linguistic examples from the Persian, Soghdian, Greek, and Syriac languages (111.1–3). With the exception of the speakers of Soghdian, a common language in Alfarabi's native region, all these peoples constituted major civilizations at some point in history, and some retain that status today. To return to the examples from another region of the world given by Ernest Gellner, Alfarabi would recognize the Czechs and Estonians as Ummas, but restrict his most serious discussion to the Germans and Italians (cf. Gellner 1997, 90–101).

Alfarabi's definition of the Umma includes what we might call tribes as well as high civilizations. Indeed, the modern term "civilization" expresses the meaning of Alfarabi's Umma rather well. To avoid confusion, it should be emphasized that Alfarabi does not develop any concept of "civilization" per se, which might be opposed to nomadic life or barbarism. However, most of the particular Ummas of which he speaks would be classified as individual "civilizations" today. We would never, in contemporary English, call ancient Egypt or India "nations," so that the common translation of Umma as "nation" appears misleading in a crucial respect.

The *Book of Letters* recounts the coming into being of the world's most splendid civilizations in considerable detail. The establishment of a separate language is only the first stage in this process. Alfarabi explains how an Umma eventually perfects its language and excels in rhetoric, poetry, oral storytelling, linguistic science, and writing (BL 148.15–20, #138). A major impetus for the development of these arts comes from the occurrence of memorable events that need to be recorded in speech (142.8–9, #129). "The wise men of the Umma," who emerge even before the advent of writing, seek to preserve recollection of these events, engaging in "the recitation of speeches and the recitation of poems, and the memorization of the reports[22] narrated by them" (143.3–5, #130). When the volume of oral material becomes too large, writing is invented, and these bards are to some extent superseded by scribes (144.12–19, #130). Finally, the formal codification of the grammar of the language by means of linguistic science completes the development of the Umma (145–48, #133–37).

For reasons that will become clearer when we turn to the study of the origins of Islam, Alfarabi does not reveal explicitly what kinds of events are recorded in the Umma's stories. But since he mentions a number of particular Ummas, such as Greece and India, by name, he invites his readers to fill in these blanks. On the basis of his account, we could say that the crowning accomplishment of these Ummas are epic poems such as the *Iliad* and the *Ramayana*, which would shape their respective civilizations as long as they endured, and the treatises of their grammarians, which would confer a fixed form upon their language. Yet at first glance the scope of Alfarabi's account appears unnecessarily limited, since the arts of civilization consist of more than just the spoken and written word. Does not this narrow focus on language and literature, to the detriment of the visual and auditory arts, risk oversimplifying the multifaceted character of the Umma and its civilization? It can certainly be shown that Alfarabi did not overlook so obvious a criticism. To respond to it fully would require a far more careful consideration of Alfarabi's writings on poetry, rhetoric, art, and music than is possible here, but I can offer some preliminary thoughts.

We cannot ignore the broader context of the *Book of Letters*, which is primarily a work about language, and not only in the second chapter. The first chapter consists mainly of a definition of philosophic terms (BL 61–130), while the third chapter consists mainly of an explanation of various logical methods and questions (162–226). It is hardly surprising that in a work thus constituted Alfarabi should emphasize the language and literature of the Umma above all else. The absence of music and poetry, as well as the extremely brief mention of the mechanical arts (138.15–17, #131, 150.2–3, #140), represents a conscious abstraction, since Alfarabi displays ample interest in these arts elsewhere. On the basis of these works, we may piece together some of his ideas about the relationship of poetry to the other arts.

Alfarabi devotes a voluminous treatise to music, in which he argues that it, too, is perfected gradually over time. The relatively few details included in these brief passages suggest some intriguing parallels with the development of language. Most notably, both emerge spontaneously from natural human qualities, crystallizing into conventional arts only through the collective efforts of many generations (BM 71, 74–75).[23] Music and poetry also strengthen one another: music becomes more moving when accompanied by words (72–73), while poetic speech becomes more vivid when accompanied by music (67). However, while Alfarabi's account of the development of poetry ignores the parallel development of music, his account of the development of music pays homage to the power of poetry. It seems that music is more dependent on poetry than poetry is on music. This impression is confirmed by a passage in the *Selected Aphorisms* where Alfarabi concludes a longer discussion of the kinds of poetry by presenting the kinds of music as derivative from them: "The sorts of melodies and songs following from these sorts of poems and divisions are equivalent to their divisions" (SA 37, #56, Ar. 65.7–8).

Alfarabi speaks less frequently about painting and sculpture: rather than devote entire treatises to the visual arts, he intersperses brief remarks about them in works ostensibly devoted to other topics. There are evident historical grounds for his reticence: unlike poetry and music, painting and sculpture were frowned upon by many Muslims, because of their association with idolatry.[24] Nonetheless, Alfarabi manages to draw strong parallels between the visual and auditory arts. While acknowledging that the visual arts have historically been linked to idolatrous worship, as took place among the ancient Greeks and still endures in distant India, Alfarabi suggests that they are in fact quite similar to music and poetry, at least with regard to their capacity to evoke passions and implant images in minds (BM 62–63). In the *Epistle on the Canons of Poetry*, Alfarabi explains that painting resembles poetry in every respect except its matter, for it imitates in color the same kinds of activities, forms, and aims that poetry imitates in words (EP 278, Ar. 272, cf. SP 183). A similar statement might apply to music, whose matter is not words, but tones (BM 85–86). Even if the matter and technique of each of the imitative arts vary, their form and purpose do not: all move human minds by providing imitations of sensible things.

With these observations in mind, we may understand why the perfection of pre-philosophic language and the stories told by it constitute the foundation of the civilization of the Umma. Since the other arts imitate the same subjects as poetry and even pursue the same goals, they adopt the material that they encounter in the Umma's poetic stories. A brief survey of the world's major civilizations should confirm this point. How could we conceive of Greek or Indian sculpture without the inspiration of Greek or Indian mythology? How could we imagine art and music in the Christian world, into the Renaissance and even beyond, without the gospel stories? Painters and musicians render in color and melody the same gods, saints, and heroes whom poets render in verse.

One might object that Alfarabi fails to grapple with the obvious differences between the various art forms and their effects. For example, music and poetry excel at stirring up passions, while painting and sculpture tend to be more meditative and serene.[25] I am not sure if Alfarabi attempts to answer such objections.[26] His purpose seems to lie more in encouraging all the imitative arts than in distinguishing between them, as I will make clear in Chapter 5.

Alfarabi's description of the Umma helps account for a phenomenon that should be familiar to visitors to any major world art museum. As we pass from one section to another, we seem to be entering an entirely different world. In the set of rooms devoted to Greece, the sculpted women are beautiful but chaste, while the male figures are muscular and handsome, with noble expressions suggestive of martial valor. The elegant, rectangular temples are mounted on evenly spaced columns. In an adjoining set of rooms devoted to India, the female figures are buxom and erotic, while their male counterparts are graceful, supple, and meditative. The sinuous temples are topped by spires that reach toward the heavens. The splendor of both exhibits resonates across space and time, yet remains entirely characteristic of its respective civilization. No half-trained eye could mistake the art or architecture of one major classical civilization for that of another. Even the very greatest art is decisively shaped by the Umma to which it belongs; this observation reveals, on the highest level, the authority of the Umma as described by Alfarabi.

Debates About the Ummas in Alfarabi's Era

Alfarabi's treatment of the Umma offers only a few scattered hints about its historical context, but this context would have been quite familiar to his readers. The ethnic Umma had become a contentious topic in the Islamic world from the eighth century onward. The Islamic empire under which Alfarabi lived ruled over subjects from a vast number of such Ummas, and it was common among Alfarabi's contemporaries to argue about the relative merits of one or another of them. I make no claim to originality here, but a brief summary of these debates, as known through primary and secondary sources, can shed some light on the distinctiveness and historical significance of Alfarabi's approach to the Umma.

The vast seventh-century conquests that brought the Islamic world into being entailed not only the triumph of Muslims over infidels, but also the victory of Arabs over non-Arabs. This inevitably gave rise to ethnic pride among the conquering Arabs, and ethnic resentment among the conquered peoples (Norris, 34). A band of desert nomads whom Persians, Romans, and Byzantines had once despised as not even worth conquering suddenly emerged as the master of vast territories that those empires had once ruled. However, the decline of the Arabs was almost as rapid as their rise. While the Umayyad dynasty (661–750) was indeed dominated by Arabs, the Abbasid dynasty that overthrew it drew its core support from the Persian region of Khorasan. By the middle of the ninth century, the Abbasid Caliphs had gradually begun to cede control over the army and the treasury to Turkish and Daylami soldiers.[27] This lengthy process culminated in the seizure of power by the Daylamis in 951, a year after Alfarabi's death, thus establishing the Buyid dynasty.

It is not difficult to imagine, on the basis of these well-known historical facts, that the early centuries of Islam were rife with ethnic tensions, as rival Ummas competed for cultural and social status within the empire as well as for royal power and patronage. The Shu'ūbiyya movement, powerful during the eighth and ninth centuries, represented the reaction of the non-Arabs against the Arabs. The movement's name is derived from Qur'ān 49.13, the only verse containing the root *sh-'-b*.[28] It advanced numerous arguments for Persian equality and, in some cases, Arab inferiority. Scholars have arrived at various opinions about the scope and aims of this movement, which seems to have found some expression in the political, literary, and religious spheres.[29] Unfortunately, none of the original Shu'ūbiyya tracts survive, so the nature of the movement can be reconstructed only through the works of authors who opposed it (Enderwitz, 515). These texts present many of the disputes as serious and others as charmingly frivolous.[30] Common themes included rhetorical skill, dexterity with arms, ancient lineage, the antiquity of their civilization, and prophecy, with each group, and especially Persians and Arabs, proclaiming its superiority to its neighbors. These debates did not always take place on a high intellectual level: it does not behoove us, let alone Alfarabi, to discuss whether ancient Arabs ate lizards, or Persians invented the game of chess.[31] Yet even the most comical charges and countercharges are indicative of genuine tension and jealousy.[32] The charged atmosphere of ethnic quarrels under which Alfarabi wrote is surely relevant to understanding his work.

The acrimony of these debates finds forceful expression in the pages of al-Jāḥiẓ (d. 869), one of the founders of classical Arabic prose and a leading opponent of the Shu'ūbiyya movement. Al-Jāḥiẓ wrote an interesting work titled "On the Virtues of the Turks."[33] Addressed to a Turkish general who held a high position in the Abbasid court, it attempts to defend the Abbasid policy of employing Turkish soldiers. The addressee has just been exposed to a long and unpleasant harangue by an Abbasid partisan who boasts about the military virtues of the Khorasanis and other founders of the Abbasid dynasty while ignoring the virtues of the Turks (al-Jāḥiẓ 1988, 177–87). The unnamed orator presents the Abbasids as the true heirs to the Arabs, devising some dubious genealogies to prove it (183–84). He takes special delight in the Khorasanis' military valor and capacity to kill in any number of gruesome ways (185–86).

Al-Jāḥiẓ himself finally steps in, invoking the mercy of God and rebuking the general's adversary for promoting needless disunity among peoples, a fault all too common among the zealots of the era (al-Jāḥiẓ 1988, 187, cf. 217). If al-Jāḥiẓ were to respond in kind with exaggerated praise of the Turks, he would fall into the same pernicious tendencies as his adversaries. His method is designed to conceal his preferences for one people over another, without depriving his readers of their capacity to develop such a preference for themselves, assuming that they are willing to engage in a long and careful consideration of the relative merits of various peoples (187–88).

Al-Jāḥiẓ does not hesitate to invoke religious arguments against excessive national pride. He argues that national differences, and in fact any kind of human difference whatsoever, must ultimately be traced to God. As al-Jāḥiẓ explains, just as God has the power to create humans male, female, or hermaphrodite, so he has the power to attach them to whatever nation he so pleases. He can create us without parents, as He did Adam and Jesus, and teach us whatever language He pleases: although Ismāʿīl was not even born an Arab, God granted him the ability to speak clear Arabic without any instruction, and endowed him with the nature[34] of Arabs in its loftiest form (al-Jāḥiẓ 1988, 188).[35] He has proclaimed Abraham the true father of all believers (cf. Qurʾān 22.78), and Muhammad's wives their mothers (cf. Qurʾān 33.6), even though the vast majority of Muslims are not literally their descendants. Furthermore, God teaches the believers of all nations[36] the language of paradise as soon as they enter (al-Jāḥiẓ 1988, 188–89), a clear indication that the righteous from all peoples are equal in God's eyes. By reminding his readers of the overwhelming power of God, al-Jāḥiẓ hopes to dissuade them from extravagant boasting about merely human genealogies and qualities. As al-Jāḥiẓ's own allusions indicate, such equanimity seems to have some basis in the Qurʾān, in which God is presented as the creator of all peoples alike.[37]

Al-Jāḥiẓ also criticizes national pride from a human point of view, arguing that nations are bound to have different but often complementary virtues and vices. Not even God will imbue an entire nation with a high degree of skill in all areas of human endeavor. The limited human energy and passion of a given people must inevitably be directed toward the cultivation of certain skills at the expense of others (al-Jāḥiẓ 1988, 206). Thus the Greeks excel in wisdom and invention, but are deficient as merchants and artisans (206–7); the Chinese excel in crafts, but not in wisdom (207); the Arabs are brave warriors, instinctive trackers, and eloquent speakers, but generally poor craftsman (207–8); the Turks are outstanding warriors and raiders, but unfamiliar with the civilized arts (208); the Persians, finally, are skilled in government, an ability inherited from their Sassanian ancestors (206, 208).[38] Much of the rest of the essay is devoted to recounting Turkish prowess in war (192 ff., 209 ff.). While flattering the addressee, a Turkish military commander, al-Jāḥiẓ also keeps a certain distance from him, attributing much of his praise of the Turks to third parties. Al-Jāḥiẓ transcribes in the speeches of others the partisan, ethnic zeal that was so prevalent in his epoch, but in his own remarks he adopts a far more measured tone. He strongly implies that the Caliph ought to employ not only Turks, but other peoples in their respective capacities as well. Couldn't Greek inventors and Chinese crafts-men also figure in his military plans? Perhaps it is up to the Caliph himself to decide which nation's skills ought to be preferred for a given task at a given moment. In doing so, he would still have to distinguish between the general characteristics of a nation and the varied qualities of the individuals that com-pose it. Al-Jāḥiẓ observes that none of the qualities and skills he mentions characterize every individual within that people, even if they do predomi-nate among the people as a whole (209).

As a critic of the Shuʿūbiyya, al-Jāḥiẓ is considerably fairer than the parti-sans whom he quotes. He appears to have a genuine sympathy and apprecia-tion for all peoples. Yet by attaching certain qualities and skills to certain nations, he indulges in what we might call "national stereotyping" in a way Alfarabi does not. His emphasis on the role of divine will and power in the formation of peoples also finds no parallel in Alfarabi, for whom the growth of Ummas may be attributed entirely to human and natural causes.

Another notable treatment of the theme occurs in Abī Ḥayyān al-Tawḥīdī, a leading tenth-century intellectual who recounts the discussions of various salons. As Joel Kraemer has documented, al-Tawḥīdī has long suf-fered from a checkered reputation: posterity never fully trusted him as a reliable raconteur (Kraemer 1986, 31–45). Yet this reproach ought not to de-ter us from considering his work. The reports of al-Tawḥīdī that concern us are discussions that took place during his lifetime, and it seems highly un-likely that he would have simply invented them out of thin air. This is not to say that every word he puts to paper ought to be deemed historically true, but merely that his colorful narrations are more or less accurate reflections of the debates current in his age.[39] I have further avoided ambiguity by focusing on what al-Tawḥīdī states in his own name.

Although al-Jāḥiẓ wrote about a century before Alfarabi, and al-Tawḥīdī a generation after him, some things had remained the same: both lament the degree to which passion, arrogance, and prejudice have skewed the debate about the merits of nations. Al-Tawḥīdī has one of his interlo-cutors, a vizier, say that "the superiority of one Umma[40] to another is chief among the subjects over which humans fight and quarrel" (al-Tawḥīdī, 1: 73).[41] Al-Tawḥīdī himself emphasizes multiple times that the truths he presents concerning the differences among Ummas would be evident to everyone if people in general were not corrupted by passion and contentiousness (74–75, 76, 78). But what are these truths? They seem to be far less flattering to any one Umma than its partisans would allow. Al-Tawḥīdī does ascribe certain characteristics to each Umma: the Persians excel in government and culture, the Greeks in wisdom and science, the Indians in cleverness and witchcraft, the Turks in courage, the Africans in patience and hard work, and the Arabs in generosity and eloquence. Yet like al-Jāḥiẓ before him, al-Tawḥīdī denies that these traits apply to every individual within each Umma (74). Furthermore, he warns against the natural tendency of each group to praise only its own (73), retorting that the virtues and vices are divided up evenly among all Ummas in accordance with a "necessity of nature" (74).

Al-Tawḥīdī proceeds to introduce an important political consideration. Every Umma enjoys its turn at political supremacy: the Greeks enjoyed theirs under Alexander the Great. This single, seemingly uncontroversial example should allow the reader to fill in the contemporary implications: just as the Arabs had their turn with the Umayyads, the Persians theirs with the Abbasids, the Turks and Daylamis are now enjoying theirs with the Buyids. Al-Tawḥīdī cites as an authority Abu Muslim, who was instrumental in founding the Abbasid dynasty: "Every group is courageous at the beginning of their dynasty" (al-Tawḥīdī, 1: 75). Not only, then, do Ummas and other human groups tend on average to have an equal amount of virtue, but the virtue of each fluctuates according to political circumstances. The fact that no one Umma or group predominates forever provides proof of God's goodness to all his creatures (75). Despite al-Tawḥīdī's earlier, provisional attribution of particular virtues and vices to particular Ummas, his apt historical observations now cast these statements into doubt, based as they are on the dubious assumption that Ummas are fixed entities immune to changing circumstances.

We conclude that al-Tawḥīdī was even more suspicious than al-Jāḥiẓ of any kind of national stereotyping. Al-Tawḥīdī was also closer to Alfarabi in his inclination to trace the causes of the differences among Ummas to nature and history, viewed apart from God's will and creative power. However, since he does not cite Alfarabi we cannot infer that he was influenced by him: he might simply have imbibed the spirit of a more sophisticated and philosophical age. In any event, Alfarabi's approach cannot be identified with al-Tawḥīdī's. Although Alfarabi shares al-Tawḥīdī's aversion to polemics among Ummas, he takes the argument one step further.

While the other authors speak more or less freely about the moral qualities and technical accomplishments particular to each Umma, Alfarabi declines to mention such details, at least in the works that have come down to
us. If each Umma, as Alfarabi suggests, is based on its language and literature, it might be expected to cultivate the moral qualities embodied by its
heroes: inspired by Achilles and Hector, the Greeks valued honor and courage, while the Indians, in emulation of Rama and Buddha, revered medita-
tion and asceticism. Alfarabi's mention of the manners (*ādāb*) cultivated by
the stories of the Umma points in this direction (BL 144.11). Yet Alfarabi is
quite scrupulous in never attaching any precise moral quality to any particular Umma.[42] With regard to the debates raging on the superiority of one
Umma to another in war, wisdom, government, and the like, Alfarabi says
absolutely nothing, as if wishing to remain above the fray. Unlike al-Jāḥiẓ
and al-Tawḥīdī, he does not even bother to lament their highly partisan
character. Generations of boasts and insults exchanged among Arabs, Persians, and Turks barely seem to have touched the mind of the philosopher
from central Asia.[43]

Alfarabi's overwhelming emphasis on the language of each and every
Umma sets him apart from his contemporaries, for whom it seems to have
been only one quality among many that distinguish Ummas from one another. Moreover, few of these contemporaries resisted the general tendency
to praise the superior eloquence of Arabic, a trope that is found in al-Jāḥiẓ
and al-Tawḥīdī as well (al-Jāḥiẓ 1988, 207; al-Tawḥīdī, 1: 76, 211). This faith
in the preeminence of Arabic, inspired by its status as the language of the
Qur'ān and of revelation, reaches even greater extremes in other authors. A
particularly telling example is Abū Ḥātim al-Rāzī's *Book of the Embellishment
of Arabic and Islamic Words*. As Jacques Langhade has pointed out, this theo-
logian and contemporary of Alfarabi, who died in 934, serves as an excellent
foil for Alfarabi's treatment of language. Al-Rāzī's treatise presents numerous arguments for the superiority of Arabic, based in large part on its status
as the language of divine revelation. Just as Muhammad excels all other
prophets, so Arabic excels all other languages in richness and clarity. Arabic
cannot be adequately translated into other languages, but other languages
can and must be translated into Arabic. Hebrew and other languages used
in revelation are also accorded a special, if secondary, rank, while merely scientific and philosophic languages such as Greek and Sanskrit are not accorded any special status at all (al-Rāzī, 1: 59–64; Langhade, 130–51).

The view articulated by al-Rāzī has some basis in the Qur'ān, with its emphasis on the marvelous clarity of the Arabic tongue (Qur'ān 16.103, 26.195; al-Rāzī, 1: 60). But Alfarabi rejects it completely: in the second chapter of the *Book of Letters* he refuses to glorify any individual languages. Alfarabi does occasionally mention specific peoples, including "the Arabs" and their language, but his account of their competent practice of linguistic science, far from proving the superiority of Arabic, illustrates a general point about the establishment of that science that applies equally to all languages and Ummas (BL 147.1–10, #135). Each and every language, revelatory Arabic and philosophic Greek included, traces its humble origins to nature, and owes its development to chance and human convention. It follows from Alfarabi's comprehensive explanation of the origin of language that no particular language has been favored over the others, either by nature or by God.[44]

I anticipate a certain objection to my interpretation, in the form of a striking passage in the *Book of Letters*, in which Alfarabi declares that certain Ummas are more moderate by nature and therefore more inclined to knowledge than others: this quality is reflected in the precision of their language (BL 138.17–139.4, #122). In the context of the *Book of Letters*, this statement may appear strangely isolated, but it is at least partially elucidated by a passage in the *Great Book of Music* (BM 107–10). Alfarabi begins by distinguishing between natural[45] and unnatural human sensation, with regard to both taste and hearing (107–8). He then suggests that the inevitable deformation of our physical organs due to the extreme weather and unwholesome food of certain climes imposes on the peoples of the far north and south immoderate natural traits unfavorable for musical development (109–10). Alfarabi goes so far as to compare this distortion of the senses and taste buds to a kind of sickness (108). The emphasis on nutrition and climate recalls the *Political Regime*, in which Alfarabi emphasizes precisely these factors as the most important natural causes of the Umma. In this passage, the physical causes of the Umma reassert their importance. It is not perverse custom, but adverse nature, that prevents certain Ummas from following a normal course of linguistic and cultural development. Yet unsurmountable natural adversity affects only remote peoples, like the Slavs in Russia, Turks in northeast Asia, or blacks in the Sudan, while leaving the Ummas of Alfarabi's own environs untouched. More significant than the Ummas Alfarabi excludes are those that he includes: all the Ummas in the median climate zone between 15 and 45 degrees latitude,[46] conquered by Alexander the Great, the Romans, and later by the Arabs, are by nature equally musical (108–9).[47] The natural group comprises all the Ummas that took part in the Shuʿūbiyya disputes and lived under the Abbasid and Byzantine empires, such as the Arabs, Greeks, Persians, and southern Turks (110).[48]

Alfarabi's views on climate and its relationship to the natural character of peoples are largely shared by his successors. Averroes assumes a similar division of climate and argues that the majority of peoples, including the Greeks, Andalusians, European Christians, and Kurds, live in the moderate fourth or fifth climate zones, endowing them with an equal capacity for acquiring the virtues (Averroes 1974, 27.3–14). A far longer discussion of the seven climate zones in Ibn Khaldūn arrives at a comparable conclusion. After describing all the regions of the world in impressive geographic detail (Ibn Khaldūn, 1: 94–166, Ar. 71–131), Ibn Khaldūn concludes that the inhabitants of pagan India and China, Christian Europe, and the heartland of Islam all benefit from a moderate climate and possess the arts of civilization (1: 167–68, Ar. 1: 133).

The Arabs who live in Syria and Iraq enjoy a moderate climate, or at least a mild winter, but what about those who remain in the Ḥijāz, the birthplace of Islam? This remote region lies at almost the same latitude as the Sudan, and was conquered by neither Alexander nor the Romans. Once the kingdom of the Arabs had been established in more hospitable climes, the Hijāz retained only religious importance. A quick Internet search reveals that Mecca boasts an annual average temperature exceeding 30 degrees Celsius, the highest of any city in Asia. Medieval Muslims lacked such technological resources, but the scorching climate of Islam's holiest city would presumably have been known to them through accounts brought back from pilgrims on the Ḥājj. Ibn Khaldūn's comprehensive account of world geography cannot avoid this sensitive issue: having placed Mecca firmly within the intemperate second climate zone, he tries to argue that the Arabian Peninsula's proximity to the sea renders it more temperate than its latitude would suggest (Ibn Khaldūn, 1: 126, 169, Ar. 1: 96, 134). Alfarabi's comparatively skeletal account permits him to avoid this question, but it is worth keeping it in mind when we turn to his views on the origin of Islam.

Alfarabi distinguishes himself from his contemporaries by refusing to draw attention to the particular qualities of particular Ummas, at least in the moderate climate zone in which the vast of majority of the peoples known to Alfarabi reside. In retrospect, he also distinguishes himself from many of the later European philosophers as well. Nietzsche, for example, titled the eighth chapter of *Beyond Good and Evil* "Nations and Fatherlands," where he explicitly discusses what each important nation in Europe could contribute to the future of the continent (Nietzsche, 179–204). The fatal consequences of the cultural and political rivalry between the various nations of Europe may induce us to think that it would have been been wiser for the philosophers to avoid stoking its flames. Alfarabi might have thought similarly about the danger inherent in the Shuʿūbiyya disputes, but such prudence alone remains insufficient for explaining his studied aversion to them. We need to reflect further on why Alfarabi might have chosen to adopt a neutral stance toward all the civilized Ummas in the moderate climate zone. This can be done only by introducing a novel consideration, philosophy, which will raise the argument to an entirely different plane.

Chapter 3

Philosophy and the Umma:
An Uneasy Coexistence

My treatment of the Umma thus far has considered the subject largely on its own terms. This was necessary in order to bring out the essential qualities of the Umma as Alfarabi understands them, but it is inadequate for appreciating the Umma's place in Alfarabi's thought as a whole. We cannot proceed any further toward this end without an examination of the Umma's relationship to other human institutions and activities. I have noted that Alfarabi's most thematic discussion of the Umma in the *Book of Letters* tends to avoid the subjects of religion and politics. It also appears to avoid the subject of philosophy, but only if the passage beginning at 134.17 and ending at 149.21 (#114–39) is abstracted from its surroundings. In fact, Alfarabi treats the relationship of philosophy to the Ummas before his account of the Umma's evolution has even begun, proclaiming it to be one of unquestioned supremacy (BL 133.6–7, #111). If this is the case, why should the philosophically inclined reader be interested in the topic of the Umma at all?

This chapter examines the reasons for Alfarabi's unusual presentation of the relationship between the Umma and philosophy. Alfarabi does indeed maintain the superiority of philosophy, but he also argues, on a number of grounds, for the continued relevance of the Umma. The simple transcendence of philosophy to the Ummas in speech cannot conceal a complex and intricate relationship between them in deed, as reflected in the *Book of Letters*, *Attainment of Happiness*, and several other of Alfarabi's works.

Philosophy and the Vulgarity of the Ummas

Alfarabi gives several accounts of the relationship between philosophy and the Umma, the gist of which is always similar. While the Umma is particular, philosophy is universal. Linguistic science, which corrects the errors that may occur in the speech of a particular Umma, varies from Umma to Umma, while logic, which corrects the errors that may occur in investigating the intelligibles and thus provides an introduction to philosophy, remains the same across the Ummas (FL 55–56, ES 77–79). Philosophy itself, although first defined in the Greek language, passes seamlessly from Umma to Umma without losing its status as the highest art, the highest virtue, and the highest wisdom (AH 38.14–39.9, Ar. 88.54).

If these statements appear sweeping and blunt, Alfarabi's claim in the *Book of Letters* is even more so: "The elite status of the philosopher holds in relation to all humans and to the Ummas" (BL 133.6–7, #111). This is the only mention of the Umma in a section of the *Book of Letters* that treats philosophy, religion, and the arts associated with them, such as dialectic, jurisprudence, and *kalām*, but ignores most of the arts later associated with the Umma, such as poetry and linguistic science (131–134.15, #108–13). Of these arts only rhetoric is mentioned, but it is demoted to a mere tool of *kalām* (132.14–17, #111). These remarks occur immediately before Alfarabi's discussion of the Umma and therefore serve as an unlikely preface to it. Paradoxical as it may seem, Alfarabi begins his memorable description of the Umma only after proclaiming its inferiority.

Alfarabi's epilogue to the evolution of the Umma is similarly derogatory: it ascribes the Umma to the vulgar and the multitude, thus repeating a claim that he had already made about the first members of the Umma (BL 148.14–149.21, #138–39, cf. 134.17, # 114). Such a claim seems appropriate with regard to the Umma's humble beginnings, when humans are only beginning to learn how to speak, but it is somewhat more surprising when repeated at even greater length in the vastly different set of circumstances that surround the flourishing of the Umma's linguistic arts. Alfarabi therefore explains his claim in some detail. It rests on the fact that these arts are ultimately dependent on the comprehension of the multitude: rhetoric must compose speeches that persuade them, poetry must coin images that move them, and linguistic science must base its analysis only on the terms that are familiar to them. The practitioners of these arts are therefore beholden to the linguistic customs of a given Umma (148.16–20, #138). As a result, they are "classed among the multitude" (149.1, #139). Confined within the arbitrary premises of their own linguistic sphere, the elite of the Umma become blind to the evidence of unmediated nature. The customary character of the Umma and its language eventually proves to be its greatest limitation

It is at this point in the text that philosophy, which has not been mentioned for a very long time (cf. BL 134.12, #113), suddenly reappears. It introduces a set of general questions that the Umma seems to have long forgotten. Philosophy investigates the natural and artificial beings common to all Ummas, but does not seem to pay any attention to the arts peculiar to each (150.1–5, #140–43). Indeed, the very term Umma disappears entirely from Alfarabi's discussion of the growth of philosophical investigation (150–52, #140), as if the splendor of the Umma has been either transcended or forgotten.

Even if philosophy transcends particular communities, it is practiced within them, and therefore cannot exist in a vacuum. In his account of the development of philosophy, Alfarabi does refer to two particular individuals, namely Plato and Aristotle, who are cited as the climax of generations of philosophic pursuits (BL 151.15–18, #142–43). These two men, as Alfarabi and everybody else know, were Greek (cf. AH 47.3, Ar. 97.65). In the account of the development of the Umma, the most important reference to any specific people concerns the Arabs, and their praiseworthy efforts in linguistic science (BL 147.1–10, #135). So while in the section on the Umma and its pre-philosophic arts the emphasis is placed on the Arabs, in the section on philosophy it seems to shift to the Greeks. Alfarabi will later acknowledge that the philosophy existing among the Arabs has been imported from the Greeks (159.1, #156). But why does Alfarabi decline to designate Plato and Aristotle as Greek in this section, as he does so willingly in the *Attainment of Happiness*?[1]

The answer may lie again in the contrast that Alfarabi is determined to draw between transnational philosophy and the Umma. Plato and Aristotle were undoubtedly Greek, at least by birth, education, and language, but is their thought inherently Greek? Alfarabi's case is even more striking: was he even an Arab? Certainly not by his Transoxanian origins and mother tongue. Philosophy among the Arabs did not develop indigenously (BL 159.1, #156, cf. 153.10–11, #146). It was first transmitted from the Greeks in the far northwest, and then practiced by a stranger from the far northeast, all of whom converged in the great cosmopolitan city of Baghdad (cf. PR 87.115,

Ar. 100.9). No example illustrates more clearly the transnational character of philosophy than Alfarabi's own.

While religious authors such as Ḥātim al-Rāzī were asserting the superiority of the Arabic language and Umma, certain partisans of philosophy indulged in exaggerated praise of the Greeks. The notion that the Greeks were superior in certain kinds of wisdom had become a commonplace that was already present in al-Jāḥiẓ (al-Jāḥiẓ 1988, 206, 208). Yet praising pagans too openly for their wisdom could be dangerous. A debate between two of Alfarabi's contemporaries, Christian logician Abū Bishr Mattā and Muslim grammarian Abū Saʿīd al-Sīrāfī, is quite instructive in this regard.[2] Recorded by al-Tawḥīdī (al-Tawḥīdī, 1: 108–28), it reads less like a debate than a monologue, in which al-Sīrāfī chides Mattā in front of a sympathetic audience led by a vizier who is clearly on his side (al-Tawḥīdī, 108, 120; Mahdi 1970, 62, 77). Al-Sīrāfī wins decisively, but since Mattā barely gets a word in edgewise one cannot but suspect that there is more to his position than happened to be expressed in the written version of the debate. Moreover, the few statements put into Mattā's mouth seem so imprudent as to cast their authenticity into doubt. Most important, Mattā declares that the Greek Umma is superior by nature in wisdom and eagerness to attain it (al-Tawḥīdī, 1: 111–13, Mahdi 1970, 67–68). The outrageous claims attributed to Mattā, which must have been particularly offensive to the vast majority of Muslims and Arabs, indicate the suspicion in which the philosophers and their new-fangled Greek wisdom were often held. But Alfarabi, for his part, refrains from displaying too much reverence for the Greeks. He does not deny the Greek origins of philosophy, but in the *Attainment of Happiness* suggests that philosophy may have existed among earlier Ummas as well (AH 38.14–17, Ar. 88.54). He never maintains that the status of certain Greeks as the fountainhead of philosophy that now exists equally among the Arabs renders their Umma in any way superior to the others. The Greeks and Arabs, as Alfarabi takes pains to emphasize, both fall within the zone of "natural" Ummas demarcated in the *Great Book of Music* (BM 109).

Alfarabi does not deny the philosophic superiority of the Greeks for reasons of prudence alone. Even though Plato and Aristotle were philosophers, Alfarabi never suggests that the Greek Umma as a whole rose to their standard. The universality of philosophy and its absolute superiority to each and every Umma, as indicated so clearly in the *Book of Letters*, is a major reason why Alfarabi declines to join the debate about the relative merits of each Umma. No Umma's conventional language and traditions, however eloquent and refined, can ever measure up to the lofty standards of philosophy. In this respect, philosophy can serve as a moderating force, putting a damper on the fruitless and potentially violent debates about the merits of each Umma. Since philosophy is so evidently superior, the question rather becomes, why does Alfarabi examine the Umma and its language at all? What justifies Alfarabi's sudden leap down from the heights of philosophy to the Umma and its vulgar beginnings (BL 134.16, #114)?

The Umma, Philosophy, and the Development of the Soul

By juxtaposing an account of the development of the Umma to an account of the rise of philosophy, Alfarabi frames the middle section of the *Book of Letters* in such a way as to urge his readers to reflect on the relation between these two phenomena. While Alfarabi does not provide any detailed discussion of this issue, he offers two important hints. First, he proclaims the unqualified superiority of philosophy to the Umma, as we have seen in the previous section. Second, he argues that the Umma is prior to philosophy in time. Consider the following quotation:

> When the practical arts and the rest of the vulgar arts that we
> have mentioned have been developed, the souls desire afterward to
> know the causes of the things perceived on earth, both what is on
> it and what is around it, and the causes of the rest of what is
> perceived and manifested in the heavens, as well as knowledge of
> many of the things that the practical arts have invented, such as
> shapes, numbers, images in mirrors, colors, and other such
> things. And they come to investigate the reasons for these things.
> (BL 150.1–6, #140)

Alfarabi states quite clearly that the desire to pursue philosophy appears only after the vulgar arts "that we have mentioned" have been fully developed. In contrast, he never ascribes the cause of anything that forms part of the Umma and its vulgar arts to this desire.[3] He also does not designate any of these arts, with the exception of linguistics, as sciences (BL 148.15, #139). The word "desire" (Arabic root *sh-w-q*) does appear once in the discussion of linguistic science, through which "humans desire to preserve individual, articulate utterances, after they have preserved poems, speeches, and composite utterances" (145.2–3, #132). The passage merits comparison to the recently cited passage concerning the emergence of philosophy (150.1–6, #140), in which Alfarabi substitutes "souls" for "humans," and the desire to understand hitherto unknown causes of natural and artificial things for the desire to preserve existing, conventional things.[4] The desires that stimulate philosophy are by no means identical in kind to those that inform linguistic science. The desire to pursue philosophy does not manifest itself in the souls of humans until they have attained a certain state, which occurs only after the full development of the Umma and its arts. It is therefore necessary to examine the changes that the development of the Umma brings to the human soul, as a result of which the characteristically human desire for knowledge finally attains its mature form.

Humans are composed of body and soul, both of which are endowed by nature with certain inclinations that drive human development forward (see Langhade, 271). I have already shown how the organs of the body, most notably the tongue, are indispensable for the emergence of human speech, but I have not yet discussed the role of the soul. The soul's inclination for knowledge manifests itself as soon as there are humans, so that the first motions of the souls toward knowledge occur even before humans have begun to speak (BL 135.1–2, 8–9, #114–15). Unfortunately, these inchoate stirrings of human curiosity do not easily translate into a philosophical desire for knowledge of the causes of things. Alfarabi gives a suitably tentative and imprecise description of these longings: "the soul is moved to know or think or formulate or imagine or reflect prudently on everything for which nature has most forcefully prepared it" (135.8–9). It is a long, hard road over which humankind must pass, before the first speechless yearnings of the soul for knowledge can ripen into passionate and methodical philosophical inquiry.

An additional obstacle to the emergence of philosophy, stated most clearly in the *Philosophy of Aristotle*, is physical necessity, on account of which the earliest humans tend to restrict themselves to seeking knowledge of necessary corporeal things, while ignoring everything else (PA 59.5 ff,[5] Mahdi 2001, 203ff.). An underlying condition of the evolution described in the *Book of Letters* is therefore the gradual perfection of the practical arts that provide for bodily necessities (BL 138.15–17, #121, 150.3–5, #140). These arts are mentioned but hardly emphasized, as if they are merely preparatory to the development of the soul. By drawing our attention to the soul on numerous occasions, Alfarabi helps us trace its lengthy evolution toward philosophy.

The initial acquisition of language lends some concreteness to the al-most formless desires of the first human souls. The Ummas endowed with moderate natures now have an inclination "to intelligence and knowledge" (BL 138.17–18, #122). Although this inclination is surely more structured than the vague instincts of the prelinguistic stage of development, it does not yet entail a conscious desire for knowledge. It leads to linguistic improvements, but not yet philosophical inquiry. These souls are now "moved by their na-tures to seek that the utterances be ordered according to the order of their meanings, insofar as this is possible with regard to utterances" (139.2–3, #122). Alfarabi does not say here that either the utterances or the meanings must necessarily be ordered according to the natural beings perceived outside the soul, which would be the goal of logic or philosophy (62.11 ff.; ES 77 ff.). The desire for articulate expression is by no means identical to the desire for clear understanding: as Alfarabi's Plato discovers, there is no strong correla-tion between the customary names of things and their substances (PP 7.1–6). During this pre-philosophical stage of human development, the longing of souls for knowledge is eclipsed by the linguistic conventions that gradu-ally establish themselves within the soul no less than on the tongue (BL 141.16–142.4, #128, 146.5–10, #134). Human energies are engrossed by the im-provement of the language, the enrichment of the words it employs, and the refinement of the stories it tells. These activities are informed by a certain natural desire for order and symmetry, which manifests itself in elegant po-etry and meter (142.12–14, #129). But while humans are preoccupied by the ordering of merely conventional signs (143.14–144.11, #130, 145ff., #132 ff.), they have little interest in the study of nature. This epoch of human develop-ment culminates in linguistic science, which seals the linguistic conventions that have arisen in the soul with firm and generally applicable rules (147.16–18, #136). The Umma's movement away from nature toward convention is mir-rored in the human soul. With the completion of linguistic science, convention seems to have triumphed. But then, quite suddenly, philosophy appears. Herein lies the puzzle: how is it that philosophy, the fullest manifestation of the soul's natural desire for knowledge, finally breaks free only after the most resounding triumph of convention?

This question defies any easy answer, especially since Alfarabi doesn't provide one, at least not in the *Book of Letters*. He never argues that the per-fection of the arts of the Umma necessitates the emergence of philosophical investigation, in the way that the pursuit of dialectic and sophistry seems to lead its practitioners inexorably toward philosophy (BL 132.8–9, #110), but he does indicate that philosophy cannot emerge except after the completion of the arts of the Umma "that we have mentioned" (150.1–2, #140). The elusive connection between the arts of the Umma and the emergence of philosophy can be pieced together, but only with the help of some passages from Alfarabi's other works.

The Arts of the Umma and Their Contribution to Philosophy

The Umma described in the previous chapter flourishes by means of five linguistic arts. At first glance, it might seem that these arts have nothing at all to contribute to the development of philosophy. The first linguistic arts to develop in the Umma are rhetoric and poetry. Throughout the *Book of Letters*, these two arts are contrasted unfavorably with philosophy. From the point of view of philosophy, the litany of their shortcomings is daunting. They do not ask proper philosophical questions, but only such questions as are useful in telling stories. They cannot explain objects that are imperceptible to the senses. They use metaphors that have at best a tenuous connection to the things themselves (BL 224.20–225.13). Poetry and rhetoric emerge only after metaphor and imagery have enriched the simpler and more direct forms of expression that characterize an earlier stage of linguistic development (141.4–15, #127). But philosophy prefers the earlier forms of expression for their precision and clarity (164.8–165.15). Alfarabi's own style is, with very few exceptions, remarkably prosaic and unadorned. The poets, rhetoricians, and linguists, for their part, seem rather unconcerned with the natural things in heaven and on the earth, which Alfarabi mentions just before and just after his treatment of the linguistic arts, but never during it (138.9–11, #121, 150.1–10, #140).

Nonetheless, the rather uncurious attitude toward nature and its causes that prevails before the emergence of the linguistic arts can in no way be equated with the avid investigation of nature that flourishes after their completion. In the earlier period, humans are concerned above all with naming the natural things according to common opinion; in the later period, they are finally impelled to seek to understand the causes of the natural things (BL 138.9–11, #121; 150.1–10, #140). How do we account for this quantum leap in human curiosity? And what is the prevailing attitude toward nature in the intervening period, during which the language and literature of the Umma is constantly evolving?

The mythology of nations is frequently associated with stories about the origin of the world and the reasons for natural phenomena. But Alfarabi, at least in the *Book of Letters*, does not emphasize this connection. His statements about the content of the early stories of the Umma are vague, or at best mildly suggestive: "Over a length of time, events occur which require rhetorical speeches or parts of speeches" (BL 142.8–9, #129). Whatever these events may be, rhetoric and then poetry emerge in order to describe them. The new sages of the Umma "recount in [these rhetorical speeches and poems] reports about past and present matters of which they have need" (143.1–2, #130). Now poetry and rhetoric do more than merely recount the events themselves: rhetoric makes extensive use of metaphor, while poetry employs images (141.4–15, #127; 142.6–14, #129). But it isn't easy to discern, on the basis of such terse and enigmatic descriptions, the character of these stories. Moreover, the first philosophers appear to ignore them, focusing instead on natural things and the products of the mechanical arts (150.1–5, #140).

It may be appropriate here to seek some help from Alfarabi's teacher Aristotle. A very famous passage in the *Metaphysics*, with which Alfarabi would most likely have been familiar, argues that humans first turned to philosophy after wondering about the heavenly bodies and the no less perplexing mythological accounts of them. Aristotle even goes so far as to equate the philosopher with the lover of myth (*Metaphysics* 982b13–20).[6] Alfarabi's own presentation of Aristotle may contain an oblique reference to this passage. Alfarabi's Aristotle examines the state of humans in his own time and describes the objects of philosophical desire:

> Then he found out that . . . the soul desires to understand the
> causes of sensible things, of what is observed in the heavens and
> on earth, and of what man sees in his own soul and the state in
> which he finds it. He desires to know the truth of what insinuates
> itself into souls and comes to the mind, be it a thing that insinu-
> ates itself into a man's own soul or a thing that has insinuated
> itself into the soul of someone who has informed him of it.
> (PA 60.1–5, trans. Mahdi)

There is considerable overlap between this passage and its counterpart in the *Book of Letters* (BL 150.2–6), especially with regard to the human desire to know the causes of the things in heaven and on earth. However, Alfarabi's Aristotle has expanded the scope of the human desire for understanding to the causes of the things that have insinuated[7] themselves into our souls, often by virtue of being heard from others. Is it hasty to infer that these insinuations consist of stories, told in a rhetorical or poetic mode, some of which describe the origins and causes of natural things? This assumption seems particularly plausible in view of the fact that Alfarabi's Aristotle also observes among humans a love of hearing and memorizing "histories of Ummas" (*akhbār al-umam*)[8] and poems, since these activities give pleasure and repose. In the same passage Alfarabi employs twice the term *khurāfāt*, translated by Mahdi as "myths," and equates them with both histories and poems (PA 61.12–18); this word never occurs in the *Book of Letters* (cf. BL 143.1–5).[9] The implication is that humans who desire knowledge must seek to know the truth about the uneasy relationship between the legends of their people that have become present in their souls, and what they themselves observe on heaven and earth. In comparison to these observations from the *Philosophy of Aristotle*, the brief indications of the content of the Umma's stories in the *Book of Letters* frustrate by their reticence. They downplay the legendary character of the Umma's stories as well as the inspiration they provide to the earliest philosophers. On this point, Alfarabi is willing to speak frankly only in Aristotle's name. The reasons behind his reticence will become clearer, I hope, when we turn to the question of the origin of religion in Chapter 4.

The evolution of humankind's orientation toward nature in the *Book of Letters* could be summarized as follows. The primordial human encounter with the natural things was mediated only by the natural faculties of the soul. It resulted in the naming of the natural things according to common opinion. These names gave some form and precision to the inchoate longings of the soul toward knowledge. Their immediate effect, however, was to inaugurate a prolonged engagement with the conventional arts of language and the Umma. This preoccupation caused humans to lose interest in their natural experience of things. The recovery of this natural interest through the emergence of philosophy occurred in response both to the natural human experience of things and to the stories about them that had been told and passed down by the Umma. It was both the inadequacy of the legendary accounts and the inherent interest of their subjects that eventually induced the first philosophers to begin their investigations.

Alfarabi attributes the emergence of philosophy not only to these stories, but also to all the other "vulgar arts that we have mentioned" (BL 150.1.2,

#140). If we may subsume both poetry and memorization of it under the aegis of those stories, the three remaining arts of the Umma are rhetoric, writing, and linguistic science (148.14–16, #138). All these arts play a useful role in Plato's investigations in the *Philosophy of Plato* (PP 7.1–8.6, 17.2–7), and evidence of their importance in the development of philosophy can also be found in the *Book of Letters* itself.

Rhetoric has the most direct relation to the development of philosophy, as indicated in both the *Book of Letters* and the *Book of Rhetoric*. The first philosophers begin to verify the opinions in their souls by employing rhetorical methods of discussion and persuasion (BL 150.11–15, #141). Even though these methods, which are entirely subservient to common speech and understanding, eventually prove inadequate (BL 150.14–16, #141, cf. 123.1–15, BRh 41.15–43.2), they pave the way for the more sophisticated methods of dialectic, sophistry, and demonstration (BL 150.15–151.15, BRh 55.5–17).

Writing and linguistic science are no less indispensable for the pursuit of philosophy. Alfarabi's account of the invention of writing as a means to compensate for the deficiencies of memory is, as Langhade has pointed out, reminiscent of Socrates's speech about writing in the *Phaedrus* (BL 141.11–19, #144; Langhade, 240–41). Alfarabi's awareness of that speech is evident in the *Philosophy of Plato*, where he reports in a passage attributed to the *Phaedrus* that Plato regarded the method of writing as inferior in certain respects to direct, oral instruction (PP 16.7–8). Given that this remark itself comes transcribed in writing, it is surely suffused with irony. Even Alfarabi's Plato acknowledges that writing sometimes succeeds where conversation fails (16.5–6). In the *Book of Letters*, Alfarabi mentions two great advantages of writing while ignoring whatever defects it might have. It provides a corrective for the unreliability of memory, which becomes ever more noticeable as the volume of oral material accumulates, and it allows this material to be transmitted to people living far away across both space and time (BL 144.12–19, #141). These increased powers of memory and communication play a vital role in the development of philosophy. Alfarabi emphasizes how much debate and argument must take place before philosophy can advance beyond the rhetorical stage (150.11 ff., #141, BRh 55.10–11). It is hard to imagine the occurrence of so vibrant and continuous an exchange of views without writing. As Alfarabi observes in the *Book of Dialectic*, philosophic inquiry progresses by means of the exchange of opinions in both writing and speech (BDi 25.13–16).

The perfection of writing paves the way for linguistic science (BL 145.1 ff., #132). Linguistic science is propelled by a desire not for knowledge but for the preservation of the existing store of language. It therefore follows closely the conventions of a given language, and belongs entirely to a given Umma. In the *Enumeration of the Sciences*, Alfarabi suggests that there are potentially as many linguistic sciences as there are Ummas (ES 57; cf. Mahdi 2001, 71–72, 90). Yet linguistic science remains the only one of the five arts of the Umma to be called a science in the *Book of Letters* (BL 148.14–16, #138). It does indeed share some important similarities with philosophy. Within the limits imposed by its conventional character, linguistic science attains a rigor and precision altogether lacking in the earlier arts of poetry and rhetoric.

It is the only pre-philosophic art or science that is concerned with giving causes (*'ilal*, BL 148.8, #137). The investigation of causes is the activity that sets philosophy in motion (150.6, #140). Even though the conventional and arbitrary causes given by linguistic science are not identical to the natural causes investigated by philosophy, the two activities do share a concern with the orderly, predictable arrangement of their subject matter. Linguistic science is therefore the first of the arts that establishes and follows clearly defined rules (*qawānīn*) in analyzing its subject matter (147.17, #136). The earlier language experts seek order (*tartīb, niẓām*) with regard to the timing and flow of poetic utterances (142.13–15), as well as words that accurately signify the meanings within the soul (144.4–5), but they do not elaborate clear and precise rules in the manner of linguistic science. In the *Enumeration of the Sciences*, five of the seven parts of linguistic science deal with the rules of language, while only two parts deal with pure memorization of utterances (ES 59 ff.). That same work emphasizes how important rules are in the correct and orderly practice of all the arts (57). Once such rules have been clearly elaborated, the task of learning and instruction (*ta'līm wa ta'līm*) is greatly simplified (BL 147.18, #136, 148.8, #137). The same emphasis on *ta'līm wa ta'līm* recurs in the ensuing account of philosophy (152.1–2, #143). It follows that the rigorous methods and rules of linguistic science, having established themselves firmly in the soul (147.16, #136), will serve humans well when they finally turn to rhetoric, dialectic, and other logical arts (150.11 ff., #141). Philosophy applies to the investigation of nature many of the same techniques that linguistic science developed for classifying conventional speech.

The comparison between linguistic science and logic is frequent in Alfarabi's logical works: logic corrects and clarifies the rules for the intelligibles in the mind just as linguistic science corrects and clarifies the rules for words (ES 79; FL 55–56). At the end of a short work titled *The Epistle Indicating the Way to Happiness*, Alfarabi argues that no one can begin to study logic without acquiring a certain grounding in the science of language and its utterances (EH 236–37). By giving linguistic science its due, Alfarabi rejects yet another outrageous statement attributed to Abū Bishr Mattā, who extolled logic and Greek wisdom while scorning Arabic linguistic science: deeming the latter unnecessary for the practice of the former, Mattā publicly refused to learn it (al-Tawḥīdī, 1: 114, Mahdi 1970, 71). Alfarabi, in contrast, is said to have made great efforts to master Arabic grammar and linguistic science under the renowned philologist Ibn al-Sarrāj (Mahdi 1971, 523).

To conclude, all the arts of the Umma play an important role in the emergence of philosophy. Poetry is indispensable for the stimulation of the desire for philosophy, while the other arts and sciences of the Umma are indispensable for its rigorous practice and development.

Philosophy Across the Ummas

The Umma and its arts set the stage for the emergence of philosophy. With the accomplishment of this purpose, the Umma appears to lose its most important role. Is the Umma anything more than a transient, or perhaps transitional, phase of human development? Does the Umma exist only for the sake of philosophy, in which case it culminates by transcending itself? What is the Umma's status after the emergence and final perfection of philosophy?

Alfarabi begins to answer these questions in the *Book of Letters*. Having ascended from the Umma to philosophy, he proceeds to gradually return to the Umma. He explains that the perfection of philosophy ought to be followed by a legislator[10] who renders its truths in a form intelligible to the multitude. The legislation derived from philosophy does not at first glance seem intrinsically bound to any one Umma or place (BL 152.7 ff., #144). Yet insofar as this legislator needs to make use of poetic and rhetorical modes of persuasion (152.4, #143, 152.9–13, #144, 153.9, #145), he would have to pay attention to the poetic and rhetorical arts of any particular Umma for which he happens to legislate. Alfarabi concludes his discussion of philosophy and philosophic legislation with an even more explicit return to the Umma, reminding his readers that "This is the order in which the syllogistic arts arise in the Ummas" (153.10, #146). Since the "syllogistic arts" include everything from rhetoric to demonstrative philosophy, Alfarabi now gives the impression that the Umma, which has not been explicitly mentioned since page 148 (#138), has somehow remained present all along, even in the account of the development of dialectical and philosophical investigation. Sure enough, this comment provides a transition to a section in which the Umma returns as a central theme (154.14 ff., #148).[11]

"Philosophy should rule, but what then?" would be an apt summary of one of Alfarabi's most characteristic teachings. However loudly and repeatedly he may proclaim the superiority of philosophy to all other human endeavors, he never forgets that such drumbeating for his most cherished activity is in fact the easy part. The *Book of Letters* illustrates this general pattern quite well. After a brief introduction neatly elevating philosophy above religion, jurisprudence, and *kalām*, Alfarabi feels compelled to give a lengthier and far more colorful description of the Umma. This was necessary, I have suggested, because the origins and preconditions of the philosophical enterprise can be understood only through the Umma. Now, however, another reason for the emphasis on the Umma begins to appear: the absolute transcendence of philosophy over the Umma exists only in speech. The perfection of philosophy does not annul the natural and customary causes that give rise to multiple Ummas. The Umma may be partially eclipsed by the emergence of philosophy, but it does not cease to count. One cannot appreciate the repeated references to the Umma in all Alfarabi's major political works without reflecting upon its uneasy coexistence with philosophy. All humans, including Alfarabi's potential disciples, remain decisively shaped by the particular Ummas to which they belong, and philosophy cannot but acknowledge this fact. Indeed, each philosopher must choose to express his most universal thoughts in the particular language of a given Umma. The qualities of this Umma are bound to vary enormously, as philosophy passes across space and time from one community to another (AH 38.14–18, Ar. 88.54). The adaptation of philosophical idiom to the language of each Umma thus emerges as a crucial theme in Alfarabi's work.

The importance of this theme follows from Alfarabi's historical circumstances. Alfarabi was the beneficiary of the translation movement of the Abbasid period, during which a large number of Greek scientific works were translated into Arabic. Dimitri Gutas's work on the subject therefore provides important background to the study of Alfarabi. Gutas emphasizes how much of the translation and recovery of the Greek tradition was in fact motivated by political, religious, and ideological concerns. For example, the Abbasid Caliph al-Manṣūr wished to please the Zoroastrians, still a large proportion of the population at that time, who claimed the Greek texts as their own (Gutas 1998b, 34–45). Al-Manṣūr's successor, al-Ma'mūn, was a sworn enemy of the Byzantines. He wished to prove that the Muslims rather than the Christianized Greeks were the true heirs to the ancient Greek sciences (83–95). Gutas even presents Alfarabi as a supporter of the latter point of view, by citing an apocryphal summary of a lost writing on the transmission of the sciences (90, 95). Having elucidated the various partisan motivations behind the translation movement very thoroughly, Gutas nevertheless acknowledges that Alfarabi and many of the writers involved in the translation movement, as distinguished from their royal patrons, "did believe in the primacy of reason" (104). Just as Alfarabi never ascribes particular qualities to particular Ummas, so he never mentions particular rulers, religious sects, or ideologies. Alfarabi's account exemplifies this interest in unfettered reason and philosophy, and a corresponding disinterest in any other motivations.

A major challenge faced by the burgeoning Arabic-speaking philosophical community was the need to develop an adequate philosophical vocabulary in their language, so that Greek works could be translated and Arabic works composed. Alfarabi argues in the first section of the *Book of Letters* that such a vocabulary can be invented for any language. One needs merely to employ the method first developed by linguistic science, through which technical terms are devised from the stock of everyday meanings (cf. BL 147.18–148.6, #136). Alfarabi gives some striking examples. The Arabic term that signifies substance is *jawhar*. It has two philosophical meanings: substance as such and substance of something. Both are clearly derived from everyday meanings. Substance as such is derived from the meaning of *jawhar* as precious stone: precious stones are the most solid and valuable thing among the multitude, just as substance is the most solid and valuable thing among the philosophers (97.20–98.9, 101.13–102.7). Substance of something is derived from the meaning of *jawhar* as ancestry or moral character. Ancestry is the most important characteristic of a human for the multitude, just as substance is the most important characteristic of a thing for the philosopher (98.10–99.12, 102.11–17).[12] It follows that inventing a term for substance should be possible in any language, assuming it has words for things that are solid and valuable, or words for qualities characteristic of a given thing. Along similar lines, inventing a word for "accident" should pose no difficulty so long as the language has words for things that are transient: Arabic, for example, has the term *'arḍ* (95.4–96.2). It is rather hard to imagine any sophisticated language that does not meet these standards.

Alfarabi's lengthier account of the invention of a term for "being" in Arabic serves to confirm this impression. Unlike languages such as Persian or Greek, Arabic does not originally have a copula, that is, an expression meaning "to be" unaccompanied by past, present, or future tense (BL 110.9–111.21). This characteristic of Arabic appears to be linked to its peculiar verb system, according to which "actions take place either in the past or in the future and . . . the present tense per se does not exist" (Abed, 128–29). The absence of the copula risks impeding the development of logic and the theoretical sciences, which require its use (BL 112.1–3). This serious deficiency in prephilosophic Arabic might appear to serve as a textbook example of how the limitations of the language of a given Umma pose an obstacle to the development of philosophy. Yet Alfarabi expounds two easy solutions to this difficulty: one involves using the personal pronoun "he" as a copula, and another involves using the passive form of the verb meaning "to find." In response to those who dispute the efficacy of either of these solutions, Alfarabi replies in the first person: "I am of the opinion that it is up to every human to use whichever he wants," provided that certain precautions are taken to ensure that the word is properly understood (114.20–115.12).[13] In the worst-case scenario, there might not exist a word in a given language suitable for transformation into a technical term that expresses a given philosophical meaning. Even this possibility does not really perturb Alfarabi. Having assured us that it "almost never happens," he nevertheless proposes the remedy of rewriting the foreign word in the letters of the new language (158.12–17, #155), as was done for the word "element" (*isṭaqis*) in Arabic, a rough transliteration of the Greek *stoicheion*. Alfarabi repeats that cases of this sort are quite rare (159.7, #156).

None of Alfarabi's examples seem to suggest any insuperable obstacles toward developing a new philosophical vocabulary within a given Umma, presuming that a group of philosophers has discovered a need for such vocabulary. The conventional character of the rules and utterances of language is never so perverse as to foil the desire to pursue logic and philosophy, once it has finally appeared. The philosophers can overcome such conventional problems by playing with the conventional rules, which, unlike certain grammarians, they do not regard as sacred (Abed, 128–30). It is a tribute to Alfarabi's foresight that his list of easily translatable words encompasses many of the technical terms that still form part of philosophical vocabulary today. "Accident," "substance," "essence," "being," "element," and "matter" (BL 95.3, 97.19, 110.8, 159.3–6, #156) retain both technical and ordinary meanings in English and other contemporary languages. These philosophical terms are relatively easy to transfer from language to language because their meanings do not vary according to historical context.[14] Yet the examples given by Alfarabi are highly technical, and therefore limited in scope. The meanings of logical and philosophical terms may not have changed, but the audience to whom they must be addressed has shifted dramatically. This affects how philosophy should be presented. Despite Alfarabi's forthright declaration, at the end of the *Attainment of Happiness*, that the philosophy of Aristotle is true (AH 46.12–47.11, Ar. 96.64–98.88), he acknowledges in other places that much of Aristotle's work needs to be rewritten.

In the *Short Book of the Syllogism*, Alfarabi decries the futility of attempting to teach logic among his contemporaries only through Aristotle, or even of writing new works that employ Aristotle's examples, many of which have long since become impossible to understand. Alfarabi blames foolhardy efforts of this sort for discrediting Aristotle as well as logic among many of his contemporaries, and recommends replacing all the Greek examples adduced by Aristotle with Arabic examples suited to his own language, place, and time (SS 68.15–70.5). The term "custom" (*'āda*) and its cognates occur frequently in this passage. If it were merely a question of linguistic custom of the sort described in the *Book of Letters*, then language could easily adjust by inventing new terms or reinterpreting old ones. But custom extends beyond language, and linguistic custom frequently reflects other customs that are deeply rooted in a given society. Alfarabi speaks both of the "customs of the speakers of this language" and the "customs of the inhabitants of this country" (SS 69.1–2). Certain concepts can be expressed easily in one language because they are familiar (*mashhūr*) to its speakers, but not at all in another language because its speakers have no notion of them (69.2). No matter how adroitly linguists attempt to coin these terms, they could never do so in a way that the majority of the speakers of the language would understand. It follows that many of Aristotle's works and examples will not be adequately understood by most Arabic learners of logic (SS 69.3–4, BD 85.22–86.1).

In the *Book of Demonstration*, Alfarabi makes the similar point, but also explains in greater detail the reasons for it. In a thinly veiled reference to revealed religion, Alfarabi observes that the rulers have instilled a new set of practical and theoretical opinions among the people, greatly affecting the kinds of things that they can imagine (BD 85.11–18). Alfarabi never suggests that Aristotle prophesied the establishment of this religion, but does maintain that Aristotle foresaw inevitable political changes that would render parts of his work obsolete (86.21–22). Since change across space and time is inevitable, Aristotle can hardly be blamed for the use of so many dated examples. On the contrary, it was precisely as a competent philosopher that Aristotle chose examples suitable to his time, and therefore unsuitable to Alfarabi's. Moreover, since Aristotle himself understood that his examples reflected the needs of his audience rather than the deepest content of his thought, their obsolescence does not entail the obsolescence of his philosophy (BD 86.19–24, SS 69.8–16).[15] It remains for Alfarabi or any other future philosopher to examine the opinions of his own time and choose examples suitable to it. But this is easier said than done. The prevailing opinions of a given time can hardly be reduced to a single doctrine, religion, or school. Every group, sect, and individual within a given society is bound to have his own, unique outlook (BD 85.1–11). Before speaking or writing, the philosopher must somehow assess the varied opinions of his intended audience. Even if, following Rémi Brague, we accept that the philosophic fish has remained the same (Brague 1996, 95), that does not make it any less slippery for the philosopher.[16]

Alfarabi places great emphasis on the changes in religion, language, and politics that have occurred since the time of Aristotle. We may therefore wonder whether he believes that Greek vocabulary in these domains can be readily transferred into Arabic. Alfarabi says relatively little about the transfer of this kind of vocabulary from Umma to Umma. He does speak briefly in the *Book of Letters* of the transfer of religious vocabulary, but suggests that the rules governing it will be extremely lax. The founder of the religion may invent whatever words he pleases, or else take terms at will from previous domestic religions or even foreign religions (BL 157.7–14, #154). There is no guarantee whatsoever that religious terms will retain their old meanings. Since religions are bound to differ from Umma to Umma (PR 74–75.90, Ar. 85.17–86.2),[17] perhaps they have no need to do so.

The transfer of rhetoric and poetry from one Umma to another, in contrast, is not mentioned in any of Alfarabi's extant works. In his *Epistle on the Canons of Poetry*, he contrasts the well-trodden paths of Arabic and Persian poetry with the more mysterious procedures of Greek poetry, leaving the impression that the former do not have that much in common with the latter

(EP 275, Ar. 269). It is difficult to believe that the rich web of poetic metaphors and associations that have evolved in one language can be easily reproduced in another (BL 140.8–141.15, #124–27). Modern scholarship confirms
that Greek poetry was virtually unknown among the Arabs. Gutas's list of
material translated into Arabic from Greek includes very little poetry (Gutas
1998b, 193–96). In a brief article on Homer and his presence in Baghdad,
G. Strohmaier argues that even though the great translator Ḥunayn Ibn Isḥāq
seems to have had direct cognizance of Homer, he translated and commented
upon only those verses that appeared in Galen's works, so that Homer was
afterward "not unknown . . . but foreign in the Islamic world" (Strohmaier,
200). The Arab scholar Iḥsān ʿAbbās confirms that Homer was translated
partially into Syriac but not at all into Arabic, so that only a highly unreliable collection of verses and proverbs attributed to Homer was available to
the Arabs (ʿAbbās, 39 ff.). Alfarabi does make scattered references to Homer,
about whom he would have learned, at the very least, from reading Plato, but
he never shows any actual familiarity with his poems (SP 172; SL 165.9, Ar.
146). In the *Book of Letters*, he points wryly to the fate of Homer in his time
by citing the statement "Homer is a poet" as a sound example of the copula
in a statement that is true but "does not now have an essence outside of the
soul" (BL 125.18–20). The nontransferability of poetry from one Umma to
another ensures that the core of the Umma will remain intact and inalienable even if some of its members turn to philosophy. The Arabs and Persians who translated and studied as much of Greek philosophy as they could
get their hands on perpetuated their own poetic traditions.[18]

As for the transfer of political vocabulary, Alfarabi does not discuss it
directly. However, certain inferences can be made from his own example.
Alfarabi does far more than merely transcribe or translate the political vocabulary of ancient Greece. The term Umma is a case in point: as I will prove
conclusively in the next chapter, it is more firmly rooted in the Arabic and
Islamic tradition than in the thought of ancient Greece. Other examples of
Arabic terms used liberally by Alfarabi that have no clear equivalents in ancient Greek include *imām*, meaning "model or leader"; *sharīʿa*, meaning "revealed law"; and *milla*, meaning "revealed religion." I will have occasion to
discuss these examples at great length in the rest of the book, as I examine
how Alfarabi restates classical political philosophy in order to make sense of
his own world.

To sum up: in the *Book of Demonstration*, Alfarabi lists several obstacles
to the transmission of Aristotelian philosophy into a new language and set-

ting. In the *Book of Letters*, he shows that these difficulties can easily be surmounted so long as they remain purely linguistic. Language is sufficiently rich and versatile to invent new terms, so long as their meanings, such as being, substance, accident, and so on, have not fundamentally changed. The challenges posed by other vicissitudes mentioned in the *Book of Demonstration*, such as a change in opinions and governments, are not so easily overcome. The meanings related to politics, religion, and culture are more deeply rooted in a given human situation. Furthermore, the terms that signify them in any given language have in many cases already been prescribed by pre-philosophic tradition. In this case, it is necessary for philosophers to have recourse to the unique, traditional vocabulary of their language while reflecting more deeply on their meaning. This, as will soon be shown in greater detail, is Alfarabi's approach to the term Umma.

In the *Book of Letters*, Alfarabi gives a splendid description of the Umma and its arts. He shows how philosophy, which comes into being only after the perfection of these arts, eventually transcends their vulgar and particular character. However, since philosophy cannot annul or overcome the differences between the various Ummas, its flourishing depends on its ability to adapt itself to the peculiar situation of each Umma, language, and epoch. Yet our discussion of these vicissitudes has barely begun. There is another kind of Umma, stricter in its laws, loftier in its doctrines, broader in its scope, and completely unknown to Plato and Aristotle. The rise of the Islamic Umma three centuries before Alfarabi's time poses a different set of problems that will be explored in the next two chapters.

Chapter 4

Another Kind of Umma: The Origin of the Islamic Umma

In the previous two chapters, I have examined the Umma as Alfarabi presents it in certain passages in the *Book of Letters* and *Political Regime*. In these passages, the Umma emerges as a civilization defined primarily by common language and literature. This definition of the Umma was hardly invented by Alfarabi: as we have seen, authors such as al-Jāḥiẓ and al-Tawḥīdī employed the term in a similar sense. But Alfarabi's treatment is deeper, with regard to both the character of the Umma's civilization and the question of its relationship with philosophy, and more strongly fortified against the temptation of ethnic bigotry. My interpretation thus far, however, has ignored another meaning of Umma, established by the Qur'ān and Islamic tradition. By Alfarabi's time, the term Umma had come to signify the entire Islamic religious community, and continues to do so today. This extremely common term is as familiar to Muslims as the term Church would be to Catholics, and has even become somewhat familiar to non-Muslims, as debates about the future of Islam percolate into the outside world, and groups like ISIS and Al-Qaeda commit acts of savage violence in the Umma's name.[1]

In order to render both these meanings into English, one might translate Umma as "community." I do not mean to contradict my earlier translation of Umma as "civilization," but to indicate that this equivocal term requires different English translations in different contexts. In this particular context, Umma signifies the two kinds of large-scale community that have historically been most prevalent in the Islamic world: the ethnic nation and the Islamic religion. It is easy to see how these two notions of community could come into conflict. The Islamic religious community consists of both one Umma and many, depending on how you define the term.

It is inconceivable that Alfarabi could have been simply ignorant of the religious meaning of Umma. But most scholars seem to think that he at least feigns ignorance of it. According to Ahmad Dallal, Alfarabi "suggested a distinction between religious forms of human association, of 'millah' and sociopolitical forms, termed 'ummah'" (Dallal, 269). Ilai Alon reaches a similar conclusion: "Alfarabi's use of the term 'community' (Umma) has no Islamic connotation whatsoever" (Alon, 12). Finally, Nāṣif Naṣṣār says that "in Alfarabi's philosophy, the concept of Umma is completely distinguished from the concept of religion" (*milla*, Naṣṣār 1978, 50–51). This interpretation appears to have a high degree of plausibility, insofar as Alfarabi never explicitly identifies the Umma with any kind of religious community.[2] But I contend that Alfarabi does allude to the religious Umma, in a subtle but highly revealing manner. The Muslim Umma may never be openly proclaimed in his work, but it is often present, especially in the *Book of Religion* and hitherto undiscussed parts of the *Book of Letters*. Just as Alfarabi gives an account of the origin of the ethnic Umma in the *Book of Letters*, so he traces the origin of the Islamic Umma in the *Book of Religion*. Alfarabi is well aware of the sensitive nature of the subject, so he avoids mentioning Islam by presenting his arguments in terms of the origin of religion in general. Even if Alfarabi's account pertains not merely to Islam, but to religion as such, it should certainly be applied to that particular faith. Since Alfarabi's own principle dictates that an author should cite mainly the examples most familiar to his readers (cf. SS 69.8–16, BD 85.6–11), his deceptively general accounts of religion may be presumed to have Islam in mind. The purpose of the following two chapters is to explore how Alfarabi understands the Islamic Umma, and its relationship to the ethnic Ummas with which it coexists.

The source of the tension between the two kinds of Umma long predates Alfarabi; indeed, it is already visible in the Qur'ān. The ambiguous understanding of the Umma presented by the Muslim holy book, and soon developed by its exegetes, already contains the germ of the dilemma that Alfarabi strives to resolve. Let us begin by examining the meaning of Umma in the Qur'ān and Islamic tradition, with the aim of bringing our particular problem into focus.

The Umma in the Qur'ān

The term Umma eventually came to signify the Islamic religious community as such. Although this meaning of Umma is already present in the Qur'ān, the usage of the term in the Muslim holy book, in which it appears dozens of times, is not nearly so precise or consistent. The great commentator al-Ṭabarī (d. 923), who lived only a generation before Alfarabi and amassed an impressive collection of exegetical material, singles out the term Umma as equivocal and lists four meanings: a group of people, a period of time, an obedient man, and a religion (al-Ṭabarī, 1: 221, commentary on Qur'ān 2.1). Other classical and modern commentators have agreed that the term is equivocal.[3]

My purpose here is not to provide a comprehensive account, philological or even semantic, of all the references to the Umma in the Qur'ān. For one thing, certain scholars have already done so. An article by F. M. Denny, devoted entirely to the term Umma as it appears in the Qur'ān, is especially thorough and useful. It attempts to classify, historically and semantically, every occurrence of the term, and the reader desiring a more comprehensive treatment is referred to this article (Denny 1975).[4] I wish to concentrate primarily on the tensions between the use of the term Umma in designating a group of any kind and its use in signifying the uniqueness of the Muslim community. This is the weightiest social, political, and religious question posed by the various meanings of Umma, and one that will be thoroughly explored by Alfarabi.

Denny has followed a long line of scholars in attributing this difference in meaning at least partly to chronology: while the general definition of Umma is prevalent in the earlier stages of the Qur'ānic revelation, the attribution of Umma to the Islamic community as such occurs only in the final Medinan period.[5] This evolution in meaning is hardly astonishing, in light of the dramatic rise in Muhammad's fortunes in the years between the earlier revelations of the 610s and later revelations of the 620s and early 630s. In the earlier period, when Muhammad and his few followers faced heavy persecution in their native Mecca, the prophet was preoccupied with, and disappointed by, the chaotic diversity of groups, tribes, and sects, as well as his failure to win over his own tribe, the Quraysh. In the later period, when Muhammad had become head of the burgeoning Muslim community of Medina, he was increasingly able to subdue Mecca, unify Arabia, and look ahead to the conquests that beckoned in Persia and Byzantium. Only then could he begin to preach the idea of a final religious community, with the hope of eventually unifying humankind.[6]

The passages identified with the Meccan period state that a prophet was sent to every Umma (Qur'ān 16.36, 35.24). Unfortunately, all these Ummas disbelieved the prophet that was sent to them (40.5, 35.25, 23.44). Yet they will face their just recompense, suffering both destruction in this world (7.34, 15.4–5, 23.40–43) and doom on the Day of Judgment, when a witness will be summoned against every Umma that disbelieved (16.84, 16.89, 28.75). These passages give the impression that Muhammad expected his own Umma to continue to reject him as implacably as the ill-fated peoples of the past, such as the 'Ād, Thamūd, and people of Nūḥ, had rejected their prophets, and that true vindication would come to him only on the Day of Judgment. Umma in these passages means simply but somewhat vaguely a distinct human community. This community may be defined by space, or even by time, so that in some passages Umma seems to mean "generation" or "period of time" (2.134, 11.8, 12.45). In most of these passages, Umma does not differ greatly in meaning from the even more common Qur'ānic term *qawm*, a generic term for "group" that appears hundreds of times and frequently designates the doomed peoples mentioned above (14.9, 15.5, cf. 23.23–24 with 23.43).[7] The concept of the Muslim Umma, with its peculiar character, has yet to be formulated (cf. Denny 1975, 54–55; 1977, 42–43).

However, several later passages, which scholars unanimously attribute to the Medinan period,[8] express the unique mission of the Islamic community. They are among the most eloquent statements in the Qur'ān, and deserve to be quoted in full:

[Ibrāhīm and Ismā'īl said,] "O Lord, make us Muslims, submissive[9] to You, and from our descendants a Muslim Umma, submissive to You." (2.128)

"We have made you (pl.) a central (*wasaṭ*) Umma, so that you may be witnesses over humankind, and the prophet a witness over you." (2.143)

"You (pl.) are the best Umma produced for humankind, commanding good, forbidding evil, and believing in Allah." (3.110)

There is an enormous difference between the self-contained and frequently impious Ummas that dominate in the earlier portions of the Qur'ān, and this newly minted Muslim Umma, entrusted with a mission for all humankind.

The shift to this Umma, although dramatic, is not without its harbingers. For one thing, the Qur'ān suggests that elements of the unified, pious Umma have existed since the origins of the human race: "What was humankind but one Umma, who then came to differ" (10.19, cf. 2.213). Although the early commentators disagree about the duration of this primordial unity, all agree that it pertained to religion (al-Ṭabarī, 4: 275–77). The disunity with which humankind was later afflicted did not entirely eliminate piety, which endured in the person of various prophets and their followers: "This Umma of yours (pl.) is a single Umma, and I am your Lord, so worship me" (Qur'ān 21.92, 23.52). Both occurrences of this statement immediately follow a list of the exploits of several prophets scattered throughout the ages and across many peoples, to which the demonstrative "this" clearly refers (23.51). Ibrāhīm himself is called "an Umma, obedient to Allah" (16.120). This verse, which attributes to a single, obedient man a term normally used to signify a group, has often puzzled commentators, both classical and modern (Denny 1975, 38–39), but it seems to accord somehow with the idea that the prophets and the righteous, of whom Ibrāhīm was the greatest progenitor, form a single Umma. A certain Umma from among the pre-Islamic People of the Book, a title commonly identified with the Jews and Christians, is praised in exactly the same terms as "the best Umma produced for humankind": it "believes in Allah . . . commands good and forbids evil" (3.113–14, cf. 3.110). Yet the People of the Book taken as a whole is never called an Umma, but rather a *qawm*, from which the pious Umma within them is clearly set apart (2.134, 2.141, 7.159: cf. 7.168, 5.66). The disparaging statements about every Umma disobeying its prophet, in whose context *qawm Nūḥ* is cited (40.5), do not apply universally to the Christians and Jews, since an Umma of them listened to their prophets and thereby became the predecessors of the Muslim Umma. Promised to the descendants of Ibrāhīm (2.128), this Umma culminates in Muhammad. The Muslim Umma is therefore not simply a new phenomenon but rather a crystallization of an old phenomenon. The spirit of piety and obedience that for much of human history has existed only in isolated prophets and small Ummas scattered among largely disobedient peoples must now accrue to a large Umma. The best among humankind and a witness over them, this Umma's mission is in principle universal.[10] It aims to gradually recover, in an entirely new setting, the primordial religious unity of humankind.

There is another link between the two major uses of Umma as well. Even when the term Umma refers to particular, pre-Islamic peoples, it often has pronounced religious undertones. The Ummas that rejected their prophets are characterized above all by unbelief (23.44, 40.5, 43.22–23, cf. Denny 1975, 58). The few instances of the term that signify a group having no religious leaning whatsoever are comparatively insignificant (cf. 6.38, 28.23). As Rudi Paret observes, the Umma refers to "ethnical, linguistic, or religious bodies of people . . . but always with the implication that these creatures are to be included in the divine scheme of salvation and are liable to judgment" (Paret, 1015). Although Paret and Denny are right to ascribe an ethnic as well as a religious meaning to the term Umma, it is noteworthy how little the former sense is examined or developed in the Qur'ān.

There are a few Qur'ānic passages that mention physical and cultural differences between peoples. But none of them employ the term Umma. The following verse is especially revealing in this respect: "Among His signs are the creation of heaven and earth, and the differences in your languages and colors: these are indeed signs for those who know" (30.22). The very same natural and conventional traits that constitute the Umma for Alfarabi, namely, physical appearance and language, are understood by the Qur'ān as divine signs. A related passage states: "O humankind! We created you from a male and a female, and we made you tribes and clans,[11] so that you may know one another" (49.13). Here, too, the division of humankind into distinct groups is simply attributed to God and his creative powers. It is presented as entirely beneficent, since God's power is beneficent: but can't these same divisions that help humans know members of their own group also cause them to hate members of foreign groups? The divine Qur'ān never stoops to consider, from a merely human perspective, the significance of the ethnic divisions of which its author was so obviously aware. It is true that God establishes different rites for each Umma (22.34, 67), but this apparent concession to human diversity does not seem to have had any great influence on Islamic doctrine. Since separate rites are not mandated for ethnic Ummas within Islam, al-Ṭabarī takes this verse to refer only to pre-Islamic peoples, such as Christians and Jews (al-Ṭabarī, 17: 198, on Qur'ān 22.67).

One struggles to find anything else in the Qur'ān that helps clarify the relation between the religious Umma and the proximate, this-worldly causes of human division.

The Qur'ān does concern itself with human linguistic diversity insofar as it poses an obstacle to the universality of prophecy: "We did not send a prophet except in the language of his people" (*qawm*, 14.4; Sayyid, 38).[12] This well-known verse raises the obvious question: was Muhammad's Arabic Qur'ān meant for all humankind, or merely the Arabs? While the verse may appear to imply the latter, another famous Qur'ānic statement eloquently reiterates the former: "O humankind (*in-nās*), I am a prophet of Allah sent to all of you" (7.158). This dilemma becomes particularly urgent with the emergence of the Muslim Umma. Even if prophets such as Nūḥ, Ibrāhīm, and Mūsā proclaimed the same message as Muhammad, their intended audience was restricted to their particular people. There would be other prophets after them, who would convey the same message to their respective peoples. Muhammad, however, is the "seal of the prophets" (Qur'ān 33.40, Sayyid, 41). As Ridwān al-Sayyid puts it, "Muhammad is the last of messengers, his prophecy is the last of the prophecies, and his Umma is the last of the Ummas. As the Qur'ān and ḥadīth say, he was sent to all humankind" (Sayyid, 48). This unique position of Muhammad can be reconciled with the claim that every Umma will have access to a prophet, but only if Muhammad's message is somehow made accessible to all present and future peoples. Yet Muhammad and his immediate audience spoke the "clear Arabic" in which the Qur'ān is revealed (16.103, 26.195). As a tradition quoted by Sayyid concisely explains, "The prophet was sent to his group (*qawm*) in particular, and to humankind (*in-nās*) in general" (Sayyid, 42). To make matters still more complicated, "clear Arabic" was soon elevated to the status of an inimitable, divine language. A partisan of the Arabic language, Ibn Faris, went so far as to say that "Arabic cannot be translated into any other language, as the gospels from the Syriac could be translated into Ethiopian and Greek, or as the Torah and Psalter . . . could be translated into Arabic" (Goldziher 1967, 1: 196). Indeed, the perceived untranslatability of Qur'ānic Arabic is a major reason for the paucity of premodern translations, and for the rule, supported by most jurists, against recitation and prayer in foreign tongues (Bobzin, 340–41).[13] The Qur'ān's status as an untranslatable Arabic work coexists uneasily with the hope that its universal message will eventually reach all non-Arabs in a pure and untainted manner. This difficulty is inherent not only in Islam, but in universalistic religions as such: how can a revelation ever be universally intelligible when expressed in the language of given people, Arab or otherwise?

The Qur'ān occasionally refers to non-Arabs, but never in a conciliatory way. It suggests that non-Arabs would never have believed the message in any case, even if it had been revealed to them (Qur'ān 26.198–99), and that the notion of a non-Arab revelation brought by an Arab prophet is absurd (41.44). It was only as the new religion spread among non-Arabs that its adherents began to grapple with the difficulty posed by its Arab roots. The influential ninth–century jurist al-Shāfi'ī sought to make it a duty for all Muslims to learn as much Arabic as possible (Druart 2012, 42). Yet how much Arabic could the majority of Muslims learn, then and even now, due to the limits imposed by geography and education? The great twelfth-century commentator Zamakshari took a more accommodating stance toward non-Arab Muslims. In his gloss on Qur'ān 14.4, Zamakshari argues that although Muhammad was indeed sent to all humankind, he was obliged to reveal his immediate message in the particular language of his kin. Translation of the Qur'ān thus becomes indispensable for conveying Muhammad's message to remote peoples and realizing the goals of Islam (Zamakshari, 2: 366–67). Yet the paucity of medieval translations of the Qur'ān indicates that Zamakshari's advice was not consistently followed.

This lack of sustained ethnological reflection in the Qur'ān[14] is consistent with the view, so forcefully expressed throughout this holy book, that piety and righteousness are the only things that really count. Shortly before acknowledging the division of humankind into tribes and clans (49.13), the Qur'ān proclaims that "the believers are a brotherhood" (49.10), while immediately afterward, it reaffirms that "the most honored by Allah are the most pious" (49.13). When the Israelites are divided into Ummas, the only significant distinction between these groups is that some are righteous while others are not (7.168). Some of the Ummas among Noah's vast progeny will be blessed, while others will be punished (11.48). Indeed, on Judgment Day entire Ummas will be sent to hell for their sins (7.38, 45.28, although cf. 27.83). The Qur'ān leaves little doubt that whatever the other differences between Ummas might be, religion and the virtues that accompany it are the only ones that truly matter in this life and the next. The Umma that commands good, forbids evil, and believes in Allah is the best of Ummas by precisely these criteria. Yet as I have argued, the difference in scale between this final Umma, produced for all humankind, and the ethnically circumscribed Ummas to whom all previous prophets were sent, should not be underestimated.

Sayyid and Naṣṣār propose some helpful ideas for resolving this dilemma. Sayyid observes the equivocal meaning of Umma in the Qurʾān, which signifies both the various, mostly unbelieving peoples to whom past prophets have been sent and the new, believing people created by Muhammad (Sayyid, 51). He suggests that the mature Umma created by Muhammad, while potentially universal, is understood by the Qurʾān to be tentative, and still in a state of becoming (Sayyid, 48, 50–52). Islamic tradition thus differentiates between the *umma ad-daʿwa*, defined as the potentially universal Umma to whom Muhammad was sent, and the *umma al-ʾijāba*, defined as the actual community of believers at any given time (Sayyid, 41; Naṣṣār 1978, 21). This distinction postpones, but does not avert, the future day of reckoning: as the *umma al-ʾijāba* strives to transform itself into the *umma ad-daʿwa*, and comes to encompass ever more ethnic Ummas, will it be able to retain its unity and cohesion through piety alone?[15] This was already a great question in Alfarabi's time, when the sprawling Islamic community had long outgrown its Arab roots and absorbed most of the peoples of the Middle East and North Africa. It is an even greater question today, when further expansion into Asia, Africa, and Europe has brought hundreds if not thousands of new Ummas into the Islamic fold. At the same time, the vigorous Muslim response to modern European thought and colonialism led by thinkers such as Jamāl al-Dīn al-Afghānī and Muhammad Iqbal has brought about a resurgence of interest in the fundamental unity of the Muslim Umma. The intensification of claims to Muslim unity, combined with the historical reality of ever-growing diversity, has led to serious conflicts within Islam, so that Muslim majority nations such as Arabs, Turks, Persians, Kurds, and Berbers have come to mistrust one another, often violently. Islamic unity is continually undermined by ethnic disunity. Alfarabi's attempt to grapple with the inherent tension between the Muslim Umma and its many constituent, ethnic Ummas is therefore of more than historical interest.

Religion Before the Umma

While Alfarabi's most important discussion of the emergence of the ethnic Umma occurs in the *Book of Letters*, his most important discussion of the emergence of the Muslim Umma occurs in the *Book of Religion*. This brief tour de force may cover only twenty-odd pages in most editions, but it manages to present an entirely new view of Islamic religion and civilization. Alfarabi intimates his response to a question that is suggested, but not fully answered, in the Qur'ān: how did the Arab Umma give rise to the Muslim Umma? His extremely subtle discussion merits a thorough line by line analysis, supplemented by references to other relevant texts. A careful analysis of the origin of religion may appear at first to lead us far away from the question of the Umma, but will eventually lead us back to the heart of it.

The title of the treatise contains the word *milla*, invariably translated as "religion." This translation is by no means inaccurate, but it requires the following qualification: while the modern English term "religion" has come to apply equally to a dazzling array of cults, creeds, and faiths, ranging from Unitarian Christianity to Native American shamanism, Alfarabi's term signifies mainly if not exclusively the prophetic religions such as Islam and Judaism. One may plausibly object that Alfarabi does indeed ascribe religion to the ancients, in one of the most famous passages of the *Attainment of Happiness* (AH 40.11–12, Ar. 90.56). That account of the phenomenon focuses heavily on images and imagination while making only a passing mention of laws (*nawāmis*; 41.16, Ar. 57.91), as if the ancients understood the relationship between religion and law to be comparatively loose. Meanwhile, the two works that Alfarabi associates most closely with the ancients, namely, the *Selected Aphorisms* and *Summary of Plato's "Laws,"* are entirely silent about *milla* and mostly silent about Umma.[16] Alfarabi does not deny that the older pagan creeds included laws, customs, beliefs, and stories, but he strongly implies that the coming together of religion, law, and Umma in a single community is characteristic of Islamic times. The *Book of Religion* provides the first philosophic account of this novel phenomenon.

Alfarabi begins his account by presenting the founding of religion as the result of a certain interaction between a first[17] ruler and his community:[18] as Alfarabi puts it, the ruler's purpose is defined "with respect to them and by means of them" (BR 93, lines 1–4, Ar. 43.3–4).[19] Even if the first ruler is free to posit and pursue his own end, the means at his disposal depend to some degree on his particular community, of which he is not the founder. While the founder of a new religion within an existing community is a major theme for Alfarabi, he never develops any equivalent to the Platonic founder who tries to shape an entirely new city from scratch. While Alfarabi attributes to Plato the idea of founding a new city (PP 19.13 ff.), in his own name he mentions only legislators (*wāḍiʿ an-nāmūs*) and lawgivers (*wāḍiʿ ash-sharīʿa*), but never the founders of Ummas or cities. Alfarabi's approach conforms to Muslim historical experience: Muhammad was the prophet of

Islam, but the founder of neither the Quraysh tribe, the cities of Mecca and Medina, nor the Arab Umma.

The founding of a new religion requires some kind of interaction between the first ruler and a preexisting community, but the character of this interaction remains vague. Does the first ruler do as he pleases with his community, or is he forced to comply with its long-standing traditions? One might infer that the truth lies somewhere in between, and that the new religion constitutes a compromise between the novel inspiration of the first ruler and the prevailing customs of the community, but at this stage of the argument Alfarabi does not resolve this question. Indeed, it is impossible to answer it when we do not even know the size or character of the first ruler's intended community, which could just as well be a tribe, city, region, great Umma, or many Ummas (BR 93.5–6, Ar. 43.4–6). In this early stage of the development of religion, the Umma does not possess any more standing than other kinds of community. As so many commentators on Alfarabi assume, Umma and *milla* are indeed separate entities at this point. It is only at a later stage in the development of religion that they will fuse together.

Apropos Islam, one could pose the question as follows: did Muhammad intend his religion for a tribe (the Quraysh), a city (Mecca or Medina),[20] a region (the Ḥijāz), a great Umma (the Arabs), or many Ummas (the Arabs, Persians, Syrians, Ethiopians, and so on)? The most widely believed account of Muhammad's life admits of each of these answers equally, in different stages of the prophet's career. Muhammad first preached to his own Quraysh tribe in Mecca but was mostly rejected, after which he fled to the city of Medina. He amassed a large following in Medina and rose to govern the city, through whose strength he conquered Mecca and became master of the entire Ḥijāz. In the last few years of his life he began to consolidate control over the rest of the Arab Umma in the peninsula, and look toward the rich and populous provinces of the Persian and Byzantine empires, which would fall to his successors within a few short years. Is Alfarabi implying that the scope of Muhammad's ambition evolved with his successes? One could object that Muhammad's prophetic visions had from the outset announced a new religion for all humankind, regardless of the vicissitudes of the moment: this is certainly how his prophetic mission came to be viewed by Muslims in later times. Yet the idea that any founder of a religion could truly have envisaged a faith for all humankind, as opposed to merely a faith for many Ummas, is implicitly rejected by Alfarabi, who never enlarges the size of the first ruler's community from many Ummas to the entire inhabited world

(BR 93.5–6, Ar. 43.4–6, Mahdi 2001, 99–100).[21] Even if Muhammad intended, in an abstract sense, a religion for all humankind, could he have foreseen the particular form that it would assume in far-flung lands such as Morocco and Afghanistan, which would have been completely unknown to him? By leaving the size of the community indeterminate, Alfarabi points to the first of a whole host of ambiguities in the standard account of Muhammad's life and prophetic mission.

Whatever the first ruler's community and his relationship to it may be, it is the ruler himself who chooses his own manner of rulership and formulates his own goals. Alfarabi lists several kinds of rulership, one of which is virtuous and the rest of which are ignorant, errant, or deceptive (BR 93.7–94.8, Ar. 43.6–44.6). The goals of the ignorant rulerships encompass the things normally sought in political life: health, money, pleasure, honor, and domination.[22] Errant and deceptive rulerships purport to pursue true happiness, but fail to do so on account of an error or deliberate deception of the ruler. By placing a description of several defective rulerships alongside a single description of a virtuous rulership, Alfarabi leaves the impression that the majority of actual human rulers may be defective. Yet only virtuous rulership seems to give rise to religion (93.10, Ar. 43.9). Alfarabi's silence about the relationship of the other kinds of rulership to religion may lead us to conclude that a religion such as Islam could only have been the product of a virtuous first ruler such as Muhammad, who stood above and apart from the myriad ignorant, errant, and deceptive rulers that surrounded him. In particular, a tyrant who views his subjects as mere tools for the attainment of his own wealth, pleasure, honor, and power (93.13–16, Ar. 43.12–14) could hardly inspire them to accept a new religion. But if the ignorant goods and rulership have nothing to do with the theme of the discussion, why does Alfarabi indulge in so lengthy a digression about them? Perhaps they are helpful for understanding the purposes even of the virtuous first ruler. Muhammad, after all, acquired wealth, wives, glory, and control over others in the course of his meteoric rise to prophecy and power.

Alfarabi also speaks of the errant and deceptive rulerships without any apparent connection to religion (BR 93.18–94.8, Ar. 43.15–44.6). Yet in this case the omission of religion seems odd, in view of both common sense and Alfarabi's other works. Only the most credulous would deny that some of the religions established by humans lack wisdom and virtue, and have been falsified, knowingly or unknowingly, by their founders. Alfarabi acknowledges this phenomenon in the *Book of Letters*, where he ascribes corrupt religion to false philosophy (BL 153.15–154.8, #147) and ignorant religion to a ruler who cares only about his own happiness and exploits his subjects as a means to this end (156.18–20, #152).[23] It seems plausible that the former statement refers to errant rulers, while the latter statement refers to ignorant or deceptive rulers. Even in the *Book of Religion* itself, Alfarabi will soon speak of "errant religions" (98.7, Ar. 46.21). Corrupt, errant, and ignorant religions appear to be at least as prevalent among humankind as virtuous religions, if not more so.[24] The disassociation of religion from false opinions and corrupt rulership in the opening paragraph of the *Book of Religion* allows Alfarabi to present religion as such as virtuous; unfortunately, this presentation of religion is not supported elsewhere in his work.[25]

If the first ruler is indeed virtuous, Alfarabi continues, then he must enjoy the help of revelation (BR 94.9–20, Ar. 44.6–13). This statement appears to confirm the genuine virtue of Muhammad, who according to Muslim tradition began to hear the voice of God in the year 610 in a cave outside Mecca. But Alfarabi is unsure about the character of this revelation. He broaches two possibilities: the first ruler could have received a revelation containing all the actions and opinions of his religion ready-made (94.11–12, Ar. 44.8–9), or he could have acquired through divine revelation the faculty by which he determined these actions and opinions (94.12–16, Ar. 44.9–11). The first possibility leaves almost nothing to human agency, while the second leaves almost everything to it. Alfarabi proceeds to suggest that the first ruler could have used a combination of the two: God dictates to the first ruler a portion of his religion, while granting him the use of his own intelligence and discernment with regard to the rest of it (94.17–19, Ar. 44.11–12). Finally, Alfarabi introduces theoretical science as indispensable for understanding revelation, but bluntly refuses to clarify the nature of this relationship, on the somewhat cryptic grounds that it has already been explained elsewhere (94–17.20, Ar. 44.12–13).[26] This omission assumes great importance in light of a passage in the *Selected Aphorisms*, where revelation informed by theoretical science is said to bear no relation, except in mere name, to revelation devoid of science (SA 63, #94, Ar. 98.9–99.2). While revelation appears to include only particular commands, theoretical science contains the general rules that encompass and justify these commands (Mahdi 2001, 103). But just as Alfarabi does not tell us whether the first ruler was virtuous, so he does not tell us whether he possessed theoretical science. In short, the role of divine revelation and theoretical science in the accomplishments of the first ruler is as murky as the other aspects of his life and career.

Since Alfarabi's account of the founding of religion in the *Book of Religion* leaves some room for human agency, it would be worth considering what the human source of religion might be. Yet the discussion of this question in the *Book of Religion* is rather cursory. Apart from blurring the link between ignorant rulers and religion, it does not explore the transmission of religion from one human group to another, or the role of philosophy in the establishment of religion. These themes are dealt with in great detail in the *Book of Letters*, to which we will now turn.

The treatment of religion in the *Book of Letters* hinges on a fundamental distinction between divine and human religion. In the rather unprepossessing section on causality that precedes the account of the Umma, Alfarabi draws our attention to the divine element of religion, stating that "*jihād*[27] is for the sake of God, and God is He for whom there is *jihād*, prayer, holy deeds, and adherence to the laws (*nawāmis*) that He legislates" (*sharraʿ*; BL 129.20–130.1). But Alfarabi immediately proceeds to discuss religion only "if it is considered (*juʿilat*) human" (131.6, #108). The subsequent section on religion and the Umma speaks of law (*nāmūs*), and a plethora of other human activities, while avoiding any reference to the root *sh-r-ʿ* and its derivatives, as well as God, *jihād*, prayer, or holy deeds.[28] It is hardly coincidental that the *Attainment of Happiness*, which also purports to describe purely human things (AH 2.1, Ar. 49.1), similarly employs only the term *nāmūs* while never mentioning revelation or *sharīʿa*.[29] Throughout both the *Book of Letters* and *Attainment of Happiness*, Alfarabi argues that religion must be derived from some kind of philosophy. In contrast, the *Book of Religion* speaks repeatedly of *sharīʿa* and its derivatives, but never of the *nāmūs* (BR 96.18, Ar. 46.11; 99.37–100.6, Ar. 50.12–51.4). It proclaims a close connection between religion and philosophy (97.9–98.8, Ar. 46.22–47.17), but says nothing about the role of philosophy in the original founding of religion, which is ascribed to some kind of revelation (cf. 94.9–20, Ar. 44. 7–13). The notion of *sharīʿa* returns briefly in the *Book of Letters*, but only in plural form, and in a passage that once again treats religion (*milla*) apart from philosophy (BL 157.5–14, #154).[30] It is striking that whenever Alfarabi speaks of a religion that has its origin in philosophy, he declines to speak of divine law.[31] Two approaches to the origin of religion emerge: one based on divine religion and law, and the other rooted in philosophy and purely human phenomena.[32]

Both approaches are marked by profound uncertainty. As we have just seen, the precise role of God in revelation, as well as its content and relationship to preexisting communities, are not determined in the *Book of*

Religion, thus rendering the origins of religion enigmatic. Treating religion from a merely human perspective has the advantage of avoiding the difficult issue of revelation, but entails serious uncertainties of its own. In the *Book of Letters*, Alfarabi conjures up several scenarios about the human origin of religion without deciding between them. The relevant variables include the domestic or foreign origin of the religion, and the truth or falsehood of the philosophy on which it is based.

The longest part of the section, which I have discussed extensively in Chapter 2, considers "the syllogistic arts when they arose in the Ummas due to their characters and innate natures" (BL 153.10–11, #146). Alfarabi then turns immediately to religion (153.13 ff., #147). He argues that religion ought to arise only after, and on the basis of, the full development of the syllogistic arts within the Umma, culminating in philosophy. Although this is the scenario "required" by Alfarabi (153.14, #147), the philosopher is not so arrogant as to expect the vagaries of human history to comply with his wishes. There are at least three ways in which the process can be disturbed. First, philosophy can arise without being followed by a legislator. Alfarabi knows that even though Plato and Aristotle completed the development of philosophy among the Greeks, a new religion based directly on that philosophy may never have been legislated: the "need" for a legislator at that historical juncture does not imply that such a figure actually appeared (151.15–18, 152.7–8, #142–44, 153.13–15, #147). Second, a religion may be legislated prematurely on the basis of rhetorical, dialectical, or sophistical philosophy: such a creed is bound to contain many false opinions (153.15–154.1, #147). Finally, religion may be transferred from a foreign nation to a people who has no knowledge of the philosophy, be it true or false, on which it was based (155.3–4, #149). This occurred most prominently in the history of the Arabs, which the reader has been urged to contemplate (147.1, #135). The development of linguistic science, which comes well before philosophy, nonetheless took place at least a century after the appearance of Islam (147.2–3, #135; Mahdi 2001, 220). Religion came to the Arabs when they possessed only rhetoric and poetry, without philosophy of any kind. If religion is always based on some kind of philosophy, then among the Arabs it must have had foreign origins.

The question then becomes, what kind of foreign origins, and on what foreign philosophy was the religion initially based? The following section of the *Book of Letters* is devoted to various scenarios for the transfer of religion from one Umma to another. Instead of providing a single, clear-cut version of the event, Alfarabi again offers several tentative scenarios. The Arabic conjunction meaning "if" (*idhā*) appears no less than nine times in the section.[33] This is not to say that Alfarabi demarcates nine separate scenarios. Some of the intertwined possibilities seem to fit together nicely with one another. I am able to discern, broadly speaking, three separate scenarios, no more than one of which can be "historically" true.

In the first scenario (BL 153.15–154.19, #147–48), a religion based on a false philosophy, which may have been Egyptian or Babylonian (cf. AH 38.17, Ar. 88.54) and did not advance beyond sophistical or dialectical arguments, was established long ago. The opinions and images of this religion were very far from the truth, without anyone being aware of it. A second legislator eventually appeared, but instead of taking his new religion from the philosophy, presumably Greek, that happened to exist in his time, he chose to rely mainly on the opinions and images of the old religion. The result was a still deeper corruption of religion. Finally, a third legislator emerged. Unlike the second legislator, he is not said to have enjoyed the benefit of any philosophy whatsoever, true or false. He simply followed his predecessor, reforming his religion to meet the needs of his Umma and devising a new vocabulary for it, thus introducing religion to a people who did not even have sophistry or dialectic (BL 154.7–19, #147–48, 157.4 ff., #154). Unfortunately, all his efforts merely served to make the religion still worse. It is by no means certain whether this chain of events takes place within a single Umma, owing to the relative ease with which religion can be transferred from one Umma to another (154.14, #148): religion arising within an Umma is merely the eventual result (154.9–10, #148).[34]

Alfarabi rarely mentions Christians or Jews by name, here in the *Book of Letters* or elsewhere in his extant works;[35] however, the selection of a sequence of exactly three legislators hardly seems accidental.[36] Far from bringing philosophy and religion closer together, this scenario serves to emphasize the distance between them. It implies that the philosophical and religious development of humankind diverged at an early stage, never to reconverge, so that religion in its most evolved form is based on false philosophy thrice removed. This account can still be reconciled with the claim of the *Attainment of Happiness* that "philosophy is prior to religion in time" (AH 41.13, Ar. 91.56), but only by admitting that in some cases the historical path from philosophy to religion is so long and tortuous that the resulting religion has very little in common with its remote, philosophic origins. Is Alfarabi inducing some readers to at least think the most rebellious thoughts about the founders of all three major monotheistic religions? But Alfarabi himself never confirms the historical validity of this account, which is couched ambiguously under three "ifs" (BL 153.15, 153.18, 154.1). It should be added that the process appears considerably more obnoxious than the results. The situation introduced by the seventh *idhā* (156.3 ff., #151), in which dialectic and sophistry arrive for the first time in an Umma whose religion is already well established, could certainly be understood as a further development of this scenario. After a prolonged struggle over the value of dialectic and sophistry within the religion, a number of people come to sympathize with, or at least be tolerant of, philosophy (156.12–13, #152).

Alfarabi then switches to a second scenario (BL 155.1–155.18, #149), which resembles a brusque demand to disregard the preceding. It feels, to be sure, altogether more palatable for both religion and philosophy. According to this scenario, religion was inspired by perfected philosophy at its inception. Yet even correct religion consists merely of similitudes of this philosophy. The connection between religion and philosophy is known to the Umma in which the religion originated, but not to the Umma to which it has just spread (155.3–7). Indeed, this Umma may be entirely unfamiliar with philosophy (156.14–15, #152). The link between philosophy and religion can be rediscovered only when philosophy reaches that Umma as well, but even then this process is not without struggle or risk. The conventional interpreters of the religion will be loath to recognize the philosophical origins of their creed (155.8–9, 12–14), while some philosophers will respond by attacking the religion, to whose roots they have long become oblivious (155.9–10). Thus the camps of both religion and philosophy will become rife with partisans who oppose the desirable cooperation between them.

Muhsin Mahdi has devoted considerable attention to this scenario (Mahdi 2001, 221–24). He infers that since the Greeks are the only Umma known to have perfected philosophy, it follows that the religion no less than the philosophy (BL 159.1, #156) that exists among the Arabs must have been transferred from the Greeks. He describes this scenario as a salutary myth, designed to persuade Muslims and especially philosophers of the essential harmony between their religion and philosophy (Mahdi 2001, 224).[37] It is true that philosophers who might have been enticed by the subversive insinuations of the first scenario are now drawn to a new scenario that neutralizes the opposition of religion to philosophy, and therefore does more to protect their own way of life. This scenario is indeed salutary, but is it a myth? Alfarabi does not explicitly declare it to be such; indeed, he never indicates the cognitive status of any of the scenarios. The improbability of the Greek origins of Islam may be inferred from the fact that the Greeks are not among the immediate neighbors of the Arabs (BL 147.9–10, #135); it is not impossible, however, that a religion based somehow on Greek philosophy might have crept into the Arab realms through Syria (BL 147.10, AH 38.18, Ar. 88.54). If this was the case, the pre-philosophic Arabs of the time would almost certainly have been unaware of its origins.

The third scenario involves a religion based on a false philosophy. In the case of the Arabs, this religion could have come from the Ethiopians, Egyptians, Indians, Syrians, or other neighboring Ummas (BL 147.9–10, #135). Once true philosophy has arrived from another source, this scenario produces the worst of results: a struggle to the death between philosophy and religion for the heart and soul of the Umma (155.19–156.2, #150). There is little evidence that Alfarabi, who advocates the cooperation and mutual interdependence of philosophy and religion rightly understood, views himself as a participant in such a struggle. As Mahdi aptly observes, Alfarabi did not take the hostile approach toward religion characteristic of his near-contemporary Abū Zakariah al-Rāzī (Mahdi 2001, 225, see Muṣbāḥ, 199). If Alfarabi regards cooperation with religious authorities as preferable to confrontation with them, he would certainly prefer the second scenario. Yet his readiness to state the third scenario as well indicates an awareness that collaboration between philosophy and religion may not always be possible. In some cases the Umma, because of the nature or bad education of its members, might simply be ill disposed toward philosophy (BL 156.13–21, #152).

On the basis of various suggestions contained in the *Book of Religion* and the *Book of Letters* concerning the origin of religion, we may derive a vast number of possibilities: the founder of the religion could have sought to establish his new faith on the scale of a tribe, city, region, great Umma, or many Ummas; he could have been virtuous, ignorant, errant, or deceptive; he could have received direct revelation or, imbued with some kind of divine inspiration, devised much of his legislation on his own; his religion could consist mainly of human *nāmūs* or mainly of divine *sharīʿa*; he could have based his religion on true philosophy, false philosophy, or mere memory of ancient creeds; he could have imported elements of his religion from the Jews, Christians, Greeks, Indians, Ethiopians, Syrians, or Persians. What does Alfarabi hope to accomplish by presenting such diverse, tantalizing, and often contradictory scenarios for the origin of religion? Mahdi's interpretation undoubtedly has a large measure of truth. In the absence of any certitude about events of the receding past, philosophers should feel free to disseminate the version of the story that best suits their aims with a clear conscience. Yet we must also account for the liberty with which Alfarabi elaborates scenarios that run contrary to such aims, by presenting religion in both its original and its current incarnation as in no way amenable to true philosophy. Alfarabi may not wish to inculcate too much complacency among philosophers, lest they underestimate the challenge of justifying philosophy to their religious community. He may also fear that persuading too many people of any dogmatic view concerning the origin of religion would restrict the freedom of their minds, even if that view happens to be extremely flattering toward philosophy. Alfarabi may encourage the majority of his readers to believe that Islam was founded as a virtuous religion inspired by philosophy, but he also sows more than enough doubt to prevent the case from becoming closed.[38]

Yet one thing remains certain, and common to all the scenarios: the new religion eventually establishes itself in an Umma (BL 154.14, #148, 155.4, #149, 156.2–3, #150–51). Why does religion come to be in an Umma, and not some other kind of community? Alfarabi's discussion of the early stages of religious legislation posit no intrinsic connection between religion and Umma, or any other community for that matter: the religion could just as well be intended for a tribe, city, region, or multinational empire (BR 93.5–6, Ar. 43.5–6, BL 152.7 ff., #144). Yet Alfarabi does draw additional attention to the Umma by means of the unusual expression "great Umma" (BR 93.5, Ar. 43.6), which appears nowhere else in his extant works.[39] The adjective could be taken to signify the large size of the Umma relative to the city or tribe. But Alfarabi ignores the fact, emphasized in the *Political Regime*, that the Umma is only intermediate in size (PR 60.64, Ar. 69.19), and does not qualify any of the other communities in the *Book of Religion* with any adjective whatsoever. The addition of "great" may point to a grander kind of Umma: at the very least, it serves to highlight the crucial role played by the Umma in the growth, spread, and eventual identity of the new religion, which sets it apart from the other communities.[40] However, the details of its role remain unclear at this point. So too does the Umma to which Alfarabi refers: is he speaking merely of the Arab Umma, or of the emerging Islamic Umma? This same ambiguity recurs in the *Book of Letters*. When Alfarabi speaks of the Umma to which the religion was initially transferred (BL 154.14, #148, 155.4, #149), he appears to mean the Arab Umma to which Muhammad initially preached. However, when he speaks of the Umma in which a struggle between religion and philosophy ensued (156.2, #150), or to which sophistry and dialectic were transferred after the establishment of religion (156.3, #151), he probably means the Islamic Umma, since these events first occurred within Islam in the ninth century, long after it had ceased to be merely an Arab phenomenon.

The *Book of Letters* points to the connection between religion and Umma and hints at the transition from the Arab to the Islamic Umma, but does not elucidate them. Alfarabi takes up this task in the *Book of Religion*, when he proceeds to describe the evolution of religion after the death of the first ruler. It is only in this account that the intimate link between religion and Umma is adequately explained.

The Expansion of the Community

The opening paragraph of the *Book of Religion* focuses on the ruler who first introduces religion. But the development of religion does not end with the death of the first ruler; on the contrary, at that moment it seems barely to have begun. The mature form of the religion will crystallize more gradually, over a period of many generations. In the following section of the *Book of Religion*, Alfarabi turns to an elucidation of this process.

Alfarabi points out that no first ruler of any description could possibly have devised legislation that anticipated all future events, given their utter unpredictability, or even covered all the events in his time, given the shortness of his life and the inevitable disturbances, such as wars, that beset it. The first ruler devotes his finite energies only to the most generally applicable legislation, or else to that legislation which is most urgent in his own particular place and time (BR 98.24–99.11, Ar. 48.6–49.8). It follows that the second ruler who succeeds him already needs to adapt the old legislation to the new era. If he does this in a way that is faithful to the intention of the first ruler, the first ruler himself would have approved. However, this can be accomplished only if the second ruler is like the first ruler in all respects. The series of equally competent rulers is allowed to continue uninterrupted down to the fourth ruler, when their succession appears to be arbitrarily cut off (99.12–25, Ar. 49.9–50.3).

This passage raises several difficult questions. By ceasing to distinguish between virtuous, ignorant, errant, and deceptive rulers, Alfarabi leaves open the possibility that he is describing competent successors to a nonvirtuous first ruler (cf. BR 108.11–12, Ar. 60.20–21). But let us assume that Alfarabi means virtuous rulers who received revelation. His arguments about the long-term imperfection of every piece of legislation on account of human finitude, as well as the inevitable, violent distractions that beleaguer the career of every first ruler, would still hold true. Yet do the second and third rulers receive up-to-date revelations of their own? Alfarabi, who ceases to speak of revelation in this section, does not explicitly take up this question, but his claim that the second and third rulers are like the first ruler in all respects (99.12–13, Ar. 49.9) would seem to imply an affirmative answer to it. By subsuming both the prophet who founded the religion and his merely pious successors into the category of ruler, and then describing the first four rulers as alike, Alfarabi blurs the conventional distinction between them. Alfarabi suggests that the alterations of the first ruler's successors may have contributed as much to the religion as his own original legislation.

Several features of this passage allude unmistakably to the history of Islam. The word translated as "succeed" (*khalaf*, BR 99.12, Ar. 49.9) is the verbal root of the term *khalīf*, rendered into English as Caliph and signifying the prophet's lawful successors as head of the Muslim community. The use of the number four, far from being arbitrary, invokes the four rightly guided Caliphs who are said to have succeeded Muhammad: Abu Bakr, 'Umar, 'Uthmān, and 'Alī. Alfarabi seems to defer, at least in these respects, to the traditional narrative of Islam. But do his numbers add up? Islam places the prophet before, and above, his four worthy successors; this should mean five rightly guided leaders, one prophet and four mere caliphs. Yet Alfarabi mentions only four virtuous rulers, into whose number the prophet is incorporated as the first ruler. Somebody seems to be missing. The question of the status of the prophet, and perhaps also of 'Alī, continues to resurface.[41]

Alfarabi places particular emphasis on change, war, and unexpected death (BR 98.29–33, Ar. 48.9–12), as factors that prevent the first rulers from perfecting their legislation. Sure enough, all three shook the Islamic community constantly during the time of Muhammad and the rightly guided Caliphs. In the span of a couple of decades, a small Meccan sect had somehow become master of a mighty empire, extending from Egypt to Iran. This astounding military success was not accompanied by political tranquility: the three Caliphs following Abū Bakr, namely, 'Umar, 'Uthmān, and 'Alī, were all assassinated. In 656, 'Uthmān's murder provoked a civil war between 'Alī and his eventual successor Mu'āwiyya,[42] in the aftermath of which the Sunni and Shī'a would split.[43] The dazzling speed of Islam's expansion, followed by its equally rapid dissolution into warring sects, might have made it especially difficult to disentangle the first tenets of Islam that were established by Muhammad from the additions of his three or four worthy successors during rapidly changing times. This question was settled within Sunni Islam by the fact that only Muhammad received the Qurʾānic revelation. Yet Alfarabi implies that the successors of the first ruler, if they were truly like him in all respects, may also have received revelation. However this may be, living revelation did cease at some point, and whatever records of it were passed down to succeeding generations would have quickly become insufficient for governing in times of tremendous flux. Even if the heirs to the religion had initially hoped to rely on the revelation of their predecessors, they soon would have discovered that only an ample dose of human ingenuity could meet the unprecedented challenges of their own time. Above all, they had to grapple with the uncharted horizons of the new imperial world. The character and size of the community for which Muhammad first intended his religion had become almost irrelevant.

The Jurists and the Birth of the Islamic Umma

The succession of qualified first rulers ends with the fourth generation. Not only does Alfarabi cease to speak of any first ruler until much later in the treatise, but he drops the word for religious succession entirely (*khalaf*, BR 99.30, Ar. 50.5, see 108.1–3, Ar. 60.14–16).[44] While the illusion of pure succession to the prophet through the caliphate was preserved in Islam throughout the Abbasid period, it rapidly disappears from the evolution of religion as understood by Alfarabi.[45] This may be because Alfarabi thought that after the ascension of Muʿāwiyya the caliphs became difficult to distinguish from ordinary human rulers.[46] Preoccupied with the profane concerns of governing an empire, they could no longer double as religious authorities. Suddenly neglected by the rulers, the religion appears to reach an impasse. Far removed from its point of origin, and recently deprived of both revelation and living wisdom, the religion must nonetheless continue to adapt to the vicissitudes of time. It does so by virtue of a new class of men, the jurists. They codify the religion, while at the same time trying to keep it as flexible as possible. It is through the jurists that the religion finally assumes its mature form.

The introduction of the jurists into the *Book of Religion* is accompanied by a noticeable change in vocabulary. Alfarabi did not determine whether the first ruler or his successors were virtuous or ignorant. On the basis of what, then, should they be proclaimed "righteous leaders" (BR 99.26, Ar. 50.4)? The statement that introduces the activity of the jurists appears to echo the opinions of the religion, which speak freely of righteous rulers (95.9–10, Ar. 45.9–10), rather than Alfarabi's own account. In designating the founder of the religion, Alfarabi replaces his original term, "first ruler," with a new expression, namely, "lawgiver" (*wāḍi' ash-sharī'a*; 99.37, Ar. 50.11). This expression is first employed by jurists, because only under them does the *sharī'a* of the first ruler and his virtuous successors become fixed.

A further change introduced by the jurists is particularly pertinent to our topic. Alfarabi does not determine the size or nature of the community for which the religion of the first ruler was intended: it could have been anything from a small tribe to a multitude of Ummas. Yet the jurists seem sure that the religion of the lawgiver was intended for an Umma, in a passage that is repeated verbatim in the *Enumeration of the Sciences* (BR 100.4, Ar. 50.13; ES 209). What is the historical basis of their certainty? Alfarabi does not provide any. He gives the impression that the Islamic Umma, no less than the doctrine of the rightly guided caliphs and the lawgiver, is the creation of the jurists.[47]

The question then becomes, what leads the jurists to associate the religion with the Umma? The original, ethnic Umma is linked inextricably to language. So are the inventors of the new Umma, who become the first group in the history of the religion to make use of refined linguistic arts. Jurists need to be experts not in the Arabic languags, but rather in the particular dialect (*lugha*) that was used in the time of the lawgiver (BR 100.18, Ar. 51.6).[48] In order to accurately interpret all the relevant reports about the life, teaching, and actions of the lawgiver, the jurists must become absolute masters of this dialect (100.17–101.8, Ar. 51.7–52.3). This dialect can plausibly be identified, at least in the Islamic context, with that of Muhammad and his tribe, the Quraysh. While physical remnants of the prophet's tribe, city, and region were gradually blurred or effaced over time, his dialect was preserved in written and oral accounts of his life and teaching (101.8, Ar. 52.2). This tribal dialect was thus transformed into a written idiom common to religious scholars of all linguistic backgrounds; as a spoken idiom, however, it did not even constitute the common language of the Arabs. In the *Book of Letters*, Alfarabi does not list the Quraysh among the tribes from whom the Arab linguists eventually distilled the purest form of Arabic (BL 147.6–7, #135).[49] It is only by virtue of the activity of the jurists that this marginal dialect becomes the language of an Umma.

The jurists use their peculiar linguistic expertise to receive reports about the lawgiver's life, allegedly witnessed and transmitted by his companions (*ṣaḥib*, BR 101.6–7, Ar. 52.1). These reports, often unwritten, are either generally known or persuasive (101.6–8, Ar. 52.1–3), qualities identified with rhetoric, or at best dialectic. Alfarabi takes care never to use the word *ḥadīth*, let alone the names of any transmitters, in this passage, but he does allude to the well-known requirement for every *ḥadīth*, that it must originate from a report by one of the Prophet's companions.[50] The reports that form the basis of *ḥadīth* are signified instead by the word *akhbār* (101.7, Ar. 52.1–2). It is striking that *akhbār* also signifies, in the *Book of Letters*, the reports on which the stories of the old kind of Umma are based, the preservation of which constitutes one of its five arts (BL 143.3, #130, 148.15, #138). Yet it is only in the *Philosophy of Aristotle* that Alfarabi speaks of both *akhbār* and *ḥadīth*, perhaps because he can hide behind Aristotle's name.[51] In emphasizing the pleasure derived from telling and listening to stories, Alfarabi's Aristotle speaks of "the myths,[52] *aḥādīth*, *akhbār* of peoples, and the *akhbār* of Ummas" (PA 61.13–14), without clearly distinguishing between them. Taken together, these passages from three different works imply that the new Umma resembles the old insofar as it acquires its mature form through storytelling. "The Umma for which [the religion] is legislated" (BR 100.4, Ar. 50.13) becomes the Umma that hears and believes the jurists' stories about the religion, just as each ethnic Umma hears and believes its bards' account of great national events.[53]

It should be emphasized that Alfarabi does not despise the jurists. On the contrary, he suggests that their accomplishments require considerable natural talent and devotion, including at least the rudiments of the logical arts (BR 100.10–101.8, Ar. 51.2–52.3). In carefully extrapolating new rules without deviating from the core principles of the religion, they also play a vital role in preserving its stability and flexibility (99.36–100.2, Ar. 50.10–12). Alfarabi's attack on the violent contentiousness of the *mutakallimūn* in the *Enumeration of the Sciences* does not extend to jurists (ES 209–19). Yet certain questions could still be asked about them. Are the materials on which they base their inferences and conclusions reliable? Does their status as standard-bearers for the religion affect their judgment? These questions are best answered by comparing the jurists' outlook with Alfarabi's own.

Alfarabi does not debunk the first ruler, but emphasizes his human limitations, such as his subjection to death and war. These inevitable disturbances to the act of lawgiving mean that the first ruler's code is necessarily incomplete and in need of revision, at least by a competent successor. The work of even the most able successor would in turn need to be revised for exactly the same reasons. The obvious implication is that no legal code can ever attain completeness or perfection (BR 98.24–99.25, Ar. 48.6–50.3). But the jurists cannot afford to dwell on the limitations of a legal code that they are supposed to expound and interpret rather than question and revise. The sanctification of the "righteous leaders" of the religion and the "lawgiver" is to a large extent the work of the jurists (99.26–27, 37, Ar. 50.4–5, 11), whose task requires not only considerable natural talent and mental dexterity, but also a firm adherence to the opinions and virtues of the religion (100.4–6, Ar. 50.13–15).

Let us consider Alfarabi's own attitude toward the past. He is not afraid to venture his own accounts of it. Unlike the jurists, Alfarabi in the *Book of Letters* goes back beyond the emergence of religion to the most remote beginnings, well before the development of written and even spoken communication (BL 134.16 ff., #114). The unlettered people of that epoch would have been unable to preserve reports of it, so Alfarabi relies on his own good sense, positing the effects of nature and custom as well as of the human body and soul on that early but crucial stage of the development of the Umma. The result is speculative and hardly detailed, but still extremely useful.[54] Its uncertain cognitive status is indicated by the highly inconsistent use of the word "clear," and the absence of terms such as "investigate" and "make known," which characterize Alfarabi's accounts of genuine science (ES passim, BR 101.20 ff., Ar. 52.10).[55] As for Alfarabi's treatment of the early development of religion, it hardly employs any words relating to knowledge, investigation, or clarity at all.[56] Conversely, none of Alfarabi's descriptions of science, in the remainder of the *Book of Religion* or in works such as the *Enumeration of the Sciences* or *Book of Demonstration*, contain any investigations into the beginnings of language, political society, or religion. Alfarabi's refusal to treat such topics under the rubric of science is in keeping with the thick veil of obscurity that envelops so remote an age.

The origin of religion may be even murkier than the origin of language because the former, unlike the latter, cannot be explained by resorting to natural human organs and capacities: the word "nature" and its derivatives (Arabic root *ṭ-b-ʿ* or *f-ṭ-r*) occur numerous times in Alfarabi's discussion of the origin of language, but remain absent from his discussion of the origin of religion. Many Muslims seek to resolve the uncertainty surrounding the origin of their religion by trusting the accounts of jurists, but Alfarabi refuses to do so. Even though he lived in an age of jurists, his account of the origin of religion does not in any way depend on them. He refers to no companions of the lawgiver, ignores the lawgiver's particular language or customs, and invokes no received reports. His version of the story contains only what can be inferred through intelligent speculation, rather than received opinion. Alfarabi's account of the origins of religion, when applied to Islam, implies that the Umma assumed its mature form over several generations under the duress of continual wars and dramatic change, with at least four rulers, and then a bevy of jurists, all contributing their part. Since the exact order of these historical accretions can no longer be traced, there is no way to proceed back from the preserved accounts of the events to the events themselves. The original intention of the lawgiver, whatever it may have been, has become irretrievable. We may contemplate several intriguing scenarios, as Alfarabi does so brilliantly in both the *Book of Religion* and the *Book of Letters*, but we cannot arrive at anything resembling certainty about it.

The jurists, by the very nature of their trade, are unable to reconcile themselves to such uncertainty. On the contrary, they need to suppress it, and insist that the religion's legal code is perfect and complete, revealed to one prophet in a single lifetime by a divine lawgiver: to do anything less would be to question the integrity of the religion and their own authority as its interpreters. Furthermore, the jurists' authority over the mass of the believers in the Umma depends in large part on their ability to tell the stories that the members of the Umma want to hear. As Alfarabi explains in the *Philosophy of Aristotle*, humans listen to stories for the sake of comfort and pleasure (PA 61.12–20). While the jurists' enchanting tales about the exalted virtue and piety of the founders of the Umma would tend to inspire such feelings, Alfarabi's unsettling insinuations about the constant war, change, and adaptation that wracked the first decades of Islam most emphatically would not. It is fair to assume that a similar distortion of events also occurred during the genesis of the ethnic Umma, whose humble origins were embellished in its early literature. The cool, detached account of the origin of the ethnic Umma presented by Alfarabi in the *Book of Letters* could never serve as the foundational story of any actual Umma, any more than the *Book of Religion* could serve as the foundational story for Islam. While casting doubt on the veracity of the jurists, Alfarabi nevertheless indicates the indispensability of the social function they perform. He therefore walks a tightrope between undermining the authority of the jurists and allowing their glorification of the past to go unchallenged.

Some recent scholarship about the origin of Islam has emphasized the extent to which jurists and their collaborators were also "storytellers" (Crone 2004b, 214 ff.; Reynolds, 12 ff.). These scholars therefore display great distrust toward the traditional Islamic narratives about the origin of their community, and try to construct their own version of events based on other historical information. Many of these sources are foreign: one of the most recent scholarly anthologies on the Qur'ān, titled *The Qur'ān in Its Historical Context* and edited in two volumes by Gabriel Said Reynolds, contains essays that discuss the role of Jewish, Christian, Syrian, and Ethiopian sources in shaping the Qur'ān (Reynolds 2008, 2011). In light of such studies, Alfarabi's hints about possible foreign origins of Islam in the *Book of Letters* appear unusually prescient. Lacking the methods and materials of modern scholarship, Alfarabi would not have anticipated all the recent findings of scholarly research or had the slightest hope of getting to the bottom of what "really" happened. Perfectly aware of the limitations of his knowledge, Alfarabi does not even pretend that his account of the origin of religion constitutes science. But he indicates, at the very least, that the true origins of the Muslim Umma are probably not what the tradition believes them to be. The impressive lucidity with which Alfarabi undermines the common Islamic narrative means that he should still be considered a forerunner to the critical approach to the Qur'ān and *ḥadīth* that has become so prominent today.[57]

Did Alfarabi's critical approach to the origin of Islam attract any followers in the medieval Islamic world? This important question would require further research. However, a certain skepticism does permeate the work of Ibn Khaldūn. Unlike Alfarabi, the great historian does not hesitate to mention by name the famous figures who fought over the rulership of Islam in its crucial, early years. His conclusion, however, is that it would be wrong to take any sides. "Consider these differences [between the early leaders of Islam] a source of divine mercy for those who came after them in the Umma, so that everyone can take whomever he chooses and make him his *imām*, guide, and leader" (Ibn Khaldūn, 1: 448, my trans., Ar. 1: 369). Like Alfarabi, Ibn Khaldūn regarded continual reflection on the political and religious tensions that characterized the early history of Islam as necessary for guaranteeing a variety of viewpoints within the Umma, thus protecting it from the temptation of rigid orthodoxy.

Chapter 5

The Mission of the Virtuous Umma: Ethnic Accommodation Within Islam

The process of the development of religion may be murky, but the result is clear: a new, religious Umma emerges alongside the older, ethnic Ummas. Do these two types of Ummas coexist, and if so, how? The rest of the *Book of Religion* provides general but compelling answers to this question, which are elaborated in greater detail in works such as the *Political Regime, Virtuous City,* and *Attainment of Happiness.*

The Two Kinds of Umma

Alfarabi concludes his treatment of jurisprudence in the *Book of Religion* by subordinating all its functions to philosophy and political science (BR 101.11–19, Ar. 52.4–9). One would expect this political science to grapple with the new kind of Umma. Yet it returns to speaking of Ummas only in a very general way. Humankind is divided into multiple Ummas and cities, the character of which the prudent statesmen must always take into account (102.27 ff., Ar. 53.20, 106.5–13, Ar. 58.9–59.2, 107.18–30, Ar. 60.5–13). There is a virtuous Umma, but it appears only as a larger version of the virtuous city, produced not by religion but by the coincidence of the right kind of governance with an Umma (103.21, Ar. 55.34, see PR 69.81, Ar. 80.5–6). As for religion, it is not even mentioned again until the very last sentence of the work. There is nothing essentially religious about the Ummas mentioned in this part of the *Book of Religion.* To be clear, there is nothing essentially ethnic about them either: by failing to distinguish between the two kinds of Umma, Alfarabi implies that his discussion pertains equally to both of them. A statesman needs to reckon with both the ethnic and the religious Umma, without privileging one over the other.

Having finished, for the time being at least, his discussion of the religious Umma, Alfarabi draws our attention back to the perseverance of human heterogeneity, on both the religious and the ethnic level. The resilience of the ethnic Ummas ought to come as no surprise, since they play a role that the religious Umma is unable to assume. Although both kinds of Umma originate from language and the stories told in it, the religious Umma has its own peculiar character and serves a distinct set of needs. Its language, now known as classical literary Arabic, is a local dialect that has been elevated into the religious lingua franca, but never becomes anybody's mother tongue. Even among the Arabs only the educated truly master it, not to mention the majority of Muslims who do not speak Arabic at all. The religious Umma does not possess the linguistic cohesion of the ethnic Umma. As for its stories, they do not overlap with the national legends. They take place among a remote people in an increasingly distant past, and are sanctified only by their universal prophetic and legal claims. The religious Umma may at times subvert, but cannot replace, the national literatures of the various Ummas that have converted to Islam.

Maimonides appears to suggest the opposite, by contrasting the vanished Ummas of the past that were governed by various *nomoi* (*nawāmis*) with the more unified humankind (*in-nās*) of his era, that is governed by divine commands (Maimonides 1996, 102, Ar. 33.12–16). We cannot examine here whether this statement represents Maimonides' final judgment on the matter, but taken at face value it acknowledges more directly than any remark of Alfarabi's the novel character of the medieval communities that have been forged by universal divine commands. Inspired by these commands, many Muslims would resist Alfarabi's arguments about the coexistence of the two types of Umma, and assert that the universal Islamic Umma necessarily takes precedence over the sundry ethnic Ummas absorbed by it. Jamāl al-Dīn al-Afghānī (1838–97), a formative figure in the birth of modern Islamic political thought, exemplifies this view. Seeking to summon his entire religious community, from Morocco to Afghanistan, to resistance against the depredations of European imperialism, Afghānī argues that the intensity of pan-Islamic feeling inspired by God greatly exceeds, and even supersedes, the merely ethnic or tribal passions that preceded it, to the point that the latter become almost irrelevant (Afghānī, 304–5, 348–49). Afghānī's eloquent declarations of the superiority of Islamic unity to any form of merely ethnic solidarity set the tone for an important strand of modern Muslim political thought, which will be considered in greater detail in Chapter 7.

Alfarabi, in contrast, implies that the two kinds of Umma endure on a more or less equal footing. The practical part of political science, which operates in particular human settings, must find a way to respond to both of them, as well as to the possible tension between them. The prescriptions for accommodating the Ummas in most of the *Book of Religion* are quite general, and do little more than confirm the arguments that I will present in greater detail in Chapter 6. Yet the treatment of the religious Umma in the penultimate section of the *Book of Religion* is unique, and finds no parallel in any of the other works that have come down to us. Let us turn to this important discussion.

Toward a Virtuous Umma

In introducing the "virtuous Umma" toward the end of the *Book of Religion*, Alfarabi recalls the new kind of Umma whose origin was described at the beginning of the work, but seemingly ignored in its center. This virtuous Umma does not possess the traits of the ethnic Umma. It is held together not by language or natural character, but by customary dispositions and voluntary traits, which induce its parts to act in tandem (BR 112.12–31, Ar. 65.4–17). In other works of Alfarabi, this kind of cohesion is often associated with a city (SA 23–24, #25, Ar. 41–42, VC 230.12 ff.). Yet this virtuous Umma is not coupled with any virtuous city. The oneness of its actions and parts approximates the oneness of the first principle of the world, as well as the oneness of the world itself, brought about by the governance of that first principle: "The Umma and the Ummas become like a single (*wāḥid*) thing performing a single action by which a single purpose is obtained" (BR 112.17–30, Ar. 65.8–17, cf. 110.1–28, Ar. 62.15–63.15). Finally, its activity benefits the other cities and Ummas, bringing them to happiness in this world and the next (113.11–12, Ar. 66.6–7). Is this not the Umma known in the Qur'ān as "one Umma" (*umma wāḥida*; Qur'ān 21.92) and the "best Umma produced for humankind, commanding good and forbidding evil" (3.110), disguised only thinly by Alfarabian vocabulary? This marvelously subtle passage,[1] intricate even by Alfarabi's standards, requires our closest attention as we endeavor to situate this Umma within both its particular context and Alfarabi's work in general.

The sequence of arguments that leads up to the introduction of the virtuous Umma begins by mentioning revelation from God to the first ruler, a theme that recalls the opening paragraph (BR 111.21–26, Ar. 64.10–14, cf. 94.9–20, Ar. 44.6–14). Alfarabi enhances that earlier discussion by elaborating further on the relation of this revelation to actual communities. He begins by stating that the first ruler who receives revelation may govern absolutely everything, from the Ummas down to the minutest parts of the city (112.1–5, Ar. 64.15–18). This grandiose declaration seems to encourage the most sweeping political ambitions of the Muslim faith. But does Alfarabi stick to it? He proceeds to state that God "is also the governor of the virtuous city, just as He is the governor of the world" (112.6–9, Ar. 64.18–65.1). He then proceeds to treat the virtuous Umma without any reference to revelation. Since Alfarabi does not speak either of God's governance of the virtuous Umma or of revelation to it, there now appears to be no direct divine guidance of any human community larger than the virtuous city.[2] The revelation sent down directly from God to Muhammad might have been perfectly suited for governing his small community of followers, up to the time of his takeover of the city of Medina, but it would have been less effective at governing the burgeoning community once it had become an Umma and empire. If God's direct guidance reaches only the city, by virtue of what qualities could any merely human governor rule the virtuous Umma or Ummas? The answer might be that he ought to govern less by means of divine guidance, than with the help of human additions to it. According to our analysis of the first section of the *Book of Religion*, these additions would seem to come mainly from the jurists. Yet Alfarabi does not indicate how the jurists could help with the task of multinational governance. Instead, he suggests that the virtuous Umma and its governor may still have some direct access to God, by means of the divinely ordained cosmic order that they are called upon to imitate (113.2–6, Ar. 65.20–66.4). God's governance of the world, however, is imitated with the help not of jurists, but of a first ruler "with thorough cognizance of theoretical philosophy" (112.2, 113.12, Ar. 64.16, 66.8). This first ruler effectively replaces the jurists, and theoretical philosophy assumes the role once played by revelation in understanding the character of divine governance. By the end of the *Book of Religion*, the transition from revelation to living, human wisdom is complete.

In light of this transition, we should hesitate to identify the first ruler introduced at the end of the *Book of Religion* with the first ruler that figured at its beginning (BR 93.2, Ar. 44.3–4). The earlier first ruler's community was not necessarily virtuous, and his influence most probably did not extend beyond that community, whereas the "first ruler of the virtuous city" (113.13–14, Ar. 66.8–9) helps to govern a virtuous community and seeks to spread happiness to the other nations and cities. Even more important, the new first ruler is distinguished not, as it may seem at first, by his access to revelation (112.2, Ar. 64.16), but by his perfect knowledge of theoretical philosophy, by virtue of which he may imitate God's governance of the world (113.12–16, Ar. 66.8–10). This knowledge was never attributed to his distant predecessor, since in the passage describing the accomplishments of the original first ruler the relationship between revelation and theoretical science was never clarified (94.17–20, Ar. 44.12–13).[3] If we accept Alfarabi's claim that first rulership absolutely requires such knowledge in order to bring happiness to the nations and cities (113.7–14, Ar. 66.4–9), then the founder of religion may well be a first ruler only in time. This penultimate first ruler represents not a lawgiver from the remote past, whose teaching has been obscured by the passage of time, but a philosopher who is alive and available in the more sophisticated intellectual environment of Alfarabi's own age. The *Book of Religion* begins at the earliest stage of the formation of the Muslim Umma, and ends at the point that this Umma could reach once it has been transformed by Alfarabi. Alfarabi proposes a collaboration between a traditional but high-minded Muslim ruler and a philosopher, with the explicit goal of helping that ruler accomplish his goal of multinational rule. The desire of the virtuous Umma to imitate divine governance can be fulfilled only with the help of the philosopher, who alone understands the complicated hierarchy through which God governs the world (108–13, Ar. 61–64). Far from being an enemy of the virtuous Umma, the philosopher emerges as an indispensable resource in realizing its goals.

Nevertheless, a basic question remains: how exactly would the first ruler of the virtuous city who has mastered theoretical philosophy instruct the governor of the virtuous Umma? Let us assume that Alfarabi is himself a philosopher, and that knowledge of theoretical philosophy might entail, among other things, knowledge of Alfarabi's writings. It is safe to say that many of these writings are at best ambivalent about the project of bringing happiness to all the Ummas under a single government. The *Attainment of*

Happiness, which I will discuss in greater detail at the beginning of Chapter 6, indicates how such a project is bound to falter owing to the difficulties Ummas have in communicating with each other, the indifference of the philosophers to governing, and the lack of popular approval of their rule. The proposal under consideration in the *Book of Religion* turns out to be no less problematic. It hinges upon the unity not only of the Umma, but of the Ummas, which come to resemble a single thing with a single act and purpose (BR 112.27–29, Ar. 65.11–13). The governor of the virtuous Umma must harmonize both his Umma and its neighbors into a single whole in order to bring about the happiness of the cities and Ummas in this life and the next (112.12–30, Ar. 65.2–14, 113. 11–2, Ar. 66.7). On this point Alfarabi arguably goes further than the Qur'ān, which demands unity only of the one, Islamic Umma, albeit for the sake of all humankind (Qur'ān 3.110, 21.92). Is such a high degree of unity among the Ummas really feasible?

Alfarabi takes the question of unity so seriously that he consecrates a whole treatise to unravelling it. This dense work, titled the *Book of One and Unity* (*Kitāb al-wāḥid wa-al-wiḥda*), does not even attempt to fulfill the high political expectations raised by the *Book of Religion*. In it Alfarabi never speaks of the unity of Ummas or even cities, but focuses mainly on logical definitions. The closest Alfarabi comes to politics in this work is to give the example of a rhetorical speech, all of whose parts are one in their goal of persuasion (BO 49, 73, 95, 100). The emphasis on "cooperation" toward "a single goal" (*gharaḍ wāḥid*; BO 95, 100) as a means of creating unity does seem to allude to the discussion in the *Book of Religion*, which uses those exact same terms (BR 112.21, 27, Ar. 65.9, 13). Yet by adducing only rhetorical speeches, syllogisms, and poems as examples of such cooperation (BO 95, 100), Alfarabi implies that it may be possible only in the realm of carefully constructed human speech, and not in the "actions" touted by the *Book of Religion* (BR 112.19, 28, Ar. 65.12, 18). If this is the case, must the idea of a single united Umma be dismissed merely as a fiction of the imagination? Not entirely, since Alfarabi still provides a category through which it may be understood: some things cannot be divided because of the prohibition of convention (*waḍ'*) and *sharī'a* (BO 54, 90). Yet Alfarabi does not elucidate either of these claims with any examples. Do convention and *sharī'a* cohere as firmly as nature? This question is raised but hardly answered in the *Book of Religion*. Its scheme depends on the essential correspondence between the natural instincts that unify the world and voluntary habits that unify the Ummas, but Alfarabi never identifies these voluntary habits as *sharī'a* (BR 112.17 ff.,

Ar. 65.60), or suggests that *sharī'a* could be the bond of any universal society. In the *Summary of Plato's "Laws"*, Alfarabi indicates that he views the prospect of a universal code of law with some dread: it would attempt to govern humans as humans keep bees, treating the free and the slave, the wicked and the lazy, as well as people living in different regions and following different rules and customs, all in the same way (SL 141.4, Ar. 131.3–4, 169.8, Ar. 148.7–149.8; Strauss 1959, 146).

Alfarabi does acknowledge that the governor of the virtuous Umma and first ruler of the virtuous city cannot implement their project without some help from convention: only a "common religion in the cities" will allow them to realize their goals (BR 113.18, Ar. 66.11). Alfarabi seems, at first glance, to credit the widespread dissemination of the Islamic religion for enabling the rulers to undertake so ambitious a project, but upon further consideration both components of this expression remain ambiguous. The "common religion" is never identified with Islam. It might be the virtuous religion elaborated toward the beginning of the treatise, but if so, why is the word "virtuous" dropped? Virtue seems to have shifted from the religion to the Umma. What, then, is the source of the Umma's virtue? Were we too quick to identify it with religion, whose actual practice in the cities may not involve virtue? Alternatively, the Umma's virtue could be based on philosophy and political science (103.20–23, Ar. 55.3–5). If that is the case, then the genuine imitation of divine governance demanded in the aftermath of revelation would move the virtuous Umma away from simple piety toward philosophy. But can philosophers rule the Ummas alone? This question remains unanswered in the *Book of Religion*. Alfarabi takes it up in the *Attainment of Happiness*, which I will discuss in Chapter 6.

The expression "the cities" is also somewhat obfuscatory. It is easy to grasp why Alfarabi does not speak of a common religion in the Ummas, since that prospect must have felt remote to him: Christian Byzantium and Ethiopia, pagan India, not to mention significant Zoroastrian remnants in Persia and a large Jewish community in Baghdad, lie well within the geographical purview of Alfarabi. But how far does the scope of "the cities" extend? In the *Political Regime*, Alfarabi states that many cities exist within a single Umma (PR 61.64, Ar. 70.4). However this may be, the continued flourishing of significant pre-Islamic communities in all the major cities of Alfarabi's time casts doubt even on the possibility of a common religion in the cities. Alfarabi points to the inconvenient fact that however much the ambitious governor of the virtuous Umma would like to benefit from a common religion among his subjects, that hope is still very far from becoming a reality.[4] As long as there is no common religion, would the governor of the virtuous Umma be advised to abandon, or at least postpone, his plans?

Let us assume that the governor of the virtuous Umma decides to pursue his plans. There is no indication that the various Ummas, religions, and rulers would consent readily to his governance. The project of bringing happiness to them under the rule of a sole virtuous Umma might therefore require war. In the *Attainment of Happiness*, Alfarabi does not hesitate to call for a war waged by the wise against all Ummas that refuse to submit to happiness (AH 32.9–17, Ar. 81.48–49).[5] In the *Book of Religion* he is noticeably more cautious. War appears explicitly only once, as a lamentable necessity that distracts the first ruler from his higher calling of making laws (BR 98.31, Ar. 48.10). Alfarabi warns the ruler of the virtuous Umma that he must provide, in full imitation of God, certain "other things" in order to consolidate the virtues and perpetuate the goods that he has established (112.40, Ar. 65.19). Do these "other things" include war and compulsion? Apart from the brief mention of war indicated above, anything requiring the use of force is consistently absent from the work.[6] But our suspicion that Alfarabi alludes to this requirement is further strengthened by the sudden addition of "arts" to "the dispositions and voluntary traits" by which the good things are perfected in the Ummas and cities (113.8, Ar. 66.5), implying that virtuous habits and intentions may come to naught unless accompanied by practical skill of the sort that could come in handy in wartime. We recall the four human things listed at the beginning of the *Attainment of Happiness* as essential for realizing happiness within the Ummas and cities: "theoretical virtues, deliberative virtues, moral virtues, and *practical arts*" (AH 2.3–5, Ar. 49.1, italics mine).

In avoiding any explicit discussion of these themes, Alfarabi reveals his extreme reluctance to advocate war in a work devoted to religion. He is well aware that many of the more obnoxious adherents of religion abuse war in order to humiliate alleged unbelievers (ES 219). The discrepancy between the *Attainment of Happiness* and the *Book of Religion* might be best explained by the differing status of philosophy and religion within these two works. In the former, Alfarabi has assured from the outset that the logicians and philosophers will be truly in charge of his project of international conquest, so that religion is reduced to a mere tool or appendage of philosophy (AH 40.3 ff., Ar. 90–91.56). In such a peculiar context, Alfarabi is willing to emphasize the role of art and advocate large-scale war. In the *Book of Religion*, Alfarabi also establishes the subordination of virtuous religion to philosophy, but he does so in a manner that explains the complexity of religion in far greater depth and acknowledges the possibility of ignorant, errant, and deceptive religions (BR 93–98, Ar. 43.3–47.17). During the collaboration of the governor of the virtuous Umma with the first ruler who knows theoretical philosophy, it is not entirely clear whether philosophy or religion is in charge. In such a context, Alfarabi is understandably reluctant to open the floodgates of war, whose potential for good is matched by its potential for ruin. But the result is that his account of a multinational empire led by the virtuous Umma cannot be regarded as a serious, practical proposal.

One final substitution may the leave the reader doubtful of whether the imitation of God required of the governor of the virtuous Umma is possible at all. The aforementioned divine "governor of the world" (BR 112.7, Ar. 64.1) suddenly assumes added responsibility: he is supposed to establish and perfect the natural goods in multiple worlds (113.6, Ar. 66.3).[7] The meaning of this change remains rather enigmatic. In the *fātiḥa* prayer, which Muslims recite daily, the Qur'ān describes God as the lord of only two worlds (Qur'ān 1.2).[8] This Islamic doctrine is reflected in Alfarabi's frequent distinction between this life and the next, which occurs in this very section (BR 113.12, Ar. 66.7). By replacing the dual Arabic form with the plural and thereby adding at least a third world, Alfarabi expands the cosmos beyond the limits of the holy book. Is he gesturing toward the possible existence of faraway planets that are familiar to God but completely unknown to us?[9] A similar ambiguity occurs in the *Selected Aphorisms*, where Alfarabi seems unable to decide exactly how many worlds there are. He speaks first of only three worlds, "spiritual, celestial, and material" (SA 45, #69, Ar. 78.17), but then enlarges his classification by introducing multiple spiritual worlds (*'awālim*, SA 48, #74, Ar. 81.9). In light of such passages, the divine governance that the virtuous Umma is supposed to imitate now appears vaster and more elusive than was previously assumed. This added complexity is also reflected in the human domain: just as God must realize the natural goods in each and every (*kul wāḥid*) world (BR 113.6, Ar. 66.3), so the virtuous Umma must realize the good things in each and every (*kul wāḥida*) city and Umma (113.9, Ar. 66.6). The word "one" (*wāḥid*) refers no longer to an association of Ummas, but only to individual cities and Ummas. Although it seemed a few lines ago that an association of Ummas led by the virtuous Umma could become a single whole (112.27–8, Ar. 65.12–13), now it seems that every city and Umma constitutes its own unity, like a world unto itself. Alfarabi concludes by suggesting that these cities and Ummas may combine to form several leagues (*jamā'āt*

al-umam wa-al-mudun, 113.11, Ar. 66.7), but never a single whole. The project
of imitating God's governance of the worlds by uniting the individual Ummas
and cities appears ever more daunting. The line between praiseworthy efforts
to imitate God, and reckless human ambition rooted in groundless preten-
sions to spiritual or divine knowledge, turns out to be quite thin.

I do not mean to say that the governor of the virtuous Umma who seeks
to imitate the governance of God should avoid collaborating with the philosopher. On the contrary, the philosopher's aid remains indispensable if the
ruler is to learn the limits of such an imitation, and thereby resist the temptation to overreach. The virtuous Umma remains, after all, a particular community, not that different from any other. If even God, when acting in the
human domain, can rule only a city (BR 112.6, Ar. 64.19), then the ruler of
the virtuous Umma should shelve his hopes of universal conquest and aim
at imitating God's order one community at a time.

Accommodating Islam to the Ummas

The *Book of Religion* concludes by implying that the goal of bringing happiness to the Ummas and cities by means of the virtuous Umma is unlikely to
be realized. Neither direct revelation from God nor human imitation of his
governance of the worlds is comprehensive and certain enough to justify the
wars that would be needed to impose religious unity over a large area. These
were surely salutary warnings in the tenth century, and they remain so today,
especially since not all Muslims have relinquished the goal of universalizing
their faith. But it would be a mistake to limit Alfarabi's critique to Islam
alone. His views on the insurmountability of human diversity endure as a
salutary warning for utopians, zealots, and Napoleons of all sorts, who hope
to trample this diversity under the feet of their imperial aspirations. Joshua
Parens has elucidated this critique of universalism in his recent book, and
I will return to it when I discuss the *Attainment of Happiness* in the next
chapter.[10]

But the question remains, what then? Islam exists, and Alfarabi displays
no hope or desire of replacing it. He speaks allusively, and at least partly in
Plato's name, of the inevitable decline of every legal code (SL 144.1, Ar. 133.1),
but gives no impression that such a decline is imminent in Islam. Over a
millennium has passed since Alfarabi's death, and Islam is indeed still with
us, making his analysis of it as timely as ever. Unlike many of the thinkers

of the European Enlightenment, Alfarabi did not envisage a society in which religion is superseded or weakened in force. In the case of Islam, a critique of the religion's tendency to reckless universalist aspirations is necessary but not sufficient, in the absence of some alternative understanding of Islam on which a more sober religious and political practice can be based. If the Islamic Umma cannot antiquate, or even subjugate, the older ethnic Ummas, it needs to find a reliable way of accommodating itself to them. Alfarabi lays out the blueprint for such a policy in the *Virtuous City* and *Political Regime*.

In both of these treatises, Alfarabi mentions the division of humankind into Ummas, but does not indicate its deeper significance immediately (VC 228.11–230.2, PR 60.64–62.67, Ar. 69.14–71.13). The true importance of the Umma becomes clear in both works only when Alfarabi lists a series of general opinions about God, the world, and humans that ought to be believed by the inhabitants of any virtuous city: in both cases these opinions closely resemble the doctrines presented in early parts of their respective books (VC 276.10–278.7; PR 73–74.88, Ar. 84.17–85.2). Alfarabi explains that these opinions should be expressed in different ways in different cities and Ummas. His argument may be summarized as follows. Sound opinions can be inculcated in the majority of humans only through images. These images vary in their closeness to the truth, as well as their familiarity to their intended audience. In disseminating the images among different Ummas, the latter consideration turns out to be the most important (VC 278.8–280.6; PR 74–75.90, Ar. 85.3–86.10). Images strive less to attain truth and exactness than to strike a chord in the souls of those who experience them. They will accomplish the desired effect only if they are taken from the environment and folklore of each particular Umma, and therefore "better known" to it (VC 280.1–4, PR 75.90, Ar. 86.4–5). Alfarabi sheds further light on this point in the *Book of Letters*, where he observes that members of some Ummas have never seen an elephant or a camel (BL 169.21–171.1). It follows that the depictions of camels that fill the souls of Arabs with majesty would have meant very little to the Greeks. Extending this same observation even further, we might infer that the common Qur'ānic description of paradise as a garden surrounded by rivers,[11] although undoubtedly appropriate to the desert Arabs, would be less effective in the steamy jungles of Borneo.

This argument that a distinct set of religious images is appropriate to each Umma seems to conflict with a passage in the *Attainment of Happiness* that urges the first ruler to coin certain images that are equally applicable to all Ummas (AH 30.16–18, 33.5–8, Ar. 79.46, 82.50). But in those same passages,

Alfarabi admits that other images are not applicable to all Ummas (30.18–31.1, Ar. 79.46). Furthermore, Alfarabi offers no examples of universally applicable images, in the *Attainment of Happiness* or elsewhere. He never says whether the images coined by Plato in the *Timaeus* are universal or applicable merely to the Greeks (41.5, Ar. 91.56). The citation of the *Timaeus* comes in the context of a passage that describes the images produced by religion, but the brief list of images hardly resolves this question. Would it make sense, for example, to imitate matter by darkness (41.6–7, Ar. 91.56) in an Umma that traditionally associates darkness with a certain deity or demon? And if darkness, as Alfarabi suggests, may be used to imitate both matter and its contrary, nothingness, doesn't that imply that many images could represent contradictory things to different peoples? Nevertheless, we should not conclude that Alfarabi completely rules out the possibility of universal images, especially in light of *Attainment of Happiness* 33.5. But even if there may be a few universal images, those of particular applicability remain far more numerous, so the claim that religious imagery varies from Umma to Umma holds true. In the *Virtuous City* and *Political Regime*, Alfarabi takes this argument a step further: "it is possible that there will be virtuous cities and virtuous Ummas that differ in their religions" (VC 280.3–5, PR 75.90, Ar. 85.17–86.1). Not merely religious imagery, but religion itself, differs from Umma to Umma. The addition of the word "possible" may give Alfarabi a slippery way out of this controversial statement.[12] Yet we may ask whether the cogency of the arguments that support this statement justifies any such disclaimer.

The implications of Alfarabi's claim are wide-ranging. The very possibility of a single religion for all humankind is discounted, implying that neither Islam nor Christianity will ever realize its universalist ambitions. However controversial this prediction may have appeared in the heyday of classical Islam, the failure of any religion to sweep over all humanity in the past millennium would seem to confirm it, at least for the foreseeable future. The import of this statement within Islam appears so shocking that it is hard to take it too literally.[13] Is Alfarabi really suggesting that the various ethnic Ummas that have converted to Islam should look for another religion, more in keeping with the peculiar character of their Umma? But what other religion is available to them? Are Persians expected to revert to the worship of Zoroaster, or Egyptians to the worship of Osiris? However implausible Alfarabi's suggestion may appear in the Islamic context, it does mirror the Christian phenomenon of national churches, which were already flourishing in

Eastern Christianity centuries before Luther and Henry VIII. Georgians, Armenians, and Copts, for example, all developed their own churches with their own unique language, liturgy, and iconography. The well-traveled Alfarabi may well have been familiar with these churches, but would also have known that there is no precedent for such institutions in Islam.

As if seeking to reassure those who fear that he is calling for the disintegration of Islam, Alfarabi promptly introduces the adjective "one" (*wāḥid*, VC 280.5–6, PR 75.90, Ar. 86.1) a term so often employed to signify the unity of God, religion, and the Umma. But this familiar adjective is used in an entirely unfamiliar way, unattested in both Islamic tradition and even Alfarabi's own *Book of Religion* and *Book on One and Unity*. It applies not to God, religion, or the Umma, but to the happiness intended for virtuous cities and Ummas. While it is extremely difficult, and indeed well beyond the scope of our analysis, to determine what Alfarabi ultimately means by happiness,[14] it is easier to imagine how many of Alfarabi's readers are likely to interpret the passage in question. Following the Qur'ān, they believe that the highest happiness can only be achieved in the next life.[15] Alfarabi's successor Averroes includes cognizance of happiness in the afterlife among the pillars of Islam (Averroes 2008, 23.9–10). Alfarabi's argument lends itself to a similar interpretation: so long as Islam preserves a unified teaching about the happiness of the afterlife, the imagery in which the religion is expressed may vary considerably from Umma to Umma. Yet it must be remembered that the afterlife is the last of the doctrines mentioned in the list of opinions in the *Virtuous City*, and barely hinted at in the shorter list in the *Political Regime* (VC 278.4–7, PR 75.88, Ar. 84.17–18). Other opinions, such as the nature of the deity, the ranks of beings in the world, and the first ruler, seem equally important. They too are one in meaning and essence, but many in imitation (PR 74.90, Ar. 85.12–15). Not just the afterlife, but every aspect of religious belief, requires a particular imitation in each and every Umma.

Alfarabi lived at a time of cultural shift within Islam. Turkish and Persian mercenaries, many of them Shī'a, had come to dominate the government in Baghdad. Alfarabi indicates that Persian and Turkish Islam may differ considerably from its Arab predecessor. Yet he is not encouraging these groups to impose the new creed on the Arabs: in the multinational setting in which Islam finds itself, no one Umma is likely to dominate the religion for long, so the religion will need to learn how to accommodate multiple ethnic Ummas.[16] If the philosophers are in fact the leading interpreters of the meaning of religion (BR 97.9–98.8, Ar. 46.22–47.17, AH 40.3–41.13,

Ar. 90–91.56), they should help to ensure that the essential doctrines of Islam are stated and imagined in each Umma in a manner appropriate to its peculiar language, character, and traditions. One of the best ways for a religion to appeal to a variety of Ummas is through the adroit use of religious art, to which we shall now turn.

Alfarabi's Encouragement of Visual Art in Islam

The passage in the *Political Regime* that argues for the multiplicity of religions places a great emphasis not merely on images, but on images of a certain kind. Alfarabi compares, not once but twice, the imagining of the opinions of religion to looking at the reflection or statue (*timthāl*) of a human, rather than the human himself (PR 74.89–90, Ar. 85.7, 16). The notion of art as images of natural and artificial things can clearly be traced to Plato's *Republic* (*Republic* 510a, 514a ff., 595a ff.). Yet this Platonic concept is bound to provoke more controversy in Islam than in classical Greece.[17] The Greeks regularly used statues in their religion, but Muslims have generally frowned upon them as idolatrous. While the Parthenon was adorned with splendid sculptures partially preserved as the Elgin marbles, the Dome of the Rock contains a single, unhewn stone. Some might assume that these well-known findings of modern historical research were unknown to Alfarabi, who lived entirely within the confines of the Islamic world. In order to dispel that impression, I quote the following passage from the *Great Book of Music:*

> One kind [of melody] provides the soul with imagination, establishing in it the forms of things, imitating matters, and inscribing them in the soul, and its effect is like the effect of paintings and statues perceived by the eyes: some produce in the sight pleasant pictures alone, but others imitate the forms of things, along with their passions, actions, moral states, and customs, as did the ancient statues (*tamāthīl*) that existed everywhere in the past, and were glorified as images of gods, and worshipped along with God or apart from God, may He be exalted [above all such things]. They were designed in shapes and forms that conveyed the actions, customs, and wills ascribed to each of them, in keeping with what Galen the physician said about several idols (*aṣnām*)

that he saw, and with what still exists now in the farthest reaches of India. (BM 62–63)

This quotation should suffice to show how clearly Alfarabi understood the historical link between statues and idolatry.

In the passage quoted above, Alfarabi employs two distinct terms for sculpted images. The first is *tamāthīl*, or "statues," which occurs many times in both the *Political Regime* and other passages about sculpture, and the second is *aṣnām*, or "idols," which as far as I know does not occur anywhere else in Alfarabi's extant writings. Both terms have Qur'ānic roots, and remain well-known to Muslims today. An ISIS video featuring the destruction of sculptures at the Mosul museum denounces *aṣnām* and *tamāthīl* with equal fervor, while invoking the actions of both Ibrāhīm, who is said to have destroyed the idols of his father, and Muhammad, who allegedly destroyed all the statues in Mecca.[18] The Qur'ānic usage is somewhat more subtle. While *aṣnām* is invariably a term of opprobrium, used to describe the idols worshipped by the Canaanites (Qur'ān 7.138) and the people of Abraham (6.74, 14.35, 21.57, 26.71), *tamāthīl* is more ambiguous: it describes not only the idols worshipped by the people of Abraham, in a manner almost synonymous with *aṣnām* (21.52, cf. 21.57), but also the sculptures made for King Solomon (34.13). It is worth noting, however, that Solomon's statues were produced not by men, but by jinn strictly subject to the command, and punishment, of Allah (34.12). This gives the impression that according to the Qur'ān it might not be wise to trust mere humans with the production of *tamāthīl*. Alfarabi's emphasis on statues in the context of purely human making displays no such suspicion of this activity, as if he means to reconsider the status of sculpture in Islam.

Alfarabi would have been quite familiar with statues, not only from the relics of ancient Egypt, Persia, and Byzantium, but also from the workshops of his own civilization. Recent research has confirmed that a vast number of automated sculptures were produced in the classical Islamic period, but unfortunately none have survived (Duggan, 230 ff.). A particularly famous Baghdadi example consisted of a rider on a horse that circled around a dome, still erect during Alfarabi's lifetime and visible to the entire city (241–42). While these statues were mounted in and around palaces in order to impress visiting dignitaries, there is no evidence of sculpture designed for religious ceremonies or places of worship (240, 266). The scholarly consensus is straightforward, and still confirmed by the experience of any traveler today: "Pictures and images were excluded from the mosques" (Grabar, 664). It follows that Alfarabi, who employs the term *timthāl* in the context of religious imagery rather than courtly pomp and protocol, goes against the norms of his civilization. One might argue that Alfarabi introduces statues of humans merely as an illustration of how the principles of the religion should be imprinted in the soul as images, without directly sanctioning their use. But this fails to explain why Alfarabi should choose so provocative an example, and repeat a version of the same example in the *Short Commentary on the "Poetics,"* by comparing poetic imitation to sculptural imitation in the form of a statue of a generic man named Zayd (SP 173, 175). The choice of a human in these examples is telling: invoking the statues of lions or horses, which are less implicated in the idolatrous worship of saints and prophets and hence more common in Islam, would almost certainly have been less polemical.

A number of passages in Alfarabi equate the effects of the various imitative arts. The passage quoted above from the *Great Book of Music* argues that sculpture and painting are just as appropriate, pleasant, and effective a means of imitating natural and artificial things as music (BM 62–63). The passage from the *Short Commentary on the "Poetics"* asserts that the imitative effects of poetry and sculpture are quite similar (SP 173, 175). In the *Epistle on the Canons of Poetry*, Alfarabi equates the ends and forms of poetry with those of painting, another visual art (EP 278, Ar. 272). Finally, in the *Philosophy of Aristotle* Alfarabi has Aristotle emphasize the pleasure that humans derive from looking at statues along with the pleasure that humans derive from hearing stories (PA 61.5–20). If this pleasure is truly universal, it should apply to Muslims no less than to the pagans known to Aristotle. Yet of all these arts, only statues were associated by Muslims with idolatry. In most of these passages, Alfarabi blurs that difficulty by speaking of statues while omitting any reference to idols (*aṣnām*). The obvious exception occurs in the *Great Book of Music*, but even there Alfarabi's tone is somewhat neutral: apart from the almost perfunctory "may God be exalted [above such things]," he makes no more effort to demonize sculpture than he does in his other works. Idolatry is consigned to Indians and ancients, people remote in space and time, so it hardly appears to be a serious temptation for contemporary Muslims.

Alfarabi describes the people who need images of the principles of the world and rulership of the city as "believers" (*mu'minūn*;[19] PR 75.90, Ar. 86.10). This extremely common Qur'ānic term signifies the Muslim community in contradiction to heretics, hypocrites, and nonbelievers. By using it, Alfarabi implies that Muslims in good standing require images of God, the world, and their religious heroes no less than members of other religious communities. Visual art emerges as one of the ways to convey these images. If, as Alfarabi argues, every representational art constitutes its own side of the same imitative coin and has comparable effects in establishing images in the soul, then sculpture does not encourage idolatry any more than its counterparts. Stories and songs about Muhammad's supreme virtue, no less than saintly icons of him, might encourage his worship in the soul. One could say, in contemporary terms, that the message is more important than the medium.

I conclude that Alfarabi favors relaxing the prohibition against the use of graven images in religion, especially in Ummas that have long been enamored of representational art. The prohibition against graven images that has been so common in Judaism and Islam ought to give way to the practical exigencies of communication with each Umma. But who would determine the images appropriate to each Umma? The most plausible candidate would be each Umma's cultural elite, who are most familiar with that Umma's traditions (BL 143.1 ff., #130). If asked by the governor of the virtuous Umma about bringing the other Ummas to happiness (BR 112–13, Ar. 65–66), Alfarabi and his fellow philosophers might encourage collaboration between the elite of each Umma and the religious authorities, in order to establish effective and unique ways of instilling the opinions of the religion in every ethnic Umma that falls within the purview of the governor's plans. This would not achieve the goal of universal empire, especially since communication with each Umma would become more difficult as the empire expanded, but it would allow for a flourishing, multinational society.

I wish to conclude my discussion of visual art by considering its importance from a still broader, comparative perspective. In Christian Europe religious authorities not only permitted, but cultivated, the painting and sculpting of religious figures. This is certainly one of the greatest differences between Christian and Islamic civilization. By portraying familiar saints and prophets countless times in a nearly infinite variety of poses and surroundings, Christian artists sanctified but also humanized them. They were forced to grapple with a vast array of questions that found no clear answer in the biblical text. What was the expression on Moses' face when he first performed miracles before Pharaoh? What was Mary doing when she first learned of the imminent birth of Jesus? What did the holy land look like in biblical times? The artists' representations of these themes were imaginative rather than scientific, but they brought the essential issue of context to the fore. By constantly adding to the sparse biblical narrative in accordance with the demands of art, they revealed the limitation of written text as such and the need for interpretation. Unlike the clerics, the artists did not possess any formal religious authority, and the images they created were by nature ambiguous. They were therefore granted far greater leeway in interpretation than the "official" guardians of Christian belief. This helped protect European Christianity from stagnant and oppressive literalism. In the language of Alfarabi, Christ's essence may have been one, but the painted and sculpted images of him were many (PR 74.90, Ar., 85.14–15).

Enriching jurisprudence, *hadīth*, and Qur'ānic interpretation with artistic license might have had similar results in Islam. Yet this never happened in any sustained manner. Muslim attitudes toward figurative representation have varied over time and place, but the general attitude has always been somewhat suspicious. While Islamic achievements in architecture, artisanship, and miniature painting rank among the world's greatest, the civilization has produced no comparable tradition of large-scale painting and sculpture, especially of religious figures. This has made it harder for most Muslims to imagine, for example, how seventh-century Arabia or its prophet might have looked to human eyes. Deprived of the human context that art provides, it became more tempting for Muslims to sanctify their prophets as unambiguously perfect, and reject Qur'ānic criticism altogether.[20] By undermining the traditional assumptions about the origin of Islam and encouraging all forms of representational art, it was precisely the ossification of religious belief that Alfarabi hoped to preempt and avoid.

Poetry, Art, and the Civilization of the Umma

Alfarabi lays special emphasis on visual images in the *Political Regime*, while seldom mentioning poetry.[21] But it would be wrong to infer that he means to exclude poetry, or even diminish its role. As I have already noted in the previous discussion, Alfarabi applies the same simile of a human being, his statue, and his image in water to poetry (SP 175). The implication is that Alfarabi could have mentioned poetry in the *Political Regime*, but for whatever reason chose to omit it.[22] Alfarabi elsewhere displays great interest in poetry, devoting two short treatises exclusively to the subject, and discussing it in most of his major works. I complete this chapter by briefly examining Alfarabi's treatment of poetry and the light it sheds on his broader teaching about art and the Umma.

Alfarabi's treatment of poetry might appear novel, especially when contrasted with the work of his predecessor Plato. I begin by observing what Alfarabi does not do. Plato concludes the *Republic*, and several other dialogues for that matter, with a poetic fable of his own (*Republic* 614b ff.). The myth of Er creates a new image of life after death, in which many of the traditional figures of Greek lore, such as Orpheus, Ajax, Agamemnon, and Odysseus, are recast in a new light (620 ff.). None of Alfarabi's extant works about Plato make any mention of these particular myths. His brief summary of the *Republic* terminates with the comparison between the just city ruled by philosophy and the cities opposite to it, which may be found in Books 8 and 9 (PP 20.12–14). Similarly, his summaries of the *Gorgias* and *Phaedo* say nothing about the stories that conclude those dialogues (PP 8.1–6, 17.7–18.2). When describing Platonic image-making in the *Attainment of Happiness*, Alfarabi cites only the cosmic imitations of the *Timaeus* (AH 41.3–5, Ar. 91.56). It would nonetheless be hasty to assume that Alfarabi is ignorant of the myth of Er, as I have already argued in Chapter 1. His successor Averroes is obviously aware of the myth, but pointedly refuses to discuss it, dismissing the famous fable as a dispute over stories that were relevant only to the ancients. Most people today, Averroes avers, obey their law without having any need for such stories (Averroes 1974, 105.15–24). But does this claim make any sense? Don't Muslims support their obedience to the law with stories from the Qur'ān and *ḥadīth*? Perhaps Averroes means that these are considered not merely stories, but the divine truth, revealed by God and only transmitted by humans. If this is the case, reworking the stories of the Islamic Umma might be extremely imprudent, inviting accusations of unbelief. Is any philosopher in Islam bold enough to transpose the myth of Er into his religious community, concocting new tales about Mūsa, Pharaoh, and Muhammad standing before God on the Day of Judgment? Alfarabi certainly isn't: he rarely tells any stories of his own,[23] and guards a resounding silence about both the prophets of Islam and their enemies. While Alfarabi lists belief in generic prophets as well as virtuous and vicious kings among the opinions of virtuous religion (BR 94.21 ff., Ar. 45.6), he never cites, in the *Book of Religion* or elsewhere, the particular names of either the righteous or the wicked. The same degree of generality characterizes Alfarabi's accounts of the afterlife, which occur in various forms throughout his works but never cite individuals (PR 70.83–72.86, Ar. 81.5–83.6, VC 258.13 ff.; SA 52–53, #81, Ar.

86–87). These descriptions of the freeing of the soul from all material constituents are presented as doctrines rather than fables, and are too terse and
general to be considered poetic in any conventional sense. The most one could
say is that Alfarabi provides templates for poetry, allowing people more poetic
and audacious than himself to fill them in.[24]

Alfarabi's reluctance to weave his own tales does not imply an indifference to the arts of poetry or storytelling. While refraining from too much
poetic invention himself, he encourages that same practice in others. Alfarabi's standard definition of poetry, repeated in any number of works, is that
it consists of imitation (EP 273, Ar. 267; SP 172–73). This seemingly banal
statement, inherited from classical sources, contains almost limitless possibilities, given the sheer number of imitable things in heaven and earth (see
Republic 596c–e). Alfarabi's own appreciation of the versatility of poetry is
evident from his *Epistle on the Canons of Poetry*. Let us take a brief look at
this work and its relation to Alfarabi's other discussions of the subject.

The treatise's central and most memorable feature consists of a colorful
list of the forms of ancient poetry, allegedly ascribed to Aristotle but not
resembling any known Aristotelian work (EP 275–76, Ar. 269–70).[25] The ostensible purpose of this list is as manifestly preposterous as its ascription to
Aristotle. Alfarabi purports to take an interest in the poetry of the Greeks
primarily because they alone matched particular meters with particular genres
of poetry (EP 275, Ar. 269). Yet in the *Short Commentary on the "Poetics,"*
Alfarabi ridicules those who claim that meter, rather than imitation, is the
defining characteristic of poetry (SP 172–73). Moreover, while Alfarabi ascribes "a known meter" to the first four types of poetry, he drops it from the
remainder of the list, with the exception of satyric poetry, whose meter was
invented by musicians in imitation of wild beasts (EP 276, Ar. 270). As his
enumeration progresses, Alfarabi loses interest in his stated reason for it.

Alfarabi may have deeper, unstated reasons for listing the various forms
and subjects of poetry in so unorthodox a manner. In the *Book of Letters*, as
we saw in Chapter 2, Alfarabi criticizes poetry as a merely popular art. Yet
as Mahdi has helpfully noted, Alfarabi's attitude toward poetry in that work
is "rather curious" (Mahdi 2001, 213): despite or perhaps on account of his
dismissal of it, Alfarabi fails to explain its relationship to religion as well as
its role in philosophic inquiry (BL 152.4, #143, 153.8–9, #145; 150.4 ff., #141).
Furthermore, in other works he undermines these criticisms, by suggesting
that the poet has a broader aim than popular adulation or propaganda. Alfarabi
expresses his dissatisfaction with conventional accounts of poetry through

the mouth of Plato, who rejects the "generally accepted poetic method" but certainly not all poetry (PP 7.20; Strauss 1945, 376 n. 48). Perhaps Alfarabi refers to the generally accepted poetic method in the *Book of Letters*, while pointing to a more unconventional type of poetry in the *Epistle on the Canons of Poetry*.

In the *Epistle on the Canons of Poetry*, Alfarabi quickly classifies the conventional divisions of poetry according to their Arabic names, without telling us anything about them (EP 275, Ar. 269). This would be superfluous, he assures us, because others have already done so in widely disseminated works. He then proceeds to give a putatively Greek classification that extends well beyond its Arabic counterpart (275–76, Ar. 269–70). This short but striking passage brings out the link between poetry and every aspect of human life. Governance, law (*nāmūs*), ethics, and music can be served and inculcated through poetic speech. Even the natural scientists have invented a brand of poetry suitable for describing their investigations (EP 276, Ar. 270). Could Alfarabi be aware of the poems of Parmenides and Empedocles (cf. VC 320.10)? However this may be, it now appears that Alfarabi's ridicule of poetry in the *Book of Letters* as a method suitable only for mere storytelling (BL 224.20–225.1) entails no small amount of exaggeration. The related claim that poets and other members of the elite of the Umma are completely subject to popular opinion (148.14–20, #138) now sounds dubious as well, since popular opinion plays no role whatsoever in the *Epistle on the Canons of Poetry*. If anything, the esteem of kings and other prominent individuals by whom poets are patronized is more important to many poets than the adulation of the people (EP 275, Ar. 269). Yet poetry can hardly be reduced to mere efforts at approval, be it popular or royal: poetic imitation, and artistic creativity more generally, surely have an inspiration of their own. Alfarabi emphasizes that the finest poetry is produced by innate talent rather than external compulsion: a natural-born panegyrist who is forced by his patron to write satire is not likely to excel at it (277, Ar. 271).

Alfarabi has good reasons to desire a poetry that is relatively free from compulsion. In Alfarabi, the Platonic notion that artists can imitate virtually everything in heaven and earth acquires a wide-ranging, highly practical application. Let us reflect again on the notion that unique images reflecting opinions about God, the world, and human politics should be coined for every Umma, city, and group (PR 74–75.90, Ar. 85.17–86.4, VC 280.1–4). Wouldn't this be a boon for imitative artists of all sorts? Painters, sculptors, and poets will fill the workshops and divans of every locality, churning out a colorful array of images of earthly and heavenly things that befit the particular nature of the inhabitants. The overwhelming fact of human diversity demands the continual use of human creative powers.

The *Book of Letters* describes the flourishing of the Umma, before turning abruptly to the appearance of philosophy. We have amply discussed the reasons for this arrangement in Chapters 2 and 3. However, it risks giving the misleading impression that the development of the Umma simply ceases after the codification of its early poetry and linguistic science. This assumption is quite obviously false. Homer and Valmiki may remain the greatest literary figures of their respective Ummas, but they did not lack worthy successors. Themes that they established were reworked according to the disposition of future poets and the times and places in which they lived. Nor had the Arab Umma ossified by Alfarabi's time: one of his most illustrious contemporaries was the poet Mutanabbi (b. 915, d. 965). Alfarabi's own teaching about the need for image making particular to all groups, Ummas, and cities surely conduces to the continued vitality of the Umma, as it adapts to the ever-changing character of its members.

At this point, another important difference between Alfarabi and Plato with regard to poetry has become clear. Plato often treats poetry with considerable irreverence, and speaks of its quarrel with philosophy (*Republic* 607b6–7). Alfarabi never mentions any such quarrel. He suggests on numerous occasions that philosophy and poetry are mutually complementary, each having its own distinct method and serving its own distinct purpose (EP 274, Ar. 268; SP 174–75; ES 103, 109–11). Poetry attains certain ends, in particular the instruction of the multitude, which could never be realized by philosophy alone (BL 152.4–5, #143). Poetry may require some political supervision insofar as it is equally capable of encouraging moderation and immoderation (SA 35–37, #55–56), but it does not represent a serious threat to philosophy. For Alfarabi, this dubious honor is assumed by false religion: inspired from the outset by untrue or limited doctrines, such a religion can never reconcile itself to philosophy and remains continually at war with it (BL 153.17–18, #147; 155.19–162.2, #150). Alfarabi seeks to enlist artistic creativity in all its diversity as a means of resisting such religion.[26] Both philosophy and art defy the narrowness of false religion by reflecting on all the things in heaven and earth, while thriving in the midst of human diversity. The relation between philosophy and poetry has been altered in a fundamental way by the triumph of revealed religion: erstwhile rivals must now become close allies. This conclusion may point to yet another reason why

Alfarabi does not attempt to weave poetic fables: if poetry and philosophy must become allied, then why would the philosopher attempt to undermine the poet by challenging him at his own game?

I have suggested in Chapter 2 that the Umma should best be understood as a high civilization, under whose aegis the various forms of art may flourish. In the final analysis, this definition of the Umma applies to some of the most admirable aspects of the Islamic Umma as well. Alfarabi could be said to have anticipated the term "Islamic civilization," insofar as it signifies the various forms of high art and literature that flourished for centuries in medieval Islam, with great local variation.[27] In modern times, however, the great medieval traditions of art and architecture have been disrupted, and their replacements are still a work in progress. The foreign-designed towers of Dubai do not compare well, except in sheer size, to old Cairo's graceful minarets. While Islamic religion has flourished over the past century, attracting new adherents from all corners of the earth, Islamic civilization often appears to have stagnated. The result is a far-flung global community imbued with a common faith but lacking any common civilization. Reduced merely to a religion, Islam becomes more vulnerable to the sweeping, obscurantist claims of religious zealots, appealing to Muslims who know only the legal, ritual, and martial aspects of their civilization. The indifference, or in some cases outright hatred, that fundamentalist Muslim groups display toward art, manifested in the demolition of Buddhist statues by the Taliban in Afghanistan,[28] the destruction of ancient Sufi shrines by Islamist rebels in Mali, and the very public obliteration of so much of Syria and Iraq's artistic heritage at the hands of ISIS, could be viewed in this light. Observations of this sort point to how Alfarabi might have understood the crisis in the Islamic Umma today, as a crisis in Islamic civilization. Alfarabi perceived that the future of the arts of the Umma, both ethnic and Islamic, and the future of philosophy within Islam, were closely linked: as they work together to preserve human variety and keep the repression of false religion at bay, the vitality of the one will help to ensure that of the other.

Chapter 6

Between City and Empire: The Political Significance of the Umma

I have shown how Alfarabi defines both the ethnic and the Islamic Umma, and strives to assure their harmonious coexistence. This requires a looser, more flexible interpretation of Islam by both artists and jurists. But the discussion to this point has yet to adequately consider the statesman's point of view. How should he handle the diversity of Ummas, ethnic and Islamic? We cannot complete this discussion without considering the political significance of the Umma more generally.

Following the pattern to which we have become accustomed, Alfarabi treats the political significance of the Umma from different perspectives in different works. Our analysis of the conclusion of the *Book of Religion* has already given a sense of what the Muslim statesman should not do. Yet this passage must be viewed in light of Alfarabi's most ambitious proposal for multinational empire, which occurs in the *Attainment of Happiness*. Examining this proposal will serve to bring the basic problem into focus. I will then turn to Alfarabi's other discussions of the political significance of the Umma and its relationship to tribe, city, and empire.

Linguistic Science, Rhetoric, and the Instruction of the Ummas

In the opening statement of the *Attainment of Happiness*, Alfarabi proclaims the ambitious scope of the work:

> The human things through which Ummas and citizens of cities
> attain earthly happiness in this life and supreme happiness in the
> life beyond are of four kinds: theoretical virtues, deliberative
> virtues, moral virtues, and practical arts. (AH 2.1–5, trans. Mahdi,
> Ar. 49.1)

Ummas and cities figure prominently in this quotation, since the lofty enterprise of attaining complete human happiness can be realized only within the framework that these lowly communities provide.[1] And yet the approach outlined by Alfarabi in his opening paragraph, and continued throughout much of work, seems to take these particular human associations for granted. They will be mentioned dozens of times, but only as an afterthought. As the wise rulers and their minions traverse the globe for the sake of spreading human happiness, they will come into contact with many Ummas and cities. But for these fleet-footed rulers, these Ummas and cities exist as mere scenery, or empty vessels to be filled with the fine wine of their wise education and rule. They require no thematic treatment or investigation whatsoever, even by political science, which is quick to equate their hierarchical structure with the structure of the world (AH 16.4–21, Ar. 63.19–64.20). But few details are given about the character of either hierarchy. In the *Attainment of Happiness*, any study of the character, aims, and parts of the Umma and city is noticeably absent.

Nonetheless, even if the Umma is not defined in this work, it is certainly defined elsewhere, and it is hard to imagine Alfarabi not having that definition in mind. Indeed, if the reader applies what he has learned from the *Book of Letters* and *Book of Religion* to the argument of the *Attainment of Happiness*, he will begin to observe some troublesome lacunae in Alfarabi's dashing enterprise.

Alfarabi espouses his plan to an addressee (AH 3.18, Ar. 50.2), who reappears at various places in the text. Following Muhsin Mahdi's cue, we must carefully observe the addressee's presence, and absence.[2] This pupil must first undergo instruction in the sciences. The list of sciences is fairly exhaustive, covering most of the "generally known sciences" presented in the *Enumeration of the Sciences*, and even following, in most cases, the order of that book (ES 49–51 passim, AH 2.6–16.21, Ar. 49.1–64.20). The glaring exception is linguistic science, which comes first in the *Enumeration of the Sciences*, but is skipped entirely in the *Attainment of Happiness*, where Alfarabi rushes his addressee ahead to logic.[3]

From a purely scientific point of view, the omission of linguistic science is understandable. We have already observed its weaknesses as a science, due to its dependence on a multiplicity of human linguistic conventions. It is telling that linguistic science appears in only some of Alfarabi's accounts of the various sciences.[4] Indeed, if there are in fact as many linguistic sciences as there are languages, then any attempt to study all of them would be absolutely futile, even for the world's greatest linguist. Yet it is the political point of view that soon comes to dominate the work (AH 15.17 ff.), and the political value of linguistic science as a means to communicate with each of the various Ummas is unquestionable. Even in the case of a local ruler, the study of the linguistic science of his own Umma would certainly be useful for governing it. However, the specific Umma to which the addressee belongs remains unspecified and unknown. Whatever his own community may be, his ambitions seem too grand for it, if he indeed aspires to rule many Ummas. The *Attainment of Happiness* operates, from the very beginning, on a transnational scale. But we do not yet know whether the first ruler has the transnational knowledge, linguistic or otherwise, that would be required to implement its scheme.

The Umma becomes an especially important theme when Alfarabi describes the first ruler's[5] conquest of the Ummas and cities. The addressee is absent from this section of the work. Not yet being a first ruler himself, he is reduced, as it were, to a mere spectator of the first ruler's successes—and struggles.[6] This conquest involves, among other things, education. Whoever wishes to become the first ruler of many Ummas must undertake the education of each of them. The vital importance of the Umma for education becomes clear when Alfarabi temporarily drops "cities" from the section devoted to the instruction of the various human communities. The formula "Ummas and cities" is reduced to simply "Ummas" (AH 34.11–36.12, Ar. 83.51–86.52).

The project of multinational rule would be easier if a common human nature allowed the same methods, images, and persuasive arguments to work for every Umma. Alfarabi acknowledges that such a common human nature exists, and that there are such universal images and arguments (AH 30.16–18, Ar. 79.46, 33.5–8, Ar. 82.50). Yet as I already observed in Chapter 5, he chooses to give specific examples neither of this nature nor of these images and arguments.[7] The description of the rhetorical arguments needed to fill the souls of the citizens with reverence toward the ruler and the virtuous, along with aversion toward his enemies and the vicious, is charming but vague. It calls for two digests of such universally applicable sayings, titled the *Book of Opinions* and the *Book of Acts* (AH 33.9–34.8, Ar. 82–83.50). Unfortunately, there is no evidence that Alfarabi ever wrote such books, as if he aspired neither to become a first ruler himself nor to help others attain that rank. On the contrary, Alfarabi's logical works contain some striking passages that bring out the difficulties associated with any universal law or morality. In order to put the argument of the *Attainment of Happiness* into context, we need to turn briefly to those passages.

A passage in the *Book of Dialectic* raises the question whether there are universal moral and ethical premises that apply to all Ummas (BDi 75.4–76.4). The universal premises include the worship owed to God, the honor due to parents, the obligation entailed by kinship, the consolation of the needy, and the debt of gratitude toward benefactors (75.16–17). These premises should not be made subjects of dialectical disputes, but simply obeyed in deed (75.11–12, 20–22). This obedience is induced not by nature or argument, but by custom and punishment, beginning in earliest childhood (75.7–11, 75.21–76.4). Now custom, we recall, is what first differentiated the Ummas and their languages in the *Book of Letters*. It follows that even the most universal ethical principles would be inculcated in different ways among different peoples: every Umma worships God and honors its parents, but none does so in exactly the same fashion. An even stronger version of the same teaching appears in one of Alfarabi's works on rhetoric. There are universal laws, such as to honor friends and never wrong anybody who has never wronged you, but these frequently come into conflict with the laws of particular groups or nations.[8] These kinds of cases, which Alfarabi never attempts to resolve, pose a formidable challenge to rhetoricians (DA, 159). Universal laws and principles may exist in theory, but they will never obtain in practice among all particular peoples.

The great concessions that Alfarabi makes to human diversity underlie many of the difficulties encountered by the first ruler in the *Attainment of Happiness*. Before launching into his most detailed discussion of how the first ruler should govern and educate the Ummas, Alfarabi reiterates the need to inquire into the human nature common to all of them (AH 34.12–15, Ar. 83.51). But once again Alfarabi fails to state any definitive result for this inquiry. This much is clear: our common nature, whatever it may be, does not eliminate the significance of the differences produced by the division of humankind into Ummas. The following section, in which Alfarabi tries to explain how to navigate these distinctions, is marked by several noticeable

equivocations. The first ruler, who may not be any more familiar with linguistic science than the addressee, must inquire into the character of each
of the Ummas, but his investigation will be able to cover only "most" of them
(34.13, Ar. 83.51). Similarly, his list of the acts and character traits that direct
the Ummas toward happiness is only "approximate" (34.16, Ar. 84.51). The
education of the Ummas toward happiness requires not only theoretical virtues, but also rhetorical persuasion and poetic image-making, as well as
"sciences extracted from these three for each Umma" (35.1–6, Ar. 84.52). But
if the number of such arts and sciences is as great as the number of Ummas
and languages, neither the first ruler nor the addressee could ever be expected
to handle them alone. The precise tasks of instruction would therefore have
to be delegated to competent subordinates within each Umma. Yet the first
ruler does not receive any answer to his question "whether or not there is a
group fit for preserving theoretical sciences" in each Umma, and is forced to
proceed hypothetically: "Provided all of these groups exist" (35.2, Ar. 84.52).
Perhaps the existence of qualified teachers within each Umma would depend
on the consummation of the growth of language and philosophy, as recounted
in the *Book of Letters*. As we have seen in Chapter 2, such progress is far from
a foregone conclusion, especially in the less hospitable climate zones.

To make things worse, the challenge of instructing diverse groups of
humans does not end with the multiplicity of Ummas. Alfarabi makes clear,
without providing much by way of specifics, that every Umma will have to
be divided into many parts, each of which will require its own teachers (AH
36.5–10, Ar. 85–86.52, cf. 34.19, Ar. 84.51). The task of carrying out this intricate and expansive education project while relying on strangers in far-flung
Ummas for all particular knowledge appears daunting.[9] Alfarabi concludes
the section with the statement that "These, then, are the modes and the
methods through which the four human things by which supreme happiness is achieved are realized in Ummas and cities" (36.12–14, Ar. 86.52). This
sounds reassuring, but one could ask whether such modes and methods will
prove feasible. The astute reader, not to mention the addressee, will hardly
have been relieved of all doubt.[10]

The Language of Philosophy

The final section of the *Attainment of Happiness* introduces two things that
are noticeably absent from the earlier portions of the work. First of all, it is

only here that Alfarabi finally speaks of, and defines, philosophy, as the science that rules all sciences and art that rules all arts (AH 38.18–39.9, Ar. 88–89.54). As in Plato's *Republic*, philosophy bursts suddenly onto the stage, dramatically altering the course of the argument. Second, it is only in connection with the transmission of philosophy that Alfarabi adduces particular Ummas. Philosophy "is said" to have existed among the Chaldeans and Egyptians. Among the Greeks, Assyrians, and now the Arabs, proof of their interest in philosophy has been preserved in their languages (38.14–17, Ar. 88.54).[11] Alfarabi's decision to cite concrete, historical examples at this precise moment, but not in his discussion of the exploits of the first ruler, is revealing: although the conquest and education of many Ummas by a wise first ruler are not attested in history, the passage of philosophy from one Umma to another is known to have occurred more than once. Most important, history shows that philosophy may be successfully transferred from the Greeks to the Arabs. The emphasis of the work begins to shift from a project that cannot be accomplished to one that can.

Shortly after the introduction of philosophy, the same addressee who has been allowed to dispense with conventional linguistic science is asked to understand "our language," in which the philosopher is identified not only with the first ruler who is supposed to conquer so many Ummas, but with the more familiar categories of the king,[12] the legislator, and the *imām* (AH 43.18–44.2, Ar. 93–94.61). The identity of "our language" is not immediately obvious. It would be tempting to identify this language with one of the three conventional languages whose terms are discussed in the *Attainment of Happiness*, namely, Greek, Syriac, and Arabic (38.18, Ar. 88.54). Since Alfarabi does not say anything about Syriac terms in the work, or suggest that either he or his reader should be familiar with them, we may rule out that possibility immediately. Alfarabi does say something about both Greek and Arabic, just enough to show that the identification of "our language" with either would entail insuperable contradictions.

The identification of "our language" with Greek faces two immediate obstacles. First, the very term *imām* has no parallel in Greek, and second, the Greek definition of philosophy as a quest for wisdom says nothing about kings, rulers, or legislators (AH 38.17–39.5, Ar. 88.89–54). Besides, it would be strange for Alfarabi to define Greek as "our language" to his mainly Arabic-speaking readers. This consideration alone makes it more plausible to identify this elusive tongue with Arabic. But here, too, a major contradiction emerges. In the "language of the Arabs" (*lughat al-'arab*)[13] the *imām* signifies a person whose aims and actions are widely imitated and accepted.[14] Alfarabi at first assumes that such universal acceptance can be obtained only by the deliberative virtues and theoretical sciences derived from philosophy (43.8–18, Ar. 93.60).[15] If this assumption holds, then the *imām* can be equated with the philosopher, and "our language" with the "language of the Arabs." However, Alfarabi later retracts his own argument, by declaring that a philosopher can still be a philosopher even if nobody listens to him, and that such indifference to the opinions of other people characterizes the *imām* as well (46.12–47.3, Ar. 96–97).[16] This preserves the identification of *imām* with philosopher, but the new definition of *imām* plainly contradicts the traditional Arabic definition, according to which an *imām* absolutely requires a large popular following. "Our language" and the "language of the Arabs" have diverged.

Alfarabi complicates the issue still further by employing terms so mutually contradictory and out of place that even Muhsin Mahdi chose to simplify them in translation. Alfarabi insists that his peculiar equation of philosopher with *imām*, king, first ruler, and legislator is upheld by "the multitude of adepts at our language" (*jumhūr ahl lughatina*, 43.18–44.2, Ar. 93–94.61), rather than, as Mahdi translates, "the majority of those who speak our language." To be fair to Mahdi, all three of these terms require more careful an interpretation than any translation can provide.

The *jumhūr* signifies the multitude, a very common term in Alfarabi, and Mahdi normally translates it as such. Since Alfarabi does not hesitate in adjacent paragraphs to distinguish sharply between the legislator, who is capable of absorbing theoretical truths directly, and the *jumhūr*, who are not (AH 44.7–8, Ar. 94.61, cf. 36.17, Ar. 86.53), how could he imagine that any multitude would speak a language that equates a philosopher such as himself with their universally beloved *imām*?[17] The traditional language of the Arabs did not even possess a word for philosopher, which had to be imported from Greek (cf. 38.18–19, Ar. 88.54). As for the word *ahl*, it has already appeared in the section on the transmission of philosophy from people to people, where it signifies those who might have practiced philosophy in Egypt and Iraq (38.15, Ar. 88.54).[18] Furthermore, the phrase *ahl al-falsafa* appears in the *Book of Letters* (BL 155.9, #149). In this context, *ahl* means something like "adepts" or "initiates." Just as only a few very talented people in each Umma could ever have practiced philosophy, so only a few very talented people could ever learn "our language." The juxtaposition of the unskilled multitude to the skilled few in a single possessive construction, placed in between two passages where the two groups are so starkly contrasted, appears extremely odd.

Finally, there is a certain difference between *lisān*, the term translated as "language" in the *Attainment of Happiness* 38.18 (Ar. 88.54), and *lugha*, the term employed here. The former represents the more common, less specialized word for language, signifying the languages of large Ummas with all their internal diversity, while the latter refers to a more particular dialect.[19] The *Attainment of Happiness* mentions three *lisān*, namely, Greek, Syriac, and Arabic, and two *lugha*, *lughat al-ʿarab* and the enigmatic *lughatuna*, "our language." If "our language" signifies no conventional tongue, then perhaps it resembles the unusual idiom passed down from Plato, according to which the philosopher, at least in theory, is best suited to rule.[20] Philosopher-*imām* thus becomes Alfarabi's supplement to the Platonic philosopher-king. Needless to say, the former would have seemed as ridiculous to most of the speakers of Arabic as the latter did to most of the speakers of Greek (cf. *Republic* 473c, 487b–d).

In devising the phrase "the multitude of the adepts of our language," Alfarabi has deliberately created a monstrous absurdity, in which the multitude willingly accepts a new dialect, fully comprehensible only to adepts, that crowns the philosopher king and consecrates him *imām*. The implausibility of this reconciliation of the Greek emphasis on the philosopher's unfettered pursuit of wisdom with the Arab emphasis on the *imām*'s acceptability to all humans leads Alfarabi to concede at the end of the *Attainment of Happiness* that the philosopher who aspires to rule may not be accepted by the people. His consolation is that he can still devote his intelligence to understanding the philosophy of Plato and Aristotle (AH 46.13–47.10, Ar. 96.64–98.66). Alfarabi emphasizes on this occasion that his two greatest teachers are Greek; in the *Book of Letters*, he chose not to specify the people to whom they belong (BL 151–15.18, #142–43; cf.159.1, #156). He concludes by reminding his readers in general, and perhaps the addressee in particular,[21] that the transmission of philosophy from one Umma to another is a genuine historical phenomenon.

There is a certain link between the inevitable failure of the original project of the *Attainment of Happiness* and the potential success of its final project. A major reason why the philosopher cannot rule is that his *lugha* is equally incomprehensible to all the various multitudes that speak each conventional *lisān* (cf. PP 7.1–9, which speaks of *lisān*). Yet it is precisely the unconventional character of the philosopher's language that helps it pass from one

Umma to another. The same universal features that render philosophy useless for governing any of the particular Ummas allow it to adapt to the inevitable rise and decline of these Ummas. Throughout these vicissitudes, philosophers continue to understand and assert their theoretical capacity to rule, in a way that conforms to the customs of their particular language, while for all practical purposes acknowledging that they will never be accepted as rulers. At the end of the *Attainment of Happiness*, Alfarabi, his addressee, and his more general audience turn away from dreams of imperial rule and devote themselves to the task they are most able to accomplish: recovering the philosophy that was passed down from the Greeks by Plato and Aristotle and restating it for their own age. The *Attainment of Happiness* serves as a most unusual prologue to remarkable presentations of the thought of the two greatest philosophers known to Alfarabi. Even if the philosophers will never succeed in ruling the Ummas, they are entrusted with the vital task of preserving their peculiar language across as many Ummas as possible. Stated in contemporary terms, philosophy can remain cosmopolitan without ever becoming imperial.

Virtuous Governance and the Umma in the *Political Regime*

The project of the *Attainment of Happiness* emerges as a grander and more philosophical version of its counterpart at the end of the *Book of Religion*: both propose the governance of many Ummas by virtuous rulers, with the aim of leading them to happiness. As we have seen, both projects are also exposed to insurmountable objections. Alfarabi does not expect the Ummas to submit so readily to such benign but distant rule, or the wise to undertake the military and educational measures necessary to secure their submission. Yet the impossibility of these projects hardly exhausts the issue of the political significance of the Umma, whose deeply rooted language and habits are sure to present a formidable challenge for statesmen, whatever their ambition might be. Even those who deal with politics on a much smaller scale are bound to brush up against the Umma. Alfarabi illustrates this problem most starkly in the *Political Regime*.

As I argued in Chapter 2, Alfarabi's thematic treatment of the Umma in the *Political Regime* explains its natural causes while neglecting its conventional causes (PR 61.65–62.67, Ar. 70.5–71.13). The rest of the discussion goes even further in separating human will and custom from the "natural"

Umma. Alfarabi elevates this distinction to cosmic proportions, ascribing will to the active intellect, while tracing nature to the heavenly bodies. The active intellect is responsible for all the voluntary human goods: without its peculiar providence, humans could not even begin to employ their intellectual faculties in attaining happiness (30.3, Ar. 32.6–7, 48–49.38, Ar. 55.5–12). The heavenly bodies, in contrast, are responsible for the production of matter and its receptivity to diverse forms (48.38, Ar. 55.3–5; 49.48, Ar. 55.13 ff.). It is the activity of the heavenly bodies that causes the natural division of humankind into Ummas, by means of a complicated but inexorable process that passes through several intermediaries, including the motion of the heavenly bodies, the climatic conditions determined by these motions, the nutrition available in each climate, and the effect that its consumption has on human bodies. All these natural causes stand equally beyond human will and control.[22] The result is the physical appearance and other hereditary characteristics of each Umma (61.65–62.67, Ar. 70.5–71.13).

The first ruler, in contrast, is the product not of nature but of voluntary acts enabled by the active intellect (PR 62.68 ff., Ar. 71.14). The dichotomy between the Umma and this ruler is at first drawn quite sharply. Between *Political Regime* 62.68 (Ar. 71.14) and 69.81 (Ar. 80.6), the Umma as well as the climate and nutrition associated with it disappears from the treatise. Alfarabi goes so far as to remove the nutritive faculty from his list of the faculties of the soul (63.71, Ar. 73.10–11, cf. 30.4, Ar. 32.14–15), even though it is included in parallel lists in other works (VC 166.1–12, SA 14–15, #7, Ar. 28–30, PA 116.4–117.12). Alfarabi never tells us what the citizens living under the first ruler eat. That they must ingest something and belong to some Umma seems obvious, but Alfarabi's refusal to discuss these details raises inevitable questions. He chooses to dump the lowly but indispensable human goods on the Umma so that the first ruler may be absolved from touching them. Is this strategy meant to be persuasive? Or it is rather meant to betray the unpleasant necessities that must at first be ignored so that the virtuous city may be constructed?

A related difficulty arises with regard to the use of the term "nature" (*ṭabʿ*) and its derivatives. At first it seems as if the heavenly bodies are identified with nature and the Umma (PR 61.65–62.67, Ar. 70.5–71.13), while the active intellect is identified with will and the intelligibles (62.68 ff., Ar. 71.14). However, nature cannot be so summarily dismissed, and it soon returns, along with the heavenly bodies (63.70 ff., Ar. 73.1). Although Alfarabi argues that the intention of the heavenly bodies and of nature does not have any bearing on the goals of the active intellect, he cannot deny that the effects of the heavenly bodies, however random, necessarily facilitate or obstruct the active intellect's ability to realize its goals (63.70, Ar. 73.1–9). The inability of the active intellect and the human will to summarily brush aside the intermittent hostility of nature casts a pall over any attempt to establish and preserve the virtuous political community. Although the governor strives to remove all evils, voluntary and natural, from the cities and the Ummas (73.88, Ar. 84.10–11), he seems unable to protect the virtuous community against natural disasters such as famine or plague (70.81, Ar. 80.10–11).[23]

I have shown that even if the Umma could be reduced to natural causes, it would still be impossible to ignore. Yet the Umma represents far more than mere nature. It is sufficient to recall the difference between the account of the Umma in the *Political Regime* and its counterpart in the *Book of Letters*. In the *Book of Letters*, Alfarabi ascribes the most significant traits of the Umma to the conventional development of language. In the *Political Regime*, Alfarabi acknowledges language as the conventional cause of the Umma in a brief sentence (PR 61.65, Ar. 70.6–7), but elaborates only on the natural causes and characteristics of the Umma. In the remainder of the *Political Regime*, he chooses never to mention language again. This significant omission allows Alfarabi to maintain, at least for a while, the fiction of the "natural" Umma versus the "willed" virtuous regime. But the absence of language has curious effects whenever Alfarabi tries to explain the city's approach to education.

The *Selected Aphorisms* is primarily a work about cities, but in it Alfarabi does not conceal from his readers that language experts, including poets, rhetoricians, linguists, and scribes, are indispensable for the education of the city (SA 37, #57, Ar. 65.9–12, see BL 143.1 ff., #130, 148.14–16, #138). The declaration of the language experts' importance follows a description of poetry and rhetoric, the popular arts of the Umma (SA 35–37, #54–56, Ar. 62.2–65.8, see BL 142.6 ff, #129). Despite the fact that the Umma is not mentioned in these passages, a reader familiar with the *Book of Letters* will immediately recognize in them an implicit acknowledgment that any city wishing to educate its citizens must do so in the language and traditions of the Umma to which it belongs. Even the *Virtuous City*, which never really discusses either poetry or rhetoric, includes facility with language among the skills required in the first ruler (VC 246.2–4, 246.16–247.1). The only account of education and government that attempts to sidestep the linguistic arts of the Umma entirely occurs in the *Political Regime*. Let us examine some of the peculiarities of this account.

Alfarabi distinguishes sharply between teachers and guides on the one hand, and those who need to be taught and guided on the other. There is a need for guides and guided, and therefore rulers and ruled, in every single kind of human activity (PR 68.78, Ar. 78.1–79.2). It would be reasonable to infer that this guidance is proffered at least in part through speech, be it technical or rhetorical, but here one runs up against Alfarabi's self-imposed silence. Not only language but poetry and rhetoric are left out of the discussion; writing appears once, but it is presented only by analogy, and as an "action" or "art" perfected through repetition and practice rather than as a form of communication (72.86, Ar. 83.1). In keeping with the pattern that we have begun to observe, the parallel discussion of writing in the *Virtuous City* does take note of the link between writing, language, and rhetoric (VC 266.11–15).

Toward the end of the discussion of the virtuous rulership in the *Political Regime,* Alfarabi finally gives imagination and imitation, both of which are closely linked to language and poetry, their due (PR 74.89, Ar. 85.3–11).[24] Yet he continues to tiptoe around the question of language. We have already explained in Chapter 5, the importance of visual imagery in this passage, and its call for artistic flexibility within Islam. But the absence of written images in it is no less striking. Alfarabi's choice of purely visual examples once again evades the issue of language, of which he speaks quite freely in his other works. In *Selected Aphorisms*, Alfarabi introduces only the imitative arts most acceptable to his community, namely poetry and music, into the city (SA 36–37, #56, Ar. 64.5–65.8). In the parallel passage in the *Virtuous City,* Alfarabi omits the example of statues altogether, leaving open the possibility that the most appropriate images might be written or oral (VC 278.8–279.6). If Alfarabi in fact regards all the imitative arts as equally suitable for disseminating religious images, as I have suggested in Chapter 5, then the discussion in the *Political Regime* could indeed allude to written images as well. But Alfarabi's reluctance to acknowledge this possibility reflects the broader silence about written communication that pervades the entire work.

Alfarabi proceeds to make the portentous claim that religion may vary from one virtuous city and Umma to another (PR 75.89, Ar. 85.18–86.1). Although there is no reason to doubt the sincerity of this statement, it is difficult to interpret it on the basis of the arguments provided in the *Political*

Regime alone, which have taught us nothing about the role of language within the Umma. In any religion based on a revealed book, the language in which that book is recited, interpreted, and discussed is bound to assume great importance. Will Persians read and interpret the Qur'ān in their own language or in Arabic? This question will remain crucial even if, following Alfarabi's suggestions, Islamic injunctions against visual image-making are relaxed in order to cater to the needs of each Umma. Alfarabi's suggestive but incomplete statement about the relation of Ummas to religion once again draws our attention to the absence of language.

The virtuous regime is grafted, somehow, on either a city or an Umma (PR 69.81, Ar. 80.6). One wonders how this can be done without a thorough examination of the structure and character of either of these two communities. We recall once more the question of the relationship between successful first rulers and the preexisting communities with which they interact. Yet in the *Political Regime*, the inadequate treatment of the Umma, along with the absence of any treatment of the city, does not permit a serious discussion of the interaction between the first ruler and his community, without which his government could never actually come into being in this world. Is the virtuous rulership, any more than the city of Plato's *Republic*, ever meant to exist anywhere on earth? Perhaps Alfarabi begins to speak of actual human situations only when describing the dispersion of this city's inhabitants following its inevitable decline on account of plague, famine, or war (69.81, Ar. 80.9–11). These inhabitants, the scattered remnants of a philosophical garden of Eden, ought to be consoled by the promise that their souls will reunite in another world. It is only among disembodied souls that the goal of the active intellect is fully realized, without the interference of heavenly bodies and therefore of the Umma (71.84–72.85, Ar 81.14–82.10). In this earthly existence, the incessant demands of the nutritive faculty, indecipherable jumble of human languages, and lingering menace of natural disasters all combine to ensure that the active intellect and heavenly bodies will never fully cooperate.[25]

I have observed in Chapter 4 that outside of Alfarabi's summaries of Plato, there is no Alfarabian equivalent to the Platonic founder of a new city, and the *Political Regime* is no exception. Yet the conflict between virtuous government and the Umma arises regardless whether the virtuous government is meant for a newly established community characteristic of the *Republic* or the preexisting community assumed in the *Political Regime*. Indeed, the relationship of virtuous rulership to the Umma in the *Political Regime* is in many respects quite reminiscent of the *Republic*: both works appear to circumvent the Umma, but in doing so tacitly acknowledge that its language and traditions cannot be ignored. Alfarabi omits the Umma, along with its language and nutrition, from his discussion of virtuous rulership. At the same time, he insinuates that without these features of the Umma the virtuous ruler can neither feed nor educate his citizens. It follows that in the absence of any effort to grapple with the obstacles posed by the Umma the virtuous community described in the *Political Regime*, like the city of the *Republic* (592a9–b4), exists only in heaven. On this earth, a prudent accommodation between the virtuous ruler and the Umma remains indispensable. But in the *Political Regime*, the path to such a compromise remains as elusive as ever.

In discussing the *Attainment of Happiness* and *Political Regime*, I have focused on two uncompromising proposals for virtuous rulership that fail partly because they attempt to circumvent the Umma. It has become patently obvious that statesmen ignore the Umma at their own peril, regardless of whether they are operating on the scale of a multinational empire or small, local community. But how should they engage it? And what is the Umma's precise relation to tribes, cities, empires, and other kinds of human community? These are the questions with which the rest of this book is concerned.

Virtuous Ummas and Ignorant Cities in the *Virtuous City*

In Chapter 1, I briefly compared Alfarabi's presentation of cities and Ummas to Aristotle's. Citing passages in the *Virtuous City* and *Political Regime*, I argued that Alfarabi did not follow Aristotle's elevation of the city above all other kinds of human community. Abandoning or at least diluting the Greek emphasis on the *polis*, Alfarabi seeks to describe communities more characteristic of the world in which he lived and wrote. I initiated this discussion in Chapter 1 in order to refute the notion that Alfarabi focuses primarily on the city, thus removing a major obstacle to the appreciation of the importance of the Umma, but I could not complete it at that stage, before I had fully defined the Umma or examined its relationship to Islam. We are ready to resume that discussion now. How does Alfarabi situate cities, Ummas, and multinational communities within his broader religious and political understanding?

Ancient Greeks often aspired to the independent *polis*, but medieval Muslims knew only monarchy and empire. Alfarabi never states the difference between ancient Greek and medieval politics directly, but quietly indicates his awareness of it. In the *Selected Aphorisms* and the *Summary of Plato's "Laws"*, works explicitly ascribed to the ancients in their titles and introductions (SA 11, Intro., Ar. 23), Alfarabi barely mentions the Umma: in the former, he does so only in the concluding aphorisms, while in the latter, he never does so at all. Both works speak of cities repeatedly, as if to reflect the fact that the ancients were concerned primarily with this type of society.

The predominant role of the city in these works must be compared to the entirely novel view of the relationship between Ummas and cities expressed by Alfarabi in the *Virtuous City*. Of all Alfarabi's major political works, the *Virtuous City*, with its emphasis on a hierarchically ordered cosmos emanating from a perfect God and imitated by a virtuous world regime governed by an *imām*, may appear the furthest removed from the spirit of antiquity. Nevertheless, the very title of the work seems to imply a certain centrality to the city, which remains, in the words of Leo Strauss, the "ancient nucleus" of political life.[26] The contents of this work vacillate between passages where the city appears as the sole political community and passages where it must share that honor with the Umma, as well as, in some instances, with the entire inhabited world (VC 228.11–230.2, 246.6–7). Most notable in the *Virtuous City* is the exclusion of the Umma and other larger associations from Alfarabi's elaborate parallels between the city, the human body, and the cosmos (VC 230.12–238.10; Mahdi 2001, 142), and from the passages treating the ignorant cities (VC 252.15–276.8).

Scholars have made some ingenious attempts to explain away these inconsistencies. Richard Walzer suggests that the term "city" is equivocal, referring in some cases to a distinct type of political community that must be contrasted with Ummas and tribes, but in other cases serving merely as a generic term for "state" (VC, trans. Walzer, 430). This solution fails to reckon with the fact that Alfarabi uses the generic term "association" (*ijtimā‘*), encompassing city and Umma, as well as other kinds of human society, whenever it suits him (VC 228.12). When Alfarabi employs the particular term "city" rather than the general term "association," we ought to assume that he does so for a reason. Nāṣif Naṣṣār suggests that the six forms of ignorant city ought to apply equally to the Umma (Naṣṣār 1978, 49–50). He cites the only passage in the work in which Alfarabi speaks of "the virtuous Ummas and the Ummas contrary to them" (VC 278.6–7). For Naṣṣār, these contrary

Ummas include not only the ignorant Ummas, but also the wicked, errant, and perverted Ummas (Naṣṣār 1978, 50; VC 256.15–258.9). Naṣṣār's assertion draws valuable attention to an important interpretative difficulty, but remains exposed to three major objections. First, why should we identify the "Ummas contrary to the [virtuous Ummas]" with the ignorant, wicked, and perverted Ummas whose existence is not even acknowledged throughout the rest of the treatise? Second, if Alfarabi had wished to designate the ignorant Ummas alongside of the ignorant cities in the *Virtuous City*, he certainly could have done so, as he does without hesitation in the *Book of Religion* (BR 103.32–33, Ar. 55.12–13). Third, these nonvirtuous Ummas are included in a list of things that "all the inhabitants of the virtuous city . . . ought to know" (VC 276.10–11). Should we share Naṣṣār's assumption that the opinions of the inhabitants of the virtuous city ought to correspond entirely with doctrines that Alfarabi expresses as his own? While I do not purport to resolve all these difficulties, I hope to have discerned the general direction in which Alfarabi's often perplexing omissions, and inclusions, of the Umma point.

The passage comparing the city to the body and cosmos omits the Umma. All three entities are endowed with a flawlessly ranked, ordered, and harmonized structure in which all their parts move together toward the same goal. Alfarabi's exclusive use of the city in such passages implies a superior cohesiveness that tends to slacken as the association expands into an Umma. This same characteristic of the city is emphasized in the *Selected Aphorisms* (SA 23–24, #25, Ar. 41–42).[27] Although such passages may appear at first glance to echo Aristotle and his emphasis on *koinōneia*, the connection between cohesiveness and virtue is not always evident, especially since cities can just as easily cooperate for a nonvirtuous end, such as wealth and honor (VC 230.5–7, 254.14–256.3, SA 26, #28, Ar. 46.10–16). In the passage treating the ignorant cities, the city is the only kind of association present (VC 252.15–276.8). The Arabic term *jāhil*, although invariably rendered as "ignorant" in translations of Alfarabi, has in Islam a more specific, historical meaning: it refers to the period of Arab paganism that preceded the prophecy of Muhammad. The ignorant cities are rife with exaggerated love of honor, wealth, pleasure, domination, false religion, and other features of pagan ignorance (254.2 ff.). Their religion is attributed to "certain corrupt ancient opinions" of unknown provenance (286.2).[28] The city may remain, in the words of Strauss, the ancient nucleus, but one may wonder whether it is a healthy nucleus.

In contrast, the passages in the *Virtuous City* that treat the virtuous city tend to include the Umma, which appears just as capable of virtue as the city (VC 228.11–13). The great prophetic and military gifts of the wise ruler (244.15–246.5) allow him to lay claim, at least in some cases, to governance of the Umma and even the entire inhabited world (246.7). Alfarabi's tendency in the *Virtuous City* is to speak of Ummas and cities in connection with the virtuous prophetic governments that many of his readers will identify with Islam, but to speak of cities alone in connection with ignorant or pre-Islamic governments. He thereby gives the impression that the extension of virtuous politics toward the Umma is characteristic of Islamic times.

This interpretation remains exposed to the one crucial difficulty indicated by Naṣṣār: why does Alfarabi speak once of both "the virtuous Ummas, and Ummas contrary to them"? According to the argument of the previous two paragraphs, it would have made more sense for Alfarabi to speak of the cities contrary to these Ummas. This is a striking case of Alfarabi not saying what we expect him to say, confounding our judgment by a sudden substitution of terms. This substitution may be best explained by considering its peculiar context, namely, the opinions of the people of the virtuous city. Why do these opinions contradict what Alfarabi says elsewhere in the work, on the question of the existence of nonvirtuous Ummas? Elsewhere in the work, Alfarabi is eager to show that despite the Greek inspiration behind his philosophy, he understands the difference between corrupt ancient cities and the virtuous Islamic Umma or multinational society that has replaced them. It is to this end that he vilifies the "ancient opinions" pervading these cities, while ignoring the existence of ignorant Ummas. Yet Alfarabi also knows that the real opponents of the virtuous community as understood in his time are not the vanished ancient cities, but the various other Ummas, religious or ethnic, that continue to resist Islam. When stating the opinions of the inhabitants of a virtuous society, he indicates that they are more likely to disparage those hostile Ummas than the half-forgotten independent cities of pre-Islamic times.

To substantiate this interpretation, let us recall our analysis of the opening paragraphs of the *Book of Religion*. The Islamic community may have begun as a small tribe, but quickly expanded into an Umma and empire, never again to return to its humble, local roots. The sweeping claims of prophecy in Islam and the generality of the religious claims inculcated by it have imbued both the rulers and the people with grander aspirations that cannot easily be contained within the bounds of a small, local community such as the city. A work such as the *Virtuous City*, which appeals to the Islamic community by presenting itself as a bulwark against any regression to the ignorant opinions of the ancients and their fractious cities, cannot possibly advocate a return to such opinions and cities.[29] This would apply to pagan Athens no less than to the pre-Islamic Arabian cities of Mecca and Medina.

City, Umma, and Deliberation in the *Selected Aphorisms*

The foregoing analysis of the *Virtuous City* shows yet again that Alfarabi neither advocates nor expects a return to the ancient city. But I have yet to elucidate what kind of political form he expects to prevail in his times. Moreover, we should not be satisfied with the claim that Alfarabi rejected the city because it did not exist among his contemporaries. He cannot be expected to accept the judgment of revelation and history without any clear, theoretical explanation.

The argument of the *Selected Aphorisms* sheds some light on these questions. It is the only known work of Alfarabi's whose introduction pays homage to the "sayings of the ancients" (SA 11, Intro., Ar. 23.3–5). By "ancients" Alfarabi probably means Socrates, Plato, and Aristotle, who are subsequently mentioned together by name (25, #28, Ar. 45.7).[30] While the ancients, or at least their opinions, are condemned in the *Virtuous City*, they are warmly praised in the *Selected Aphorisms*. Given the connection between ancients and cities, it is fitting that such a work should contain Alfarabi's most thorough analysis of the city. In keeping with the preferences of Plato and Aristotle, no kind of political community other than the city is even mentioned, all the way through Aphorism 94. But in the second-to-last aphorism, the Umma finally appears (63–64, #95, Ar. 99.3–8). Why? Let us examine this work with this question in mind.[31]

Throughout much of the treatise, Alfarabi takes some pains to remain within the bounds of a city, passing up some excellent occasions to introduce the Umma. First, he discusses the role of rhetoric and poetry in the city's education, and assigns the language experts an important rank within it (SA 35–37, #54–57, Ar. 62.14–65.8). Despite this open acknowledgment of the city's dependence on the Umma's arts, Alfarabi does not cite the Umma at this point. The fact that the city needs the Umma for purposes of education does not necessarily mean that its political life should extend to it.

Somewhat more puzzling is Alfarabi's discussion of war and international politics (SA 43–44, #67, Ar. 76.11–78.2). As we know from works like the *Book of Religion* and the *Attainment of Happiness*, these activities take place on the scale of Ummas, and entail sweeping, multinational ambitions (BR 112–13, Ar. 64.14–66.13; AH 32.11–17, Ar. 81.49). Here, however, Alfarabi implies that all legitimate wars are waged by the city: while the city is mentioned repeatedly in the first half of the aphorism, it falls out of the discussion of unjust war.[32] Apart from the city, Alfarabi speaks only of anonymous enemies (*'adu*) and foreign groups (*qawm*)[33] with which the city often comes into conflict. As I explained in Chapters 1 and 5, *qawm* is a generic term for "group" in the Qu'rān that is employed rather sparingly by Alfarabi, and has none of the linguistic or cultural significance of the Umma. While Alfarabi in the *Attainment of Happiness* speaks freely of just war in connection with virtuous communities and human happiness, here he is loath to do so: virtue and happiness do not figure in the account, and justice is mentioned only once as the outcome of certain kinds of war.[34] Alfarabi does speak of war for the sake of some good, conferred on either the city or its foe (SA 43–44, #67, Ar. 76.12–77.9), but it is not clear whether he means a virtuous or ignorant good (cf. VC 294.14–15).[35] The result of all these omissions is a much more cautious, even cynical account of international politics, according to which the one city exists in a state of hostility with the many *qawm* outside its borders. Indeed, the distinction here between the one city and the many *qawm* seems almost to recall Aristotle's usage of the rare *polis* and many, indefinite *ethnē*. War under these circumstances does not, at least as Alfarabi presents it, possess the aura of virtue or piety that came to surround *jihād* after the rise and early conquests of the Islamic Umma.

The high walls Alfarabi has constructed around the city in the *Selected Aphorisms* are barely punctured by his discussion of education and war. Yet they are resoundingly shattered by his definition of deliberative virtue. When Alfarabi introduces this concept in the second-to-last aphorism,[36] he acknowledges that it is exercised within the domain of Ummas as well as cities (SA 63–64, #95, Ar. 99.3–8). Alfarabi's argument in the *Selected Aphorisms* eventually finds its way into the same, multinational sphere that characterizes the *Book of Religion* and the *Attainment of Happiness*. Since the turn to the Ummas in the *Selected Aphorisms* is so closely linked to deliberative virtue, it behooves us to examine the development of this concept more closely. What is it about deliberative virtue that finally induces Alfarabi to stray beyond the bounds of the city?

Alfarabi establishes at an early stage of the work that sound political judgment, like sound moral and medical judgment, depends on finding the mean. But while the mean in mathematics is fixed, in medicine, morals, and politics it is constantly shifting, and subject to five or more external variables (SA 20–22, #19, Ar. 39.4–10). Among these variables are the size and character of the community in which the king or governor acts: as Alfarabi puts it, the mean varies from "group to group" (*ṭā'ifa*, SA 22, #20, Ar. 39.8–9).[37] The word "group," as opposed to tribe, city, and Umma, tends to designate smaller groups within the city, with whom the king or governor of the city has to cooperate (AH 22.8–10, Ar. 70.31, see SA 22, #21, Ar. 39.8–14). This is indeed the meaning that best fits the immediate context, in which Alfarabi is silent about any community larger than the city (SA 20, #22, Ar. 40.1).

Alfarabi eventually introduces a definition of prudence, but in it he continues to avoid the Umma. The several kinds of prudence do not seem to operate within any political associations larger than the city (SA 32–33, #42, Ar. 57.10–58.10). This restriction corresponds to Aristotle's in the *Nicomachean Ethics*, where the list of the kinds of prudence ends with the "political" and "legislative prudence" practiced within the city (*Nicomachean Ethics* 1141b23–34). In the *Selected Aphorisms*, the narrower scope of prudence appears to contrast starkly with the broader scope of deliberate virtue.

The difficulty with this conclusion, however, is that it is contradicted by the *Book of Religion* and *Book of Letters*, in which prudence as understood by the philosophers and the ancients already operates on a multinational scale (BR 106.10–16, Ar. 58.14–59.2; BL 133.8–13, #112). Even the deceptively "Aristotelian" account of prudence discussed above is not attributed directly to Aristotle, and the definition of prudence that is so attributed, which comes somewhat later in the *Aphorisms*, neglects to define the size of the community in which it operates (SA 55, #85, Ar. 89.8–10). Upon further examination, one may discern two points in this aphorism where Alfarabi appears slightly uncomfortable with the limited scope of prudence. He speaks of "advisory prudence" as applying to the government of "a household, a city, or something else" (32, #42, Ar. 58.3–4). Does this "something else," which Alfarabi hardly seems obliged to add, refer to the Umma, or to some other community larger in size than the city? Alfarabi also recognizes that greater (*'aẓīm*) matters require "a more powerful and complete prudence" (33, #42, Ar. 58.6–8). But since the Umma and multinational associations are larger (*'aẓma*) than the city (VC 228.12–13), might not the governance of Ummas be greater than the governance of a city? In the section of the *Attainment of*

Happiness that refers to deliberative virtue, Alfarabi speaks again of the most powerful (*'aẓīm al-qūwwa*) of these virtues, ascribing it to cities, nations, and multinational associations alike (AH 21.10–22.2, Ar. 69.29, 23.7–12, Ar. 71.33). To return to the *Selected Aphorisms*, it seems that even there Alfarabi manages to raise the specter of the Umma or even a multinational empire, by hinting at some other kind of prudence and ascribing greater prudence to matters of greater size. Yet this apparition remains neatly concealed until Aphorism 95. Why does deliberative virtue, rather than prudence, require an explicit acknowledgment of the Umma? This question is especially perplexing because the two qualities themselves appear to be so similar: both consist mainly of the capacity to discover specific actions that serve a virtuous end (SA 31, #39, Ar. 55.6–9; 63, #95, Ar. 99.3–4).

Some of the peculiarities of the discussion of prudence in the middle of the *Selected Aphorisms* might be due to its inadequacy. While the account of prudence in the *Book of Religion*, as well as the later definition of deliberative virtue in the *Selected Aphorisms*, include the ability to react and adjust to external accidents (BR 106.5–6, Ar. 58.15–17, SA 55, #85, Ar. 89.12–15, 63–64, #95, Ar. 99.3–5), such accidents do not figure in Aphorisms 39 or 42. This omission gives rise to a somewhat inflexible definition of prudence that doggedly pursues noble ends leading to happiness without making the adjustments required by external events (SA 31, #39, Ar. 55.6–9). Alfarabi indicates in this subtle way that the restriction of prudence to the city comes at the expense of its ability to react effectively to the vicissitudes of political life, which risk drawing it beyond the city's narrow boundaries.

The middle section of the *Selected Aphorisms* is also characterized by an unsatisfactory account of the relationship between theory and practice. Knowledge and wisdom concern the unchanging things, such as God and numbers, of which we can acquire certainty (SA 29–31, #36–37, Ar. 52.3–54.9). Since we possess no such enduring certainty about whether a given man is standing or sitting, this does not fall within the realm of knowledge (29, #36, Ar. 52.8–9). The implications of this argument for our ability to acquire any scientific knowledge of politics are stark. Political prudence would seem to deal with a Protean, ever-changing realm in which our mind can find no sure anchor. Alfarabi concludes the discussion by attempting to unite prudence and wisdom: while wisdom posits the end, namely, "true happiness," and prudence discovers the means to happiness (35, #53, Ar. 62.2–13), neither capacity appears to inform or enrich the other. So long as wisdom refuses to descend into the realm of particular things, it is unclear how prudence could receive guidance from it; and so long as prudence fails to acquire any idea of true happiness, it is unclear how wisdom can make use of it in the pursuit of that end. Alfarabi's definition of deliberative virtue, in contrast, comes after a much fuller attempt to unite theory and practice. Without further ado, let us turn to this definition and its relation to the discussion of science that precedes it.

Alfarabi prefaces Aphorism 94 with a summary of its content: "on the use of the theoretical part of philosophy and its necessity in the practical part in [different] ways" (SA 61, #94, Ar. 95.14–15).[38] This introductory comment heralds a major deviation from the doctrine expressed in the middle of the work, according to which the objects grasped by theoretical intellect have little bearing on practice. Alfarabi now proceeds to argue that only the pursuit of logical demonstration, natural science, and theoretical science studied according to their proper order confers the principles on which sound practice is based (61, #94, Ar. 96.5–11). Alfarabi proceeds to state that order, suggesting that the student begin with mathematics, which seems to possess more certainty than the other theoretical arts (61, #94, Ar. 96.11–16; see 20–21, #19, Ar. 5–7; 30, #36, Ar. 52.2–3). He should then proceed gradually to subjects that involve more and more matter, such as optics, music, and the heavenly bodies. He thus becomes aware of natural science (62, #94, Ar. 97.2–4). Since this science alone turns out to be insufficient for human perfection (62, #94, Ar. 97.14–16), the student also needs to inquire into divine and metaphysical beings as well as the ends for which humans aim (62–63, #94, Ar. 97.8–98.2). Only then is he ready to engage in the right kind of practical activity, by transferring his knowledge of the sciences to the practical part of the soul (63, #94, Ar. 98.7–8). Alfarabi never suggests that we can attain a high degree of certainty in these investigations: the word "certain" is absent from the account, and the investigation into the human ends and perfections so necessary for practical activity is ongoing (63, #94, Ar. 98.5–7). While the student may not attain theoretical certainty, he does learn two crucial things. First, theoretical science[39] allows him to contemplate rational principles and approach the human end of happiness, toward which all human activity must be directed (62, #94. Ar. 97.17–18): in this manner, theoretical science assumes the role that was filled provisionally by wisdom in the middle of the work (35, #53, Ar. 62.10). And natural science allows him to define the "nature of the possible," precious knowledge that not even revelation can give us (63, #94, Ar. 98.10–20). Perhaps the absence of any clear articulation of natural science in the earlier portions of the work left prudence unable to grapple with possible, accidental things, while the absence of theoretical science left wisdom unable to begin to actualize its insights into true happiness in the realm of practical affairs.

It is in the following aphorism that Alfarabi introduces the Umma in his definition of deliberative virtue, along with the idea that this virtue responds to various accidental events (SA 63–64, #95, Ar. 99.3–5). The close proximity of this new definition of deliberative virtue to the discussion of theoretical science hardly seems accidental. The clearest difference between prudence and deliberative virtue in the *Selected Aphorisms* is that the latter is informed by theoretical science while the former is not. We may wonder whether there is any connection between deliberative virtue's foundation in theoretical science and its turn from the city to the Ummas. Further textual evidence for this suspicion comes from the *Attainment of Happiness*, whose account of deliberative virtue also includes the Ummas while following shortly after an account of theoretical science (AH 20.3 ff., Ar. 68.26). The two definitions of deliberative virtue converge despite the dissimilar beginnings of these works: the *Selected Aphorisms* opens with a promise to move only the cities toward happiness, while the *Attainment of Happiness* opens with a promise to bring happiness to an unspecified number of cities and Ummas. With regard to the scope of deliberative virtue, theoretical science proves to be a great equalizer. It enlarges the sphere of political activity, dissolving all purely local differences in a whirlpool of abstract speculation, so that both the city and Umma are reduced to small parts of a cosmic whole (see AH 16.4–16, Ar. 64.20; BR 108–13, Ar. 61–66). Furthermore, it forces the statesman to grapple with the entirety of the accidents that might affect him, presumably occurring over a very large area. In the *Selected Aphorisms*, Alfarabi contrasts the soothsayer or prophet, whose decisions concern only "cities or a city" (SA 63, #94, Ar. 98.19), with a ruler informed by science, whose deliberations extend to the Ummas (63, #95, Ar. 99.3–5).

If science and not mere historical contingency determines Alfarabi's political turn to the Ummas, we may doubt that he suspected the ancient philosophers of artificially limiting politics to the city. They too, after all, were men of science. Alfarabi may suppose that the ancients took the city as their starting point, but he does not suggest that they never looked beyond it. The last ancient mentioned by name in the *Selected Aphorisms* is Alexander the Great (SA 56, #86, Ar. 90.12–18), still famous among Alfarabi and his contemporaries for his great imperial exploits (cf. BM 109). Even if ancient politics tended to focus on the city, it proved to be more than capable of empire.

We recall that Alfarabi attributed two definitions of prudence directly to the ancients: Aristotle's definition does not restrict itself to any particular community at all (SA 55, #85, Ar. 89.13–15), while the ancients in general define prudence as dealing with Ummas as well as cities (BR 106.1–14, Ar. 58.7–59.2). Not only does Alfarabi expand political deliberation to the Ummas, but he gives some strong indications that the ancient political philosophers would gladly have followed him there.[40]

The Ummas and the Sphere of Deliberation

We have seen that deliberation extends to the Ummas, but does this include the entire world? Not only the standard doctrine of Islam, but a certain abstract, comprehensive understanding of science, might tend in that direction: just as there is one God, one world, and one human species, so there should be one society and government. Alfarabi does speak of the entire inhabited world (*ma'mūra*), but only in certain contexts. Let us briefly examine his use of this term and its relationship to political deliberation.[41]

The definition of a certain kind of deliberative virtue in the *Attainment of Happiness* is remarkably similar to its counterpart in the *Selected Aphorisms*.[42] Both describe this virtue as operating within "Ummas, an Umma, or a city" (SA 63, #95, Ar. 99.4; AH 21.10–12, Ar. 69.29). With regard to the scope of deliberative virtue, both works arrive at the same conclusion. Yet in both definitions, as well as in the account of prudence in the *Book of Religion*, Alfarabi is silent about the entire inhabited world. While theoretical science does push the deliberator to consider many Ummas, it does not suffice to put the entire inhabited world at his fingertips.

The inhabited world is entirely absent from many of Alfarabi's political works, such as the *Selected Aphorisms*, *Enumeration of the Sciences*, and *Book of Religion*. On the other hand, it is present in the *Attainment of Happiness*, *Virtuous City*, and *Political Regime*. In the *Attainment of Happiness*, Alfarabi observes that the voluntary intelligibles worthy of investigation occur throughout the inhabited world (AH 20.1, Ar. 67.26).[43] Yet the statesman who strives to bring these intelligibles into existence in the inhabited world does so only in "a determined place" within it (19.10–14, Ar. 67.25). Political knowledge ought to encompass, as much as possible, the accidents that occur throughout the inhabited world, but political action must restrict itself to the carefully defined portion of it that is relevant to its goals. Therefore the subject of the inhabited world is immediately dropped (AH 20.2 ff., Ar. 67.26), never to return, shortly before the introduction of deliberative virtue. By speaking thereafter of Ummas and cities but never the inhabited world, Alfarabi strongly implies that the first ruler who strives to rule an indeterminate number of Ummas and cities will not even attempt to rule all of them.[44]

In the *Virtuous City*, Alfarabi does indeed speak of a single government in the inhabitable world (VC 230.10–11, 246.7). Yet in the absence of any discussion of deliberation in that work, it is difficult to ascertain how such a government is to be realized. Furthermore, the very idea of such a project is severely undermined in the *Political Regime*. In its parallel listing of the communities in which virtuous governments take root, the single government in the entire inhabitable world is replaced by a government encompassing only several Ummas (PR 60–61.64, Ar. 69.16–70.4; 69.81–70.82, Ar. 80.5–14). The inhabitable world is mentioned in the work, but only in the context of the savage, ungovernable peoples who live on its edges, and cannot be integrated into any kind of political society (76.92, Ar. 87.12–14). If such peoples could never be tamed by a project of the sort envisaged in the *Attainment of Happiness*, how could the entire inhabited world ever be brought under a single political rule? The implication is that the limit of the actual statesman's purview is many Ummas. In the *Book of Religion*, Alfarabi maintains that the same limit holds even for the founder of a religion, as if Islam's aspirations to rule the entire world must have postdated Muhammad and its founders (BR 93.5–6, Ar. 43.5–6; Mahdi 2001, 99–100).

The point made by Alfarabi is really rather commonsensical. For every actual founder, statesman, or prophet, there will be, as Socrates so memorably put it, "barbarian places far outside our range of vision" (*Republic* 499e), be they in the South Pacific or Central Asia. Muhammad may somehow have imagined that his religion would, in the indeterminate future, cover the entire world, but this abstract hope would not have given him the slightest clue about the form that his creed would actually assume in, say, Indonesia or Albania. Even those cosmopolitan prophets and statesmen whose ambitions extend in theory to all humanity are limited by circumstance to acting and legislating only for the cities and Ummas in their relative vicinity. Rule of the inhabited world may be discussed or imagined by jurists in their study halls, but it has little place in the assembly hall where actual deliberation occurs. However abstract or theoretical Alfarabi's understanding of politics may sometimes appear to be, he was never blind to the inevitable, local limitations of political life and practice.

Alfarabi's enlargement of the sphere of deliberation to many Ummas reflects both his theoretical understanding of politics and his practical realization that the major political units of the Islamic world would never shrink back to the size of a city. The birth of the new Umma and empire during the rapid expansion of Islam signaled the obsolescence of the city as a meaningful political unit. The decline and disintegration of that empire, more or less complete by Alfarabi's time, heralded the emergence of smaller empires but not the resurgence of cities. Arbitrarily confining his political understanding to the ancient city in a world where that city no longer existed would have been pointlessly anachronistic, and no more justified by theoretical science than by contemporary practice. However, Alfarabi's refusal to expand the sphere of deliberation to the inhabited world expresses his view of the unfeasibility of universal government in the face of immense geographical distance and human diversity. This particular insight of Alfarabi's retains its force even in our globalized age: despite massive recent increases in global interconnectivity and the success of large federations and states, the prospect of establishing a unified world government in the face of geographical distance and human diversity remains extremely remote. Alfarabi rightly foresaw that politics would continue to be conducted on the scale of many Ummas, somewhere in between the city and the inhabited world.

Linguistic Diversity and the Unity of the Umma

Up to this point, we have focused on the political approaches to the Umma that in Alfarabi's view will not work. Neither a multinational empire ruled by philosophers, as proposed in the *Attainment of Happiness*, nor a virtuous city, as proposed in the *Political Regime*, can simply impose itself on the Ummas. Attempting to shrink the domain of politics to the size of a city, following a certain nostalgic attachment to antiquity, is also doomed to failure, given the broader religious and intellectual attachments of Alfarabi's time. The remaining alternatives all involve some kind of accommodation with the Umma. Before we assess these accommodations, we need to examine more thoroughly what the political claim of the Umma might be. Let us revisit the relevant discussions in the *Book of Letters* and *Political*

Regime, considering them this time from a more overtly political standpoint. Does the Umma constitute a unified political entity, and if not, what kind of political significance should it have?

I determined in Chapter 2 that the development of language as recounted in the *Book of Letters* is not inherently political, since neither cities nor governments figure in it. Nevertheless, it has major political consequences, in establishing both common characteristics and significant divisions within the Umma. True equality among humans is characteristic only of that primordial stage when they can neither practice any of the specialized arts nor speak with any fluency. Alfarabi prefaces his account of that development with the observation that "The vulgar and the multitude are prior in time to the elite, and knowledge common to the unexamined opinion of all is prior in time to the practical arts and the knowledge which is particular[45] to each of these arts" (BL 134.17–20, #114). The growth of the Umma entails the increasing specialization of language and the arts, and is therefore accompanied by the emergence of inequality.[46] In tracing the development of this inequality within the Umma, we need to ponder its political implications.

Related to the development of inequality within the Umma is its movement away from nature toward custom. In the *Book of Letters,* nature appears initially as a collective force affecting a large group of people, thereby helping to determine the character of each Umma (BL 134.21 ff., #114; 136.16, #118). Although Alfarabi does not mention climate specifically, his account of nature at the beginning of the *Book of Letters* does recall the climatic conditions engendered by the motions of the heavenly bodies described in the *Political Regime* (PR 61.65–62.67, Ar. 70.5–71.13). Once nature has determined the Umma's physiognomy and the first sounds of its language, it remains largely static, while human ingenuity and custom acquire ever greater weight. Stated in the terms of the *Political Regime,* the heavenly bodies dominate the initial stage of the formation of the Umma, while conventional human language exercises a decisive influence on its evolution (PR 61.65, Ar. 70.5–7; BL 135.10–14, #115). These customary traits affect everybody, but they also accrue disproportionately to certain individuals, leading to an increase in inequality (BL 134.17–20, # 114).

We should not assume, however, that the development of the Umma permits its members to ignore nature. As we have already observed earlier in this chapter, nature can never be thrust neatly aside. It is not merely that the effects of climate and nutrition on each Umma endure, but also that nature continues to affect the souls of its individual members, as Alfarabi indicates in the *Book of Letters* (BL 135.6–8, #115). This point is developed further in the *Political Regime*, in which Alfarabi emphasizes the enormous natural differences among humans with regard to their capacity to receive the first intelligibles. Some humans are brilliant, while others are insane or hopelessly defective, and most are somewhere in between. Some are well endowed by nature for grasping certain kinds of knowledge, and poorly endowed for grasping other kinds (PR 65.74–67.77, Ar. 75.4–77.17). This inequality in natural ability among individuals affects the practice of every conceivable human art. Nature is underestimated if it is regarded merely as the material cause that predominates at the birth of the Umma. It reasserts itself with every single human birth, demarcating to a significant but not universal degree the accomplishments of which each human is capable: it provides limitation and direction without compulsion and tyranny. Custom must build upon nature and on occasion struggle against it, but cannot hope to fully annul its effects (66.75, Ar. 76.3–10, 74.90, Ar. 85.12). The best summary of this teaching occurs in the *Selected Aphorisms*, according to which the complex and unpredictable interplay of nature and custom determines every human's proficiency with regard to every human art and moral quality (SA 17–18, #10–13, Ar. 31.1–34.5).

Natural inequality, unlike the Umma, does not develop and change over time. Alfarabi argues that nature endows individual humans with unequal talents at all times, including the epoch of the formation of the Umma, when some actions are already bound to be naturally easier for some people than for others (BL 135.6–8, #115). But the absence of arts and even of speech prevents the primordial humans from making use of that natural inequality in any meaningful way. The particular effects of nature on individuals become manifest only in the context of developed civilization and organized political society. The importance of this second aspect of nature means that our treatment of the theme in Chapter 2, which presented the development of the Umma as a general movement away from nature toward custom, requires modification. As shown in Chapter 2, the advance of custom at the expense of nature occurs most consistently in the specific realm of conventional human speech. Yet in the *Virtuous City*, Alfarabi indicates that even advances in speech depend on the natural eloquence of certain individuals (cf. VC 246.8–9, 246.16–247.1). Besides, Alfarabi never speaks of the advance of custom at the expense of nature in the realm of politics or morals. No degree of development in the linguistic arts and sciences can blur the innate differences in natural capacities among humans with regard to all aspects of human life; on the contrary, such progress serves only to make them more manifest, by increasing the number of activities in which talented individuals may excel. In this respect the growth of the Umma, far from overcoming nature, brings natural talents—and limitations—into focus.

In the *Book of Letters*, signs of the budding inequality within the Umma become visible in a relatively early stage of its development. Language begins by naming the natural beings observable to all, such as the sun, stars, and earth, and proceeds to name the natural powers common to all. It then gradually finds words for arts, actions, and states of character acquired only through custom, and for knowledge attained only through experience. Alfarabi insists that all these notions fall within the domain of the "matters common to all": every human surely has some general knowledge as well as some basic experiences and abilities (BL 138.9–15, #121). But words for particular (*kh-ṣ-ṣ*) arts and their tools develop immediately thereafter, according to the needs of the Umma (138.15–17, #121, cf. 134.18–19, #114). Specialized arts, and therefore inequality of knowledge and ability, arise in every Umma from an early stage.

Alfarabi proceeds to show how the inequality within the Umma is dramatically enhanced by the further refinement of language. The gradual emergence of synonyms, equivocal terms, metaphors, and finally the syllogistic arts of poetry and rhetoric dramatically increases the vocabulary of the language (BL 140.8–141.15, #134–37), demanding an entirely new degree of linguistic specialization. This need is filled by the emergence of language experts. They are the "wise men of the Umma, their governors and authorities on matters of language" (143.5–6, #130). They use words that are unknown to the rest of the Umma (143.6–13, #130). Superior to the other members of the Umma in eloquence and knowledge of the language, they strive to beautify, and on occasion simplify, the language (144.14–145.6, #130). Their linguistic reforms, which are initially passed down only among themselves (143.8–9, #130), do eventually influence the rest of the Umma (144.6–11, #130). This diminishes the gap between the language experts and the people, without dismantling the basic hierarchy.

The work of the language experts helps to consolidate the Umma's official language (*lisān*; BR 143.5, #130). Before the language was touched by these new authorities, it was called a dialect (*lugha*; 142.3, #128). The distinction between the official *lisān* and informal *lugha* becomes even more crucial when the first grammarians, assisted by the advent of writing, set about collecting the material for the codification of the language. They encounter a great diversity of *lugha* (146.12–20, #134; 147.4, #133), from which they have to gather the *lisān* of the Arabs (147.7, #133). They base the *lisān* on the *lugha* least exposed to the foreign *lugha* that inevitably leave their mark on the speech of the people by virtue of the geographical proximity of their speakers and long-standing commercial relations with them (146.5–20, #134; 147.4–7, #135). In the case of Arabs, much of their official language (*lisān al-'arab*) was taken from the five tribes who lived in the geographical center of the Arab homeland and were thus deemed freest from any foreign influence (147.6–10, #135). The one official *lisān* that is developed from the many *lugha* does not render these dialects obsolete, but rather coexists with them, so that every mature Umma has both *lugha* and *lisān* (144.7, #130). Not even the most adroit and determined language experts could preserve the Arabs who lived in Iraq from the enduring influence of Persian, as long as they continued to have interactions with people who spoke it (146.14, #134).

The standardization of language around which the Umma crystallizes produces neither unity nor equality. The natural hierarchy of human talents thrives with the increasing sophistication of language and the arts. These vertical differences are accompanied by horizontal differences: distinct dialects emerge under various foreign influences, as a result of which clear communication across the entire Umma cannot always be guaranteed. The important political point is that Alfarabi does not assume any fundamental unity among the people of the Umma, beyond a common physique and a certain official language and literature. This is certainly not a compelling argument for any national will or consciousness on the popular level.[47]

Nevertheless, I do not mean to suggest that the Umma is without political authority. The Umma's common characteristics may not suffice for political autonomy or independence, but they should not be underestimated by rulers. It would be particularly foolish to ignore the Umma's linguistic elite. Unlike the scattered people of the Umma, this elite represents a cohesive, educated group that wields a large measure of authority over each particular Umma, so that any attempt to govern humankind Umma by Umma would likely depend on them. The realization of the right kind of rulership within the Umma thus requires cooperation between the philosophers and the linguistic elite. The question then becomes, is such cooperation feasible?

To answer this question, we must first consider the character of the linguistic elite and its authority in greater detail.

The Uncertain Political Role of the Umma and Its Elite

There is a clear discrepancy between how Alfarabi views the language experts, and how the language experts view themselves. The language experts themselves claim a place among the elite (BL 149.20, #139). But Alfarabi wryly observes that all people who possess political skills, arts, or even ancestry and wealth not shared by most of their fellows are inclined to consider themselves elite (BL 133.16–134.4, #113, AH 37.3–13, Ar. 86–87.53). To attempt to honor all these claims would be to invite political chaos. Yet would anybody deny that rhetoricians, poets, and scribes, who are indispensable to rulers in all large, well-organized societies, possess some measure of political authority? Alfarabi himself does not deny it: although he never speaks of first rulers or cities while tracing the development of the Umma in the *Book of Letters*, he does treat the language experts as governors and men of authority (BL 138.4, #120; 143.5, #130). Nevertheless, when Alfarabi begins to discuss rulers in the highest sense, he consigns the linguistic elites to the multitude (149.1, #139). They are excluded from the list of the genuine elites, which is restricted to the philosophers, dialecticians, sophists, legislators, *mutakallimūn*,[48] and jurists (134.12–13, #113). This unusual ranking of intellectual professions, along with its relation to Alfarabi's broader hierarchy of the human arts and sciences in general, merits careful consideration.

As we have seen, Alfarabi does not shy away from proclaiming the absolute superiority of philosophy. Nor is he squeamish about proclaiming the inferiority of the multitude, in a manner that may seem shocking in our democratic age. Yet Alfarabi harbors no illusions about the ability of philosophers to rule the people directly: the two groups simply do not have enough in common. The wisdom of the philosophers can trickle down to the people only through a complicated series of intermediaries, among whom language experts would seem to play a role. However, it is the dialecticians, sophists, legislators, jurists, and *mutakallimūn* who have something in common with philosophy, and occupy, as it were, the higher rungs of the ladder (BL 134.12–15, #113; 133.14–16, #113).[49] Alfarabi illustrates the link between these syllogistic arts and philosophy in various places in the *Book of Letters*. The dialecticians and sophists engage in investigations of the world that eventually give rise to philosophy (150.11–151.6, #141). If philosophy is the fruit of the tree, than these lesser arts are both its nourishment and its bud (132.7–9, #110). Even after the perfection of philosophy, they play an important role in philosophic training, thus nourishing future generations of philosophers (151.6, #141, 151.13–15, #142). If properly instructed, dialecticians and sophists can be made to advance the same goals as the philosophers.

The case of the *mutakallimūn* is already somewhat more complex. Like the sophists and dialecticians, they are concerned with theoretical things (BL 132.18, #111; 153.2, #145). They engage in some dialectical discussions among themselves and even make the knowledge acquired in these discussions the goal of their life, thus setting them apart from the multitude (132.21–23, #111). However, they use mainly rhetorical arguments with the people (132.14–15, #111; 153.9–10, #145). So long as the *mutakallimūn* serve a philosophically inspired religion, Alfarabi is able to imagine a scenario where they advance the same goals as philosophy (132.23–133.7, #111–12; 152.16–153.9, #145). But if they serve the wrong kind of religion, they become the inveterate enemies of philosophy (157.1–3, #153). This brings us back to the question that we were unable to resolve: is the religion of Alfarabi's time inspired by philosophy? If not, the prospects of cooperation with the *mutakallimūn* might be rather dim. Unlike the *mutakallimūn*, the jurists seem uninterested in theoretical things. But in the realm of practical deliberation, they serve the same goal as prudence and practical philosophy (133.8–13, #112; 152.17–153.2, #145). In general, Alfarabi evinces greater concern over hostile *mutakallimūn* than recalcitrant jurists, since he says nothing about jurists' enmity toward philosophy.

Alfarabi never makes any comparable statement about the amenability of the language experts to the service of philosophy. Caught somewhere between the genuine elite and the people, the language experts fit uneasily into the ruling hierarchy. Their shaky situation is articulated in the *Book of Letters*. As we have seen, Alfarabi eloquently describes the linguistic experts and their authority within the Umma, but then leaves them out of the ruling hierarchy and emphasizes their remoteness from philosophy. The language experts are thoroughly dependent on the speech of the multitude (BL 148.14–20, #138), and therefore ignorant of the philosophical language articulated in the *Book of Letters* and the *Attainment of Happiness* (BL 157.19 ff., #155, AH 43.18–44.2, Ar. 93–94.61). Like conventional kings and farmers, they serve only the aims of the multitude and have no interest whatsoever in theoretical things (BL 149.1–21, #139). They could be said to occupy the lower rungs of the ladder, gazing downward toward the multitude rather than upward toward philosophy. And yet how could the teaching of the philosophers, *mutakallimūn*, and jurists be transmitted to the people of each Umma in their own language without the language experts' help? This step in the transmission of knowledge is more difficult than it initially appears, because of the difference in character and education between the transmitters and the recipients. Can the philosopher's wisdom survive its communication from religious authorities who know something of wisdom and theoretical science to language experts who know only popular opinion and particular conventions? Or is the ladder of transmission split irremediably in two? This same dilemma is reflected today in the suspicion that scientific experts of all sorts tend to harbor toward the journalists and media personalities who are responsible for communicating their findings to the mass public.

The works of Alfarabi that have come down to us not only fail to offer any solution to this difficulty, but often seem to amplify it. The most complete version of Alfarabi's plan for the diffusion of knowledge is formulated in the *Attainment of Happiness* (AH 34.12–36.13, Ar. 83.51–86.2). The unwieldiness of this scheme has already been discussed earlier in this chapter. Some of the most serious problems associated with it stem from the vast number of Ummas. But it might be easier to think of implementing it on a smaller scale, involving one or maybe just a few Ummas. In a passage that we have yet to fully consider, Alfarabi discusses how the first ruler should establish the sciences in each Umma. Yet Alfarabi does not seem to include the language experts in his scheme. He asks, inconclusively, "whether or not there is a group fit for preserving the theoretical sciences" (34.19–35.1, Ar. 84.51). Since the language experts have nothing to do with theoretical science, this query can hardly refer to them. Alfarabi also inquires, just as inconclusively, about potential guardians of "popular theoretical sciences and image-making theoretical sciences" (35.1, Ar. 84.51). It turns out that pure theoretical science is but one of the four sciences required in each Umma. The second and third sciences involve persuasive methods, which are normally the preserve of rhetoricians, while the fourth is extracted for a given Umma (35.2–8, 84.52). Does Alfarabi enlist the language experts in the mastery and dissemination of these sciences? As tempting as an affirmative answer might be, it is striking that Alfarabi never speaks of these experts in the text. Rather, Alfarabi assigns the preservation of these sciences to an anonymous "man or group (*qawm*)" (35.12–16, Ar. 84–85.2). If Alfarabi is unable to determine whether the practitioners of these sciences are one man or an entire group, he probably does not have the entire class of language experts in mind. Perhaps he means rather men of science familiar with the language and customs of their given Ummas and willing to advance his scheme, but who may exist only in very small numbers in certain Ummas. The absence of the language experts in the *Attainment of Happiness* follows quite naturally from the absence of linguistic science from the education expounded in the beginning of the work. This rigorous scientific training does not suffice to tackle the challenges posed by the diversity of languages and Ummas. The first ruler never quite manages to descend from the summit of philosophy to the lush, exuberant valleys of human particularity below it.

The dilemma of the relationship between the genuine elite and language experts is not unique to the *Attainment of Happiness*: none of Alfarabi's other works give a persuasive account of their cooperation either. If philosophers cannot communicate their ideas to the language experts directly, one might expect them to do so with the help of religious authorities. In the previous chapter, I suggested that the passages in the *Political Regime* and *Virtuous City* about the diversity of religion in each and every Umma imply a need for cooperation between religious authorities and the elite of each Umma. Yet I am unable to find any account in Alfarabi of the relationship between jurists or *mutakallimūn* and the language experts.

On the one hand, there are works such as the *Book of Letters* and the *Book of Religion* that describe the harmonious cooperation of philosophers, dialecticians, legislators, jurists, and *mutakallimūn* (BL 152.7–153.9, #144–145, BR 98.9–23, Ar. 47.18–48.5, 99.26–101.19, Ar. 50.4–52.9). However, Alfarabi neglects to mention linguistic experts or particular Ummas in his discussion of legislation in the *Book of Letters* (BL 150.1–153.9, #140–45). Their absence is particularly glaring given the evident importance of Ummas to the development and transmission of the syllogistic arts (153.10–11, #146). Alfarabi does acknowledge that poetic and rhetorical methods need to be employed in the instruction of the multitude, but never explains who will employ them (152.4, #143). The omission of poetry but not rhetoric from the arts employed by the jurists and *mutakallimūn* at the end of the section (153.9, #145) implies that while the religious authorities may on occasion be competent rhetoricians, one should hardly expect them to be poets. The reader is left with very little idea about how to communicate the universal legislation, as interpreted by the jurists and defended by the *mutakallimūn*, to the particular Ummas. As for the *Book of Religion*, it speaks repeatedly of the Ummas but tells us little about their arts. It is completely silent about poetry and linguistic science, while rhetoric comes up only briefly in the context of dialectic (BR

98.24, Ar. 48.2). The various exhortations for the prudent statesman to engage with the individual Ummas (106.5–16, Ar. 58.10–59.1; 107.22–28, Ar. 60.5–13) are therefore noticeably lacking in details: does the statesman enlist the help of the Ummas' elite, and if so, how?

On the other hand, books such as the *Political Regime*, *Virtuous City*, and *Attainment of Happiness* allude, however incompletely, to a collaboration between the virtuous rulers and the elite of each Umma. Yet one is astonished to observe that none of these three works ever speaks directly of jurisprudence or *kalām*. In the *Political Regime*, Alfarabi touches upon the question of succession and the need for a traditional king (*malik al-sunna*) who follows the demise of the chain of first rulers and governs the city according to written *sharī'a* (PR 70.82, Ar. 81.2–4). In the *Virtuous City*, he presents a somewhat more detailed account of the second ruler, who follows the *sharī'a* laid down by the first ruler and even infers new laws from it (VC 250.6–252.4).[50] Both of these rulers would seem to perform the functions of the jurists or at least collaborate with them. Yet the term "jurisprudence" and its derivatives are not employed in either of these schematic passages. Does Alfarabi expect these rulers to have the time to interpret the *sharī'a* themselves? In the *Attainment of Happiness*, Alfarabi speaks of religion as a tool of philosophy, but says nothing about the jurists and *mutakallimūn* who would presumably be needed to interpret and defend religion (AH 40.9–41.13, Ar. 90–91.56). In all three books Alfarabi discusses religion and therefore points to the need for jurisprudence and *kalām*, but never takes the trouble to discuss them.

The passage that alludes most clearly to some sort of collaboration between religious authorities and language experts occurs in the *Selected Aphorisms*. Even by the terse standards of aphorisms, this statement is cryptic and concise. Alfarabi at first lists the language experts, clearly identified as rhetoricians, scribes, and poets, as second in rank in the city, beneath only the virtuous and wise, but then combines them with the "transmitters of the creed" (SA 37, #57, Ar. 65.11).[51] This addition hints again at what we have suspected all along: in a virtuous city, the language experts of each Umma will have to ally with religious authorities in order to have a share in rule. Yet it hardly suffices to explain how these two groups, who are supposed to possess the same rank within the city, will share power. Alfarabi's brief comment in the *Selected Aphorisms* points to the heart of the problem: virtuous governance based on the gradual diffusion of philosophic knowledge to the people requires collaboration between religious authorities and language experts, but none of Alfarabi's extant works elucidate how such a partnership could come about. We can never discount the possibility that Alfarabi did deal adequately with this theme in a work that has been lost. Yet the surviving passages that touch upon this question are all evasive, obscure, and characterized by at least one flagrant omission. We may doubt that so recurrent a tendency is purely accidental. Let us venture to explain it on the basis of the works available to us.

The *mutakallimūn* are sandwiched between the particular religious Umma that they represent and the various ethnic Ummas among whom they must perform their trade (BL 133.5–7, #111). Alfarabi describes two kinds of religious *kalām*.[52] In the *Enumeration of the Sciences*, *kalām* merely defends existing tenets of the religion against various opponents (ES 211).[53] This sterile, defensive kind of *kalām* would not need the assistance of the philosophers, nor would it have to adapt itself to the peculiar character of the various Ummas subject to it. The ultimate consequence of such *kalām* is not the sustenance of religion, but war and *jihād* against real or imagined opponents (219). This spirited attack on a certain perverse form of *kalām* is nevertheless not Alfarabi's last word on the subject. In the *Book of Letters*, he presents a healthier, more dynamic sort of *kalām* that not only defends existing tenets of the religion but also infers new ones (*istanbaṭ*; BL 153.2–8, #145): in this latter respect it resembles jurisprudence (BL 152.17–153.2, #145; ES 80–81, Ar. 131–32).

The jurists and *mutakallimūn* who are expected to issue new rulings and opinions according to changing circumstances require the continual guidance of living wisdom. It is in this context that Alfarabi urges both the jurists and the *mutakallimūn* to hearken to the philosophers. Alfarabi shows that the actions covered by jurisprudence ought to be subordinate to political science and philosophy (BR 101.11–19, Ar. 52.4–9): so, too, should the best kind of *kalām* (BL 133.1–4, #111). Jurisprudence, whenever it infers new rules and opinions, needs to make use of prudence (133.8–13, #111), consisting of a continual response to unexpected events and adaptation to particular communities (BR 105.36–106.18, Ar. 58.7–59.2). The creative kind of *kalām* might also depend on prudence, although Alfarabi never says so explicitly: how could it successfully infer new opinions without tailoring them to their particular time and place? It follows that not only the images employed by religious authorities, but also the opinions and actions they prescribe (BR 93.1, Ar. 43.3; PR 89.74, Ar. 85.1), should vary from Umma to Umma. But since prudence deals with an infinite number of variables, the most philosophical kind of political science is compelled to acknowledge its incapacity to determine particular rules (BR 106.17–25, Ar. 59.3–8). It is the immeasurable flexibility required by prudence, along with the uncertain relationship between the religious allies of philosophy and the language experts who are indifferent to it, that renders any exact, "scientific" account of the relations between religious authorities and the Ummas impossible. Still, one may hope that the force of Alfarabi's general warning against the thoughtless imposition of the laws and dogmas of the Islamic Umma on disparate ethnic Ummas would render such an account superfluous. Jurists and *mutakallimūn* who obey the philosophers are not likely to undertake any kind of arrogant or oppressive action toward the Ummas, even if they lack precise guidelines for dealing with them.

Among the most difficult variables will be the pride of the language experts, who "consider themselves among the elite" (BL 149.20, # 139). It is worth asking how inclined these language experts would be to obey religious authorities, regardless of whether the latter serve philosophy or not. It is entirely plausible that many of the language experts would prefer maintaining an independent prestige within their own ethnic Ummas to becoming surrogates of cosmopolitan outsiders whose teachings they may not fully appreciate or understand. The language experts are, after all, figures of some stature within their respective Ummas (BL 143.5, #130). Even if they are not the political rulers of their Ummas, they might still possess enough power and eloquence to thwart attempts by foreigners to rule them. In some cases, the elite of the Umma might be inclined to accept the new religion only in exchange for the preservation of their ancestral language and culture. A version of this compromise has been adopted in Iran and large parts of India, whose elite converted to Islam but continued to speak and write in Farsi, Urdu, and Bengali.

The extent to which the ethnic Ummas can be made to cooperate with the overarching goals of the philosophers and religious authorities remains up in the air: it would presumably vary from Umma to Umma, whose almost unlimited diversity defies the application of any one theory. Paul Heck argues that Alfarabi's account results in "endless diversity i.e. anarchy, at the *milla* level" (Heck, 201). I agree concerning the diversity allowed by Alfarabi's view of religion, but would not quite call it anarchy. The number of distinct groups, although numerous, remains definite, and Alfarabi argues that the prudent men can and should try to grapple with the particular needs of every kind of community (BR 106.5–16, Ar. 58.15–59.1; 107.18–29, Ar. 60.5–13).

Yet since these communities are subject to accidents that cannot even be counted (106.23–25, Ar. 59.7–8), he will simply have to do so on a case-by-case basis, with varying degrees of success. Indeed, the absence of clearly defined ways of cooperation between the authorities of the religious and ethnic Ummas represents a formidable challenge to the plan of accommodation outlined at the end of the previous chapter. In his ultimate display of moderation, Alfarabi indicates that even his moderate policy of accommodation between the authorities of the two major kinds of Umma cannot be universally advocated or even described. Besides, there may indeed be some cases that call for the rigid imposition of the norms of the Islamic Umma on the ethnic Umma. For example, should the Muslim authorities tolerate the interment of the living with their dead spouses, cannibalism, or other atrocious folk practices reported in Sindbad's travels (*Arabian Nights II*, 18–19, 28–29)? One looks in vain for any concrete answer to this question in Alfarabi, although he does suggest on one occasion that certain peoples are so menacing for other peoples that they might have to be completely destroyed (see SA 44, #67, Ar. 77.8–9). Difficulties of this sort, I surmise, might help explain why Alfarabi never sets down any formal doctrine of religious or communal toleration. But it cannot be denied that he supports such toleration in the overwhelming majority of ordinary circumstances.

The religious authorities who learn from Alfarabi may not emerge with any dogmatic policy toward the ethnic Ummas, but perhaps this is the point: they will come to appreciate the innumerable and unpredictable difficulties involved in dealing with each Umma and strive to avoid unnecessary conflicts. They will become appropriately selective in the images they disseminate, the opinions they inculcate, and the actions they prescribe, for each Umma, all while attempting to accommodate, or even cooperate with, the Umma's elite. They will become voices of political compromise and cultural enrichment rather than war and *jihād*.

Chapter 7

The Umma Among the Ignorant Associations: Nationalism and the Threat of War

Alfarabi devotes much of his oeuvre to virtuous opinions and associations, so we may be tempted to dismiss, or at least downplay, his accounts of ignorant opinions and associations. But it would be rash to do so. We have seen how many of Alfarabi's accounts of the virtuous associations are wistful and ironic. The previous chapter has revealed considerable obstacles to the plan of establishing virtuous government in the Ummas. Such government is impossible without the cooperation of the Ummas, but both the philosophers and the elite of the Umma seem less than enthusiastic about unleashing the brute force and relentless propaganda that would be needed to bend recalcitrant Ummas to their will. The best that one could reasonably hope for would be cooperation between the philosophers, religious authorities, and the elite of the Ummas, but even this wish is exposed to great uncertainties. If the establishment of Alfarabi's virtuous rulership cannot be guaranteed or even expected, then his two substantial accounts of ignorant opinions and associations merit serious attention. Besides, Alfarabi would never have given so lengthy and eloquent an account of the ignorant associations if he regarded all of them as equally beneath contempt. On the contrary, he is concerned with ranking these associations, and displays a preference for some over others (BR 93.17–18, Ar. 43.14–15; PR 79.100–80.101, Ar. 92.1–7; VC 314.7–10). Alfarabi's remarkable analysis of politics as interpreted and practiced in most actual human situations jolts his readers down from wistful hopes of perfection, and into the tumultuous political conflicts that wracked the imperfect societies of his time. Looking at the Umma from a this-worldly point of view is indispensable for completing my analysis of it, and demonstrating the claim made in the Introduction that the seemingly abstract and aloof Alfarabi is never oblivious to how this world works.

The Umma and the Ignorant Opinions

In the accounts of virtuous governance and opinion, the city and the Umma predominate over all other kinds of human community. This applies equally to all Alfarabi's major works on the subject. The laws of the city, along with the languages and ways of life of the Umma (PP 22.19–23.1), make them essential for the realization of human happiness through education (AH 29.6 ff., Ar. 78.43), in a way that other kinds of human community are not. Yet Alfarabi is hardly blind to the existence of these other kinds of community. They appear even in those works that are primarily devoted to virtuous governance, and tend to lose their significance only with the introduction of virtuous governance or the philosophy that lies behind it. For example, in the *Book of Religion*, Alfarabi introduces tribal and regional communities, but only before determining whether the religion is virtuous or ignorant (BR 93.4–5, Ar. 43.4–5). In the *Philosophy of Plato*, Alfarabi lists "having a large tribe . . . [and] ruling over a group (*ṭā'ifa*) or a city" (PP 3.5–8) as one of the supposed goods, but this inclusion of tribe and an undefined "group" in place of the Umma comes in a survey of pre-philosophic opinions. Both of these works, once they have turned to philosophy and virtuous governance, display a consistent emphasis on the city and the Umma at the expense of the other human associations. This being said, the other types of community are never entirely absent. In the *Political Regime*, religion requires a different imitation for every "group (*ṭā'ifa*) and Umma" (PR 74.90, Ar. 85.17–18). This group could refer to the city mentioned shortly thereafter, but the use of the vaguer, broader term implies other meanings as well, such as faction, sect, or tribe. The importance of these other groups is confirmed in the *Book of Religion*, where Alfarabi admits that political prudence needs to take into account not only cities and Ummas, but certain undefined "communities" (*jam'*, BR 106.12, Ar. 58.16, 107.21–31, Ar. 60.8). These presumably include the tribes and regional associations that were defined as communities at the beginning of the work (93.1–5, Ar. 43.3–5), but we learn nothing else about them in the *Book of Religion*. Indeed, any substantial discussion of these other kinds of community is reserved for Alfarabi's treatment of ignorant associations and opinions, many of which derive their political authority from them. If even the wisest statesman and philosopher must operate at times within communities other than cities and Ummas, he needs to examine these communities, as well as the ignorant kinds of governments and opinions to which they are linked.

In the section of the *Virtuous City* devoted exclusively to the goals and practices of the ignorant cities, no community other than the city is mentioned. I have already explained in Chapter 6 why Alfarabi might want to appeal to his Islamic audience by associating ignorant governments and opinions with the cities of the ancients. But the link between ignorant governments and cities is not corroborated by his broader account of the ignorant opinions, in which neither the city nor the Umma enjoys any great predominance. Among the large diversity of ignorant opinions and the variety of human attachments reflected in them, the city and Umma are demoted to just two associations among many. By cataloguing all the major ignorant opinions with such thoroughness, Alfarabi acknowledges that most humans view political life in terms of attachments that are essentially ignored by the virtuous governments. The list of political bonds, as understood by the ignorant opinions, includes shared ancestry, marriage ties, a first ruler who caused the group ruled by him to prosper in ignorant goods, and confederacies based on agreements sworn under oath (VC 292.16–296.3). It is easy to see how these types of bonds, which have little to do with either the languages of Ummas or laws of cities, may just as well produce governments based on tribes and confederacies rather than cities and Ummas (298.4–6).

Nevertheless, cities and Ummas figure in the ignorant opinions as well. The bond of the city is based on merely living together in a single place, an extended and therefore diluted version of the ties among households and neighbors (VC 296.8–12, cf. 228.14–230.1, PR 60.64, Ar. 69.20–70.3). According to the adherents of ignorant opinions, who care nothing about law and virtue, the intrinsic bond of the city turns out to be extremely weak. Yet a group of them is unable to deny the substantial bond of the Umma:

> Others hold the opinion that the bond lies in the similarity of
> natural character traits and customs, and sharing in dialect and
> language, and difference in these things causes them to differ.
> And this is the bond of every Umma, through which there ought

to be love amongst themselves and aversion to others. For the
Ummas differ due to these three things. (VC 296.4–7)

This statement agrees with Alfarabi's own description of the Umma in his
treatment of virtuous cities, which also emphasizes both language and natural character traits (PR 37.65, Ar. 70.6–7). It acknowledges the political significance of human tendencies toward ethnic identification, which modern
nationalism would eventually bring to the fore.[1] Alfarabi himself can hardly
be accused of fostering such sentiments, which he lumps together with the
other ignorant opinions, but neither does he explain, at least in the immediate context, why they are mistaken. The bond of the Umma remains in
many respects tighter than the other ignorant bonds. Some of these bonds
are based merely on temporary accidents, like eating, drinking, suffering, or
traveling together: these could never hold together a large number of people
over a long period of time (VC 296.13–298.3). Others are based on kinship or
living together in the same place. Such bonds tend to weaken as communities expand: a clan is less close-knit than a family, just as a city or region is
less cohesive than a neighborhood or household (294.2–9, 296.8–12).[2] A sworn
confederation might also be quite limited in scope, if in fact every member
is expected to personally contribute to it (294.16–296.3). The bond of the
Umma, based less on accident or immediate acquaintance than on enduring
qualities shared by a vast number of people, would have a better chance of
holding larger associations together.

There is one other ignorant bond that may be capable of uniting large
communities. A first ruler who helps an indefinite group of people attain
one or more of the ignorant goods (VC 294.13–15) could rule a community
of indefinite size. However, among the goods bestowed by the first ruler is
the domination of others (Arabic root *gh–l–b*). Such aggression is also encouraged by the bonds of shared ancestry (294.4) and sworn confederacy
(296.2). The bond of the Umma, on the other hand, does not lead so plainly
in that direction. The members of the Umma love one another and are averse
to outsiders, but display no manifest desire to conquer them (296.6–7). The
combination of internal cohesion and relative gentleness toward outsiders
makes the Umma among the most attractive of the ignorant communities.

However, the bond of the Umma fails to motivate not only conquest, but
also defensive war (VC 296.6–7): in this respect, it is weaker than the bonds
of shared ancestry or sworn confederacy (294.4, 296.2–3). It is possible that
the Umma's aversion to its neighbors would induce it to muster the force

necessary to defend itself, especially in the case of an emergency (cf. 294.8–9), but how the Umma would do this of its own accord is by no means clear. If surrounded by warring empires, the free and independent Umma might find itself especially hard-pressed.[3]

The brief summary of the political bonds of the Umma in the *Virtuous City* draws our attention yet again to the importance of dialect and language (*lugha wa-lisān*, VC 296.5) in defining the Umma. We might therefore become more able to understand the inadequacy of the bonds of the Umma by reconsidering the bond of language, this time from the perspective of the ignorant cities. Alfarabi hints at some of the inadequacies of the language experts with regard to the attainment of the ignorant goods in the *Book of Letters*. He compares them to the rulers of farmers and to kings, both of whom are also part of the multitude (BL 149.7–21, #139). Alfarabi argues that all three types (language experts, rulers of farmers, and kings) share the goals of the multitude, which they serve and advance in their respective domains (149.10–15, #139). At first glance, neither of these offices seems to have much to do with the language experts or even with each other. Such examples are nonetheless not chosen randomly. They point to certain aspects of human life that the description of the Umma in the *Book of Letters* has hitherto ignored.

The Umma is associated with food and nutrition in the *Political Regime*, but before the introduction of the farmer this aspect of it is absent from the *Book of Letters*. The office of the king is also absent from Alfarabi's account of the development of the Umma. While the farmer provides humans with their most basic need, the king is the person endowed with actual political power and authority. It may safely be asserted that the language experts possess neither of these qualities. They cannot deliver the goods of the necessary cities (cf. PR 77.94, Ar. 88.4–13) any more than they can govern the kingly cities of honor (cf. 79.99, Ar. 91.11).[4] They can influence the multitude of the Umma only in tandem with the patronage of the king and the food of the farmer. The power of poets and scribes is highly dependent on the ruling dynasty. As in the virtuous governments, the language experts may form a part of the ruling class, but certainly not the strongest part.

The Umma and the Wars of the Ignorant Associations

To this point, the discussion of the relation between Ummas and ignorant governments has focused mainly on opinions about governments and their internal bonds. But we cannot complete that discussion without examining the actual operation of governments, in both the domestic and the international sphere. For opinions do not always reflect reality. If certain ignorant opinions describe governments that seem ineffectual in prosecuting wars, that may point to a discrepancy between what some people hope and think about political solidarity and how political solidarity actually works. Indeed, the ignorant opinions about government listed in the *Virtuous City* bear a very tenuous relation to the actual functioning of those associations, as described in the *Political Regime*.

The association based on the Umma does not occur in the detailed account of the ignorant associations in the *Political Regime* (PR 76.92 ff., Ar. 87.5). Furthermore, the arts associated with the Umma, such as rhetoric and poetry, appear only in the context of a democracy, where the efflorescence of these arts is neither encouraged nor hindered by a weak government (PR 87.115, Ar. 101–1.2). Neither the Umma nor its elite seem to serve any political role. But the same could be said about the associations based on descent, kinship, oaths, or living in the same place, which are equally absent from the discussion. All the associations discussed in the *Political Regime* are based on only one of the ignorant opinions, namely, that of a first ruler who helps his people attain the ignorant goods, often through conquest (VC 294.13–15). The good that he obtains depends on the principle of the city: in the association of wealth, he attains wealth for himself and his subjects (PR 77.95, Ar. 88.14–89.6), while in the association of honor, he attains honor for them (80.101, Ar. 92.6–13), and so on. Alfarabi thus implies that despite the variety of ignorant opinions, all of which must have some small bearing on ignorant political practice, the only truly effective ignorant associations are sustained by the concrete acquisition of the ignorant goods rather than by any familial, ethnic, or communal attachment. The *Political Regime* does contain occasional references to some of the other ignorant bonds, especially marriage and kinship (PR 79.98, Ar. 91.1–2, 79.100, Ar. 91.13–16, 80.102, Ar. 93.1–2, 87.115, Ar. 100.14–16), but these factors influence the politics of the ignorant associations without ever constituting their main principle. The inherent tribal solidarity of groups such as Arabs and Turks should not be summarily dismissed, but it will only develop into empire if these groups succeed in distributing power, honor, wealth, and pleasure among themselves and others (cf. 89.119, Ar. 103.6).

Considerations of this sort might explain why the concept of ʿaṣabiyya, made famous by Ibn Khaldūn, occurs only rarely in Alfarabi, and never in the *Political Regime.* In the *Summary of Plato's "Laws,"* Alfarabi presents *'aṣabiyya* as a clannish, disorderly passion that legislation has to overcome (SL 145.2, Ar. 133.2–3; Parens 1995, 74). In the absence of laws and policies guaranteeing the broader acquisition and distribution of goods, no clan can successfully unite a large society. Ibn Khaldūn does not conceal the narrow origin of *'aṣabiyya,* which arises from the lengthy personal acquaintance characteristic of blood or client relationships (Ibn Khaldūn, 1: 264–65, Ar. 1: 207–8). It therefore resides not in the whole of an Umma, but in small and sometimes alternating branches thereof, which are better described as *shu'ūb* (1: 296–99, Ar. 239–41). How this intense but narrow bond translates into the establishment of large-scale societies is a question well worth considering in the study of Ibn Khaldūn.

Most of the ignorant opinions err in overestimating the political importance of traditional human attachments, while underestimating the importance of the acquisition of goods such as money, pleasure, honor, and power. But they can hardly be characterized as naive about war. The ignorant bonds that they posit result in the formation of political communities of various sorts, most of which tend to be hostile to one another. The result is a world of tribes, cities, confederacies, and Ummas vying with one another for supremacy in the ignorant goods, often by means of war (VC 298.4 ff.).[5] The prevalence of war, whose naturalness and justice are not questioned by most of the ignorant opinions (VC 298.13–300.10), is yet another reason why the political form of the ignorant governments remains so fluid. War upsets the balance of communities and alters their form. A tribe, city, or Umma that is too successful in conquest may eventually find itself dispersed among the vast territories of a multinational empire, as happened to the Arabs in the early Islamic centuries. The political weakness of the Umma, and the other ignorant bonds for that matter, becomes clearer when considered from the point of view of the wars in which the ignorant associations are continually engaged. To better understand the significance of this dynamic, we need to turn to the *Political Regime,* in which Alfarabi describes the conduct of the ignorant associations and their wars in some detail.

Alfarabi introduces the ignorant cities in the *Political Regime* by contrasting them to the virtuous city, without mentioning any political form other than the city (PR 76.92, Ar. 87.5). This echoes some of the passages in the *Virtuous City,* which present the ignorant governments as subsisting only in cities (VC 254.2–256.14). Yet subsequent passages in the *Political Regime* do not maintain this pattern, for the cities of necessity, wealth, pleasure, honor, and tyranny are all called associations as well (*ijtimāʿ*, PR 76.93, Ar. 87.18–88.3, 77.94, Ar. 88.4, 77.95, Ar. 88.14, 77.96, Ar. 89.7, 78.97, Ar. 89.14, 81.104, Ar. 94.5). Associations can signify not only cities but also communities larger and smaller than them (PR 60–61.64, Ar. 69.14–70.4; VC 228.11–13). By adding the term "associations" to his account of ignorant governments, while associating the "ancients" only with the "king in truth" who rules the virtuous communities (PR 69.80, Ar. 79.12), Alfarabi rejects the assumption of the *Virtuous City*, which appeared to link ignorant governments to the cities and opinions of the ancients. He shows how ignorant opinions and governments, far from being limited to the cities of the ancients, also provide cohesion to contemporary societies, most of which are much larger than cities.

The one exception is democracy,[6] which is introduced as a city but not as an association (PR 86.113, Ar. 99.7). The original list of these associations follows a similar pattern: all of them except democracy are said to exist "in cities," as if they are larger than one city (76.93, Ar. 87.18–88.3).[7] If this interpretation holds, then democracy is singled out among the ignorant associations as the only one restricted to a single city.[8] This anomaly requires some careful consideration. It should be considered in conjunction with Alfarabi's two references to the Umma, an association known to be larger than the city. One occurs in the context of the association of honor (80.101, Ar. 92.9), and the other in the context of democracy (87.115, Ar. 100.14).

Of the ignorant associations, the associations of honor and domination are treated in the greatest detail. I wish to elaborate here on a point that has already been made by Joshua Parens, concerning the proclivity of the ignorant governments for the conquest and domination of foreigners (Parens 2006a, 83). This tendency is particularly obvious in the case of the associations of honor and domination. The noblest of the rulers of the city of honor seeks both present and future fame among the Ummas for his magnificent and generous deeds (PR 80.101, Ar. 6.13; VC 256.4). These extravagances will have to be funded somehow. Alfarabi suggests taxation, and, when that fails, attacking neighboring groups for the sake of plunder (PR 80.102, Ar. 92.14–17).[9] Alfarabi displays here the impeccable realism for which he is rarely given credit.[10] He perceives the link between honor among the Ummas and conquest: how many ancient and medieval rulers ever attained great glory without becoming great conquerors? Yet the line between honorable and tyrannical acts seems at times to be rather thin, as indicated by the association of honor's proclivity for imperious behavior (78–79.98, Ar. 90.10–15; 81.103, Ar. 94.2–4; Parens 2006a, 82). The city of domination is, not surprisingly, even more addicted to the conquest of its neighbors than the city of honor: in a city whose principle is domination, joining together to dominate others is certainly more appealing to its inhabitants than being dominated themselves (PR 81.104–83.107, Ar. 94.5–96.16).

The associations of necessity, wealth, and pleasure appear in their initial presentation to be relatively benign. However, nothing about their foreign policy can be inferred from these brief summaries, beyond the disturbing hint that their inhabitants often regard banditry as a legitimate means of subsistence and profit (PR 77.94–78.96, Ar. 88.5–6, 89.5–6). Alfarabi reintroduces these associations, rather ominously, in the section devoted to tyranny, and they all turn out to be engaged in the domination of others (85.110–86.112, Ar. 98.1–99.6). These cities are driven to conquest by a lively sense of the superiority of their own way of life (85.111, Ar. 98.6–7), and the simple fact that the pursuit of wealth, pleasure, and even necessary goods is best sustained by conquest (85.110, Ar. 98.1; 85–86.112, Ar. 98.14–16). Conversely, a city of domination that succeeds in conquest will surely acquire wealth and indulge in pleasure (86.112, Ar. 98.19–99.6). Alfarabi reiterates in the conclusion of the section that the associations of necessity, wealth, pleasure, and honor often obtain their goods primarily through war and domination, and have a corresponding need for warlike men (88.118, Ar. 102.5–11).

While Alfarabi accepts the inevitability of war and conquest, he is by no means an apologist for them. In the *Virtuous City*, he recognizes that some of the ignorant opinions favor the "voluntary transactions" of trade over war (VC 312.2–5), and engage in the latter only in cases of defensive necessity (312.7–15). Alfarabi goes so far as to state that the souls of the inhabitants of the peaceful ignorant cities are healthier than the souls of their warring counterparts (314.7). Yet trade is overshadowed by war in Alfarabi's own account of the functioning of the ignorant associations in the *Political Regime*. While commerce and the peaceful arts may indeed serve as a means of obtaining the goals sought by the inhabitants of the ignorant cities, Alfarabi seems to regard war as more generally effective (PR 77.95, Ar. 89.5–6, 85.112, Ar. 98.14–16, 88.118, Ar. 103.4–6). In the ignorant governments, the demands of politics and the health of the soul do not usually coincide.[11]

In the somewhat disturbing account of ignorant associations in the *Political Regime*, war seems to prevail over peace, and the distinction between the various ignorant associations becomes quite blurred. Alfarabi suggests elsewhere that all actual ignorant regimes consist of an indefinite mixture of the major prototypes, none of which ever exists in its pure form (SA 58, #90, Ar. 92.13–17). His last word on the ignorant associations suggests one such possible mixture. They are often ruled by peoples such as Turks and Arabs, whose sybaritic habits developed in the wilderness. Even when transplanted to the city, they never overcome their addiction to pleasure and women. They consecrate, and eventually dissipate, much of their public bravado as glorious conquerors for the sake of this low, private end, so that they and their households are eventually ruled by women (PR 89.119, Ar. 102.13–103.13).[12] Alfarabi alludes here unmistakably to the harem, an especially ancient institution in his part of the world. The four "associations in cities" are in the final analysis rather similar: their love of pleasure, wealth, and honor among the Ummas, as well as the habits of the Ummas from which their rulers come, all tend to push them toward imperial designs that recognize neither political nor ethnic boundaries, and then to their eventual decline. The multinational scope of Islam may contribute to the obsolescence of the city as a political association, but so too do the decidedly profane habits and ambitions of the Abbasid caliphs and their Turkish successors.

Where does this leave democracy? Among the ignorant regimes, it is very much an outlier. To repeat, democracy alone is not called an association, but merely a city, or else described as an association limited to a single city (PR 76.93, Ar. 88.3; 86.113, 99.7). Why can't a democracy expand to include an Umma or many Ummas? This question looms especially large because Alfarabi presents the democratic city as continually growing (87.115, Ar. 100.14).

The democratic city does attain extraordinary success in a certain sense. On this score a bit of Arabic wordplay is revealing. Although this city is never called an association (*ijtimā'*), the expression rendered "democratic city" is *madīna jimā'iyya*, which could literally be translated as "associative city."[13] The verb derived from the same root "associate" (*j-m-'*) appears multiple times in the treatment of democracy (PR 86.113, Ar. 99.12; 87.115, Ar. 100.18; VC 314.2).[14] All the cities, human passions, and ways of life will associate with one another in this city. In this respect, it is not merely one city, but many different cities, mixed together and barely distinguished from one another. Many Ummas will flock to live in it, and its size will increase beyond bounds (PR 87.115, Ar. 100.14–101.5). This emphasis on untrammeled population growth and immigration shows that Alfarabi equated democracy not with the small cities of the ancients, but with large metropolises such as Baghdad,[15] which had hundreds of thousands of inhabitants.[16] The flocking of the Ummas to a burgeoning democratic city represents yet another allusion to Alfarabi's own journey to Baghdad[17] from his remote non-Arab origins.

We recall that the Umma is mentioned only twice in the discussion of ignorant cities. Both instances are in the plural, one in connection with the city of honor, and the other in connection with the democratic city. The city of honor and democratic city both overcome ethnic boundaries in gaining fame among the Ummas. The former does so by means of its great military exploits (PR 80.101, Ar. 92.9); the latter, by means of its freedom and openness to newcomers (87.115, Ar. 100.14). Rather than subjugate the Ummas, the democratic city receives them into its bosom with open arms. Unfortunately, democracy's illustrious reputation for tolerance does not ensure its political or military success. Alone among ignorant governments, democracy remains restricted to a single city.

Parens asserts that all the ignorant governments engage in conquest and domination (Parens 2006a, 83). This observation is generally both apt and true, but does it hold in the case of democracy? Alfarabi is well aware that no democracy could maintain itself without mustering enough force to combat its enemies. He speaks twice of resistance to these enemies (PR 86.114, Ar. 100.1, 88.117, Ar. 101.13). In both cases, the context is clearly defensive: the ruler must guard the goods that the city already possesses, rather than acquire new ones. Offensive war is not encouraged by democracy's guiding principle, freedom, which is left out of the list of the ignorant goods that impel their seekers to conquest (88.118, Ar. 102.5). Furthermore, the city's openness to all things foreign (87.115, Ar. 100.18) is sure to weaken its desire for the domination of foreigners. Despite its frenetic internal growth and cosmopolitan character, democracy's external expansion is limited by its indifference toward offensive war. One might object that all the ignorant cities, ways of life, and rulerships are said to exist in the democratic city (87.115, Ar. 100.16–17): this would have to include, among others, the city of domination. But even if the desire for conquest and domination remains present in some of the city's inhabitants, it might risk being crowded out by other, more pacific inclinations, such as love of freedom and the arts. Although democracy does not adopt love of peace as an official doctrine, it is the ignorant city closest to the ignorant opinion described in the *Virtuous City*, which champions peace among all humans and authorizes only defensive war (VC 310.12 ff.).

Alfarabi is in many ways sympathetic to the multiethnic, democratic city. He presents it as disorganized and sometimes licentious, but anarchic only in the most extreme case (PR 86.113, Ar. 99.14–17). The most exaggerated Platonic accusations against democracy, such as disobedient slaves, unenforced death penalties, and recalcitrant mules (*Republic* 562e–563c), are not repeated by Alfarabi. He emphasizes at least as much as Plato the flourishing of the arts, including poetry, rhetoric, and wisdom in all their forms, as well as the presence of virtuous elements within the city (PR 87.115, Ar. 101.1–2).[18] Yet Alfarabi's praise of democracy retains a certain wistful air. The virtuous city or Umma cannot defend itself from enemies any more than it can protect itself from plagues (70.81, Ar. 80.10–11). Would a democratic city that prefers a plethora of peaceful activities to offensive war be able to defend itself? In a world abounding in associations of honor and domination, this is not merely a theoretical question. The Baghdad of Alfarabi's day, despite its intellectual vibrancy, was in terminal political decline, in the process of being taken over by Turkish and Daylami mercenaries (Kraemer 1992, 31ff., cf. PR 89.119, Ar. 103.6). The only genuine, independent cities that are likely to exist in the Near Eastern regions known to Alfarabi would resemble Abbasid Baghdad and Byzantine Constantinople in their later centuries, vast imperial capitals that had attracted inhabitants from half the world but lost their own military genius, governing the ever-shrinking remnants of a decaying empire and struggling to defend themselves against the repeated encroachments of enemies.[19] Considerations of this sort lead one to suspect that however much Alfarabi may have cherished the freedom and intellectual ferment of the democratic city, he did not regard it as a permanent solution to the dangers posed by the love of honor and domination. Perhaps Alfarabi hoped that his praise of democracy's unique capacity for intellectual freedom would somehow penetrate the harems of the military rulers as well, and convince the men and women who would rule the Islamic world for the foreseeable future to tolerate philosophy and related activities even while devoting most of their time to pleasure and war.

The weakness of democracy as presented by Alfarabi resembles the weakness of an association based on an Umma. When stating the bond of the Umma among the ignorant opinions, Alfarabi hints by omission that it is insufficient for waging war. Neither the democratic city nor the association based on the Umma has the cohesiveness or ambition to succeed in aggressive or even defensive wars against predatory neighbors. The associations most likely to endure would have to triumph repeatedly in war, and therefore eventually encompass many Ummas (cf. PR 80.101, Ar. 92.9). In their incessant quest for the ignorant goods of victory, honor, and plunder, ignorant rulers and their armies have no reason to respect ethnic boundaries. Whenever political boundaries correspond to national boundaries, they do so only by accident. For entirely different reasons, this conclusion applies equally to both virtuous and ignorant governments. The Umma possesses neither the wisdom required of the one, nor the military might required of the other.

Alfarabi and the New Kind of Umma

I have thus far emphasized the degree to which Alfarabi's presentation of the Umma does not support modern nationalism. From the point of view of the modern nationalist, his understanding of the Umma is too imperfectly political, and his notion of ethnic cohesion too weak. Both wisdom and war, the most vital springs of government in the virtuous and ignorant associations, respectively, operate on a transnational scale, thereby undermining any claims for national autonomy. This being said, there exists a certain affinity between Alfarabi's Umma and some of the tendencies of modern nationalism, as they appear in the thought of Rousseau. Let us take a closer look.

The political claim of the Umma with regard to the virtuous associations is rather weak. The mostly pre-philosophic Umma is best understood as a recipient of wise and virtuous rule, rather than as its source. Compromise with the recipient may be inevitable, but that does not mean that it should be granted any independent political authority. The Umma's claim with regard to the ignorant associations may be somewhat stronger. After all, the ethnic and linguistic bond of the Umma creates more genuine fellow-feeling than the merely spatial proximity of the city. The problem is that it does not suffice to rouse its members to war (VC 296.4–7). Yet while Alfarabi recognizes the pervasiveness of war, he does not glorify it. On the contrary, he displays some sympathy for the naïveté of the inhabitants of the peace-loving cities, whose souls are described as healthy, in contrast to the wicked souls of the war-loving conquerors (314.7–8).[20] It is perhaps not merely coincidental that those who love peace regard "Ummas and groups" as the most prevalent political associations (312.8–9). The implication seems to be that the Umma might emerge as the most natural political association if it could somehow avoid war or become capable of national defense (312.9–15). Alfarabi thus appears quite sympathetic to the prospect of a peaceful community of nations based on the independence of the ethnic Ummas, but he has no illusions about its coming to pass. With regard to his own part of the world, such skepticism was certainly well grounded. Nationalism arrived in the Middle East only in the twentieth century, when it was imported from Europe. And it has hardly brought peace.

The political situation in nineteenth-century Europe, however, may not have warranted such skepticism. It was the scene of the emergence of nationalism. The next major political philosopher who took the nation as seriously as Alfarabi did was probably Rousseau, who lived on the eve of that epoch. His *Considerations of the Government of Poland* provides an early blueprint for modern nationalism. Without ever having read Alfarabi, Rousseau takes up many of the questions concerning national autonomy that were left unanswered by his tenth-century predecessor. Most importantly, Rousseau is well aware that a nation can neither attain nor retain its independence unless it acquires enough cohesion to succeed in war.

Broadly speaking, Alfarabi speaks of two crucial steps in the emergence of the Umma. The first step is the simple development of language. We have seen that language in itself, which varies considerably from region to region and class to class, is woefully insufficient for sustaining political unity and cohesion. Rousseau's agreement on this point is indicated by his virtual silence about language in his nationalistic proposals for Poland. This silence cannot be explained by any general disinterest in the topic, since works like the *Discourse on Inequality* and *Essay on the Origin of Languages* display a manifest concern with it.[21] But neither of these works contains any discussion of nationalism. The only mention of language with regard to Poland occurs, almost as an afterthought, in a discussion of military matters (Rousseau 1990, 229). It is obvious that Rousseau does not perceive a very strong link between nationalism and language, since he tends to talk about either one or the other in several of his major works.

The second important step in the development of Alfarabi's Umma is the creation of its literature. This literature is based on memorable events recorded in speech. In speaking about the nature of such events himself, Alfarabi is deliberately vague. Our examination of the issue in Chapters 2 and 3 led to the conclusion that the most frequently recorded events probably involve legendary feats of human strength and courage, interactions with gods, and accounts of the origin of natural things. This is the stuff out of which most early national literature is formed. The civilization of the Umma coalesces around preserved accounts of these events. Such stories would seem to produce greater political unity, but they remain insufficient to that end. The assortment of tales that form the basis of the Umma may involve political events, but they are not tailored to any specific political goal. Homer gave Greece much of its literary heritage, but he did not bring about its political unity. Socrates mocks Homer for not giving any city its laws or regime, or improving the government of cities in any significant way (Plato, *Republic* 599c–e).

Rousseau seems to agree with both Socrates and Alfarabi about the doubtful claims to political autonomy of the nation as traditionally understood. Its shared language and customs suffice to establish cultural uniqueness, but not to forge the bonds of political solidarity. While claiming no great familiarity with prevailing Polish customs (Rousseau 1990, 173), Rousseau is quite sure that the Polish nation in its current form is not well suited to the preservation of long-term political independence: he asks how "a state so strangely constituted, was able to last for so long" (164, cf. 170, 184). The pre-political nation can serve as the point of departure for a nationalist political identity, but it will reach the finish line only if it has been transformed in the novel manner proposed by Rousseau.[22]

On the basis of Alfarabi's understanding of the evolution of the Umma it is not difficult to imagine this third step, which makes use of the Umma's common language and literature yet proceeds well beyond them. A new sequence of events, primarily political or military in nature, is recorded. Heroic accounts of these events then serve as the basis of national education and political unity. Rousseau's proposals for Poland point in this direction. He suggests that national cohesion may be firmly established through a new and aggressive form of education. In Poland this education should include, among other things, a glorification of the Confederates who are waging war against the Russian invaders (Rousseau 1990, 170). The great events and deeds of the war for independence, even if ultimately unsuccessful, can serve as a trigger for the development of a durable national identity. Rousseau extends the national education still further. Every great man ever born, and every great act ever done, in Poland, as well as the more mundane geography of the country, must already be engraved in the heart of every Polish adolescent (178). As for the various errors and humiliations of Polish history, the national education is silent about them. The intense love of the fatherland produced by the inculcation of national memory will protect the country from foreign conquest. It will eventually inspire a militia fearsome enough to fend off foreign invaders (230 ff.), but such an institution is sure to be years in the making. Meanwhile, a firm national identity can preserve even a conquered people from foreign subjugation or absorption. As Rousseau memorably puts it, "If you act so that a Pole can never become a Russian, I respond that Russia will not subjugate Poland" (171, cf. 230). The fact that Poland would gain its independence from Russia only in 1918, and then manage to do so again in 1989, renders Rousseau's suggestion quite prescient.

Despite Rousseau's emphasis on the strong militia necessary for self-defense (1990, 230 ff.), he shares Alfarabi's suspicion of the conquest and domination of neighbors. Indeed, he takes it a step farther. Alfarabi seems to have grudgingly accepted such aggressive pursuits as inseparable from political life, but Rousseau makes a serious effort to discourage them. Invoking the negative example of Rome, whose successful conquests eventually destroyed its own political freedom, he attempts to convince the Poles that "Whoever wants to be free ought not to want to be a conqueror" (230, cf. 234). The new national education is meant, among other things, to discourage foreign military adventures. A people endowed with a distinctive national identity will have no more desire for the excitement of such excursions than Spartans had for the soft, luxurious life of Persia (171). Rousseau's new national education strives to fill the people and leaders of the nation with an aversion to foreign things that includes an aversion to foreign conquests. He attempts to render each nation firmly at home only in its own country, and thereby provide the peaceful stability to international borders that consistently eludes Alfarabi, but appears in some way to be desired by him.

The influence of Rousseau appears clearly and succinctly in the work of his nineteenth-century successor Ernest Renan, author of perhaps the single most famous speech on the nation, titled "What Is a Nation?" This famous scholar of Averroes would unfortunately have been quite unfamiliar with Averroes's predecessor, most of whose works were unavailable in the nineteenth century. Yet he displays a partial agreement with Alfarabi. Writing in the late nineteenth-century heyday of nationalism, Renan takes the political understanding of the nation for granted. He therefore treats the nation as a modern European phenomenon, and denies that any of the ancient Ummas mentioned by Alfarabi, such as the Egyptians and Arabs, deserve the name of "nation" at all (Renan, 223–24). He goes on to show, with great lucidity and numerous empirical examples, how neither race, language, religion, nor geography, alone or in combination, suffices to define a nation properly understood (231–40). Similar factors also shape Alfarabi's Umma, and on their inadequacy for establishing political unity and independence, he agrees with Renan. But Renan proceeds to explain the phenomena on which the political nation is actually based, namely, shared memory and a will to live together (240–43). He emphasizes the role of shared memory, and the salutary distortion of history through which it is formed: France could not become a nation until it had forgotten the savagery of the medieval wars that had united it (227–28). This emphasis on memory, and its selective application, follow from Rousseau and his proposed Polish national education. It may not have surprised Alfarabi, who suggests that the stories remembered and eventually written down during the formation of both the ethnic and religious Ummas have but a tenuous and unknowable relation to the events themselves. As we saw in Chapter 4, Alfarabi implies in the opening pages of the *Book of Religion* that the hallowed period of early Islam was in fact a time of savage conflict. Religious and national solidarity both require a rewriting of the bloody events that gave rise to them. But Alfarabi did not aspect this kind of storytelling ever to produce an effective political bond, on the national or religious level.

In the nineteenth century, the flimsy cultural and linguistic ties of the traditional ethnic Umma were tightened into the firmer shackles of the nation-state, possessing formidable political, military, and economic force. Can Alfarabi be blamed for overlooking the possibility of this new kind of Umma and new kind of national education, the germ of which may even be present in his own thought? I would defend Alfarabi on two grounds. First of all, nothing of the experience of Alfarabi's epoch would have suggested such a possibility: both the religion and habits of its rulers encouraged large, multiethnic political units. Alfarabi is more concerned with dissuading rulers from excessive expansion and oppression of ethnic groups within their borders than with attempting to dissolve empires into their component parts. Renan disparages the Ottoman arrangement of separate and unassimilated ethnic or religious communities living side by side within the same cities as "the ruin of the Orient" (Renan, 228); Alfarabi might have considered such an arrangement quite satisfactory, so long as there was minimal persecution or ethnic strife. Imperial diversity and tolerance, rather than national self-determination, are in Alfarabi's view the most practical arrangement for limiting national or religious conflict.

The foregoing observations are relevant to the American context as well. One may argue, with the Gettysburg Address, that the American Revolution "gave birth to a new nation, conceived in liberty," whose national identity coalesced around stories of the heroic deeds of the Revolution. Lincoln himself, in his speech at the Young Men's Lyceum, ascribed to these stories a continued role in fostering American national identity, even as they fade from living memory: "The scenes of the revolution . . . we hope . . . will be read of, and recounted, so long as the bible shall be read" (Lincoln, 84). The English-speaking peoples, while maintaining a single language, came to establish several successful nations. But this fact does not refute Alfarabi's teaching, if that teaching is flexibly understood. Members of a single linguistic group may migrate in various directions across the ocean and eventually splinter into several distinct peoples, each formed around accounts of their own particular national events. Once again, tracing the formation of the Umma to stories recorded about heroic events proves far more tenable than reducing it simply to language. This applies equally to peoples as diverse as the Greek *ethnos*, Islamic Umma, French *état-nation*, and American federation: in each case, the character of the people will reflect the traits embodied in its national narrative.

Alfarabi and the Modern Restoration of the Muslim Umma

The nationalism that developed in Europe eventually reached the Muslim world as well. It manifested itself in a variety of forms, some pan-Islamic, some pan-Arab, others more strictly local. Attempting to track the varied careers of these movements lies well beyond the scope of the present work. I therefore wish to limit myself to one particular aspect of the problem that relates closely to Alfarabi's teaching. As I suggested in Chapter 4, certain pioneers of modern Islamic thought, such as Jamāl al-Dīn al-Afghānī and Muhammad Iqbal, restated the claims of the Islamic Umma, thus bringing the old tension between the Islamic and ethnic Ummas to the fore. Examining their new visions for Islamic unity and contrasting them with Alfarabi's greater skepticism on the topic will help make the case for Alfarabi's continued significance in modern times.

The most important figure in the formation of modern Islamic thought was arguably Jamāl al-Dīn al-Afghānī (1838–1897). His life and career bear more than a superficial resemblance to Alfarabi's. He too was born on the eastern fringes of the Islamic world, in either Afghanistan or Iran, but ended a lifetime of wandering in Istanbul, the imperial capital at its center.[23]

Despite a troubled relationship with the Muslim powers that be, whose internecine quarrels and impotence in the face of European imperialism
aroused his disgust and contempt, Afghānī left an indelible imprint on the
minds of his contemporaries and their successors, forever changing how
Muslims viewed themselves. Yet while the effect of Alfarabi's odyssey was
the recovery of classical Greek philosophy and its introduction into Islamic
civilization, the effect of Afghānī's pilgrimage was the emergence of a
powerful political ideology informed by both Islam and modern European
Enlightenment. Afghānī devoted his life to resurrecting the power of Islam
in this world, putting an end to centuries of decay that had culminated in
the humiliation of foreign rule. He knew something of the medieval Islamic
philosophical tradition, but suspected it of being excessively beholden to
Greek thought, and insufficient for attaining his goals (Afghānī 1968, 107,
115). He resembled less a latter-day Alfarabi than a Muslim Herzl, whose
indefatigable energy was directed toward restoring the long-lost dignity
and independence of his people. The result of Afghānī's worldliness was
that his practical expectations for the Islamic Umma greatly exceeded
Alfarabi's.

These hopes are expressed quite forcefully in the monumental Qur'ānic
commentary of Afghānī's student and associate Muhammad 'Abduh. 'Abduh devotes many pages to the analysis of a single Qur'ānic verse, 3.104, in
which the new Umma, "commanding good and forbidding evil," is proclaimed. His ingenious interpretation contains many elements that are difficult to find in the original Qur'ān. To be sure, 'Abduh builds on Qur'ānic
precedent, laying great emphasis on the unity of the Umma. He defines
Umma as a particular form of community (*jamā'a*) characterized by an especially high degree of unity (*waḥda*) and cohesion, so that it resembles a
single, healthy body with a collection of well-functioning organs ('Abduh, 5:
66). Like Alfarabi in the *Attainment of Happiness*, 'Abduh recognizes that this
Umma will have to function locally. Leaders will need to be chosen, prefer-
ably by the vote of the entire community, at a village as well as at an international level (67, 71–72). Moreover, 'Abduh emphasizes that these leaders
will require knowledge of the particular people to whom their mission is
entrusted (68). 'Abduh's overwhelming emphasis on knowledge, or science
(*'ilm*), expands greatly on the Qur'ān, and in a sense brings him closer to
Alfarabi. Geography, ethics, psychology, history, political science, and linguistics all become indispensable for the mission of the Umma (68–71). Yet
it is difficult if not impossible to detect in 'Abduh any of Alfarabi's irony.

'Abduh does not speak of a virtuous city of philosophers that cannot exist anywhere on earth, but of his own novel understanding of the mission of Islam. In 'Abduh's attempt to fuse Islam with modern thought, the line between Islam and Enlightenment becomes blurred. The old, universal Umma of faith is not only resurrected, but also transformed, so as to become compatible with European thought and its *mission civilisatrice*.

Afghānī paves the way for this more ambitious understanding of the Umma in three crucial steps. First, he adopts as his starting point the political view of the Umma presented in the ignorant opinions of Alfarabi's *Virtuous City*. Second, he strengthens its political bond. Alfarabi, we recall, did not emphasize military solidarity of the Umma, even in his ignorant opinions. Afghānī attaches a new term, namely, *'aṣabiyya* and its derivatives, to the Umma. Made famous by Ibn Khaldūn, this word may be roughly translated as "group solidarity." But while Ibn Khaldūn defines *'aṣabiyya* as the solidarity of a clan or small tribe, Afghānī greatly expands the scope of this sentiment, calling the related term *ta'aṣub* the "bond" and "form" that induces every Umma to vigorously defend its territory and rights (Afghānī 1981, 40–41). Third, Afghānī argues that such feeling is strongest not in the ethnic Ummas, but in the Muslim Umma, since the Islamic religion is the "holiest of bonds" (42). Shared Muslim devotion to the one true God constitutes a bond so strong that as long as it retains its force, merely national bonds become superfluous (34–35). Despite his elevation of Islam above all else, Afghānī cannot be identified with Islamic fundamentalism, at least in its more savage, atavistic form. Deploring the excessive religious *'aṣabiyya* that leads to the persecution of other faiths, he reassures us that such injustices have been comparatively rare in the history of Islam, as proven by the continued flourishing of religious minorities in the Islamic world (42–43). Although Afghānī can hardly be blamed for not foreseeing the steep decline of most of these communities, his faith in the benevolence of Muslim religious fervor may in retrospect appear somewhat naive.

Afghānī's argument for the superiority of divine attachments over merely human ones possesses a certain logic, rooted in the teaching of the Qur'ān, according to which piety is the only thing that truly counts. Afghānī was fond of quoting the Quranic verse stating that "All believers are a brotherhood" (Qur'ān 49.10, Afghānī 1981, 28, 31). Yet by Afghānī's time such a doctrine had been challenged by centuries of experience. The Islamic Umma had not, in the millennium since Alfarabi, regained its political or cultural unity. A multiplicity of empires, languages, and cultures had become an enduring feature of Islamic civilization. As Nāṣif Naṣṣār puts it, Afghānī speaks of an ideal Islamic Umma, not Islamic as they are but Muslims as they ought to be (Naṣṣār 1986, 50). To discover any such unity, Afghānī must point to the ancient stories about the concord that prevailed at the origin of Islam, continuing from the time of the prophet to that of the famous ninth-century Abbasid sultan Harūn al-Rashīd (Afghānī 1981, 37–38). The present reality, which Afghānī laments countless times, was the gradual subjugation of most of the Islamic world to European imperial rule, often by means of a "divide and conquer" strategy. Afghānī evidently thought that restating the ideal unity of the Islamic Umma would help resist colonialism, but to what extent did he expect this unity to be realized?

On this point, Afghānī was not as demanding as one might expect. He acknowledged that complete political unity was unlikely: "I am not attempting with my words to make the ruler of all affairs one person, since that might be quite difficult" (Afghānī 1981, 29; Naṣṣār 1986, 54). Yet Afghānī did believe that the aggressive dissemination of his new, pan-Islamic political doctrine combined with the menace of European rule would eventually induce the various remnants of the Islamic empires to cooperate. He continues: "But I hope that the Qur'ān will be the sultan of all of them, and religion the cause of their unity, and that everyone possessing rulership will strive to protect one another as much as possible, since in the life and survival of the one lies the life and survival of the other" (Afghānī 1981, 29). Afghānī's writings include two pleas for the Persians and Afghans to unite in resistance to British and Russian encroachments on their territory (265–71).

Afghānī was also not so zealous as to hope for an end to linguistic and cultural differences among Muslims. Yet he did adhere to the principle that religious unity always ought to take precedence over them. "The religious Muslim who is sound in his beliefs refuses all kinds of *'aṣabiyya* apart from Islamic *'aṣabiyya*, and ignores his nationality and tribe" (Afghānī 1981, 35). Declarations of this sort might explain Afghānī's rather harsh judgment of the Ottoman Turks for not adopting Arabic, "the language of religion," as their official language (13–14, 320). This linguistic adjustment, Afghānī contests, would have helped the Ottomans to consolidate their empire by unifying Turks and Arabs. Yet we may invoke themes that are prominent in Alfarabi, in asking whether such a policy would have been feasible. Can Ummas be expected to jettison their ancestral language for the sake of mere political or religious expediency? Afghānī himself does not expect all Muslims to take such a step: to the best of my knowledge, he never blames Persians or Mughals for clinging to Farsi and Urdu. Afghānī seems to prefer Arabic over other tongues, insofar as it is the language of Islam, while accepting the practical inevitability of a multiplicity of languages within the faith. Yet he fails to give a persuasive account of how religious unity will calm linguistic or ethnic tension, beyond expressing the mere hope. "The influence of dislike and aversion between tribes, clans, indeed between nationalities that differ in their birthplaces, languages, and customs, will be erased" by the holy tie of Islam (Afghānī 1981, 42). Yet can one name a single Muslim society, past or present, where this has actually occurred? The most that Afghānī can claim, in considering "the ways of Muslims, from the birth of their religion until today," is that "the Arab does not shun the rule of the Turk, the Persian accepts the rule of the Arab, while the Indian subjects himself to the rule of the Afghan" (35). Under the multinational Ottoman, Abbasid, and Mughal empires, each nationality yielded to the rule of the dominant race, but is there any proof that they did so willingly? And how can we be sure that these disparate nations will continue to get along after the disintegration of these empires? These questions point to a major historical limitation of Afghānī, with regard to present-day affairs. Living at the end of the nineteenth century, he did not clearly foresee the collapse of empires and their replacement by states. Muhammad Iqbal, another important Muslim reformer who lived a generation later, did experience the development of the new international system, which his theory of the unity of Islam is obliged to take into account.

Iqbal's comments on Islam and nationalism are interspersed throughout his books and speeches. The most ample discussion is also the last, composed just before his death in 1938. Addressing a contemporary Indian Muslim who had been influenced by European views of nationalism, Iqbal reiterates his lifelong conviction that genuine Islam rejects that mode of political organization (Iqbal 2015, 301). Islam as a religion is not rooted in land, race, or genealogy, but in a universal, spiritual idea that applies equally to all humans in all climes (311; cf. 121). Iqbal supports this view with a thorough analysis of the use of *umma*, *milla*, and *qawm* in the Qur'ān, in which he concludes that there are many ethnic *qawm*, but only two Ummas, those who embrace the *milla* of Ibrāhīm and those who do not (308–9). Nationalism falsely divides human beings according to nation and territory, destroying the universality of religion and eventually leading to the skeptical conclusion that "the religion of a land belongs to that land alone and does not suit the temperament of other nations" (311–12). Iqbal follows Afghānī in alleging that nationalism has been promoted by the Europeans in Islamic lands in order to "shatter the religious unity of Islam to pieces" and advance their own imperialistic designs (Iqbal 2015, 301; Afghānī 1981, 44). Relying on these comments alone, one might imagine Iqbal to be a zealous supporter of a universal Muslim state. Yet like Afghānī before him, Iqbal did not unleash the political power of Islam without simultaneously seeking to rein it in. He observes that the notion of political pan-Islamism does not even exist in any traditional Muslim language, and cites Afghānī as someone who "never dreamt of a unification of Muslims into a political state" (Iqbal 2015, 283). Unifying the world by force is impossible, even for the Muslims, whose attempt to conquer the nations met the same end as that of their Greek and Roman predecessors (141). Iqbal therefore has to articulate how the grand ideal of Islamic unity can coexist with the inevitable dispersion of Muslims into different nations and states.

Iqbal admits that despite Islam's universal teaching, "the differences of nations, tribe, colours, and language are at the same time acknowledged" (Iqbal 2015, 311). This remark alludes to Qur'ānic verses such as 49.13 and 30.22, which Iqbal cites verbatim on another occasion (cf. 237). Yet what does his acknowledgment entail in practice? Iqbal proceeds to argue that despite the unparalleled progress made by Islam in unifying the nations, tribes, races, colors, and languages under the aegis of a sole "Muslim Umma, obedient to You" (309), this enterprise remains a work in progress, to be consummated sometime in the indefinite future (311). The "mutual conflicts, sanguine [sic] battles and civil wars" that have characterized the "infinite process" of history will not culminate easily in the peace desired by Islam (312).

Iqbal already anticipates major changes in Islam in the near future. In his own time, the religion is undergoing a period of transition, as it gradually adapts to the modern world. The old, unifying institution of the Caliphate has been abolished. While some of the bloodiest Muslim fanatics of today pine for the Caliphate, Iqbal welcomes its abolition, as a way to bring Islam more in line with the contemporary, post-imperial system (Iqbal 2015, 244, 2012, 124–25). Yet isn't it precisely an international system of nation-states, none of which are supposed to have universal political or religious ambitions, that might have trouble adjusting to the most comprehensive claims of Islam? Iqbal is hardly oblivious to this difficulty. He admits that in the present period of transition and uncertainty, the result of the interaction of the universal Muslim ideal with actual nation-states is yet to be ascertained. The following passage is quite striking in this regard:

> I do not know what will be the final fate of the national idea in
> the world of Islam. Whether Islam will assimilate and transform
> it, as it has assimilated and transformed before many ideas
> expressive of a different spirit, or allow a radical transformation
> of its own structure by the force of this idea, is hard to predict.
> (Iqbal 2015, 6)

Despite Iqbal's apparent rejection of nationalism, he makes his peace with the fact that it will somehow influence Islam. Alfarabi and Iqbal both argue that Islam would flourish only by respecting human diversity and evolving over time: on this point, the medieval philosopher and modern internationalist are of one mind.

This is not to say that Iqbal does not express definite opinions or hopes about the future of the national idea in Islam. He distinguishes between Muslim majority countries such as Egypt, Turkey, and Iran, and Muslim minority countries such as India. With regard to the former, he supposes that Islam is so thoroughly embedded in their cultural and national identity that among their inhabitants love of country will never come into conflict with Islam (Iqbal 2015, 238). But the question of the relations between these different states remains. Iqbal is again hopeful, but only cautiously so: he explains that Islam "is shifting from one form of political solidarity to some other form which the forces of history have yet to determine" (239). While a world-state sustained by the common spiritual atmosphere inherent in Islam would be ideal, a league of Muslim states, or even a number of independent Muslim states enjoying peaceful, commercial relations among themselves, seems more likely (238). Iqbal's most enduring hope, expressed in his most famous book on the reconstruction of Islam, is that Islam will come to be understood as advocating a League of Nations that recognizes the inevitable heterogeneity of humankind while serving as a bulwark against the nationalist and imperialist excesses to which such heterogeneity gives rise (Iqbal 2012, 126). This international arrangement among Muslims would presumably rest on Afghānī's basic assumption that the devotion of Muslims to their religious community exceeds in force all merely national attachments.

As far as Indian politics was concerned, Iqbal was actively involved in the fight for Muslim autonomy. He argues that while the Hindus of India, divided as they are by caste, region, and language, do not constitute a unified nation, the Muslims have received "the free gift" of nationhood by virtue of their religion (Iqbal 2015, 13–14, 26). He therefore proposes that the Muslim-majority regions of Sindh, Punjab, Baluchistan, and the Northwest Frontier be united into a single province, as "the final destiny of Muslims, at least of Northwest India" (11–12). Perhaps Iqbal hoped that this Muslim province, or nation, would eventually join his anticipated Muslim league. Unfortunately, his claim encounters several obvious difficulties at the local level. Muslims in India remain no less divided than Hindus by language and region. Hundreds of miles separate Sindh from the Northwest Frontier, and over a thousand miles stand between what is now Pakistan and Bangladesh. Outside the Muslim majority regions, significant Muslim minorities belong to almost every major linguistic group in India. Iqbal's claim that the Muslims "are far more homogeneous than any other people in India" and "a nation in the modern sense of the word" (26) can only be understood in light of the religious Umma of the Qur'ān, whose universal spiritual ideal transcends these lesser forms of human differentiation. In proposing a separate Muslim autonomous region in the northwest part of India, Iqbal is inspired by this Umma. Yet he seems somewhat aware of the problem posed by the diverse ethnic composition of this region. Is this the difficulty alleged by his critics, who believe that the proposed state will be "very unwieldy" (11)? Iqbal responds to this criticism by reassuring his audience that Muslims, when guaranteed a clear majority in their respective region, will defend India faithfully and not oppress Hindu minorities (11–12), but he does not speak very cogently about the considerable ethnic differences within their own ranks. Since Iqbal acknowledges that Islam in India has yet to shed the intricacies of caste, which it inherited from the Hindus (115–16), why does he refuse to admit the same with regard to Islam's absorption of the various Indian nationalities? We should not imagine that a man as intelligent as Iqbal was blind to obvious empirical facts, but rather that like Afghānī before him he had faith in the overwhelming power of the Islamic Umma to eventually unify, in India and elsewhere, the sundry ethnic Ummas of which it is composed. Iqbal's frequent claims that Islam's "peculiar conception of nationality" consists of a "purely abstract idea," detached from all territorial and racial considerations (Iqbal 2015, 121–22, cf. 141, Iqbal 2012, 124, 142), points strongly in this direction.

I wish to make some brief observations on the basis of later historical experience. Even if Iqbal did not foresee Pakistan as a separate, independent state, the recurrent communal problems that have plagued its existence from the very beginning suggest that he may have underestimated the power of ethnic attachments. It has turned out that Bengalis, Punjabis, Baluchis,

Pushtuns, Sindhis, and Muhajirs from elsewhere in India do not flourish together in a single state, despite its pronounced Muslim identity. Bengal has broken away, leaving the Punjabis with a large plurality, of which the numerous other ethnic groups are constantly suspicious. Iqbal might regard these problems as ephemeral, part of the stormy transition of Islam to the era of nation-states and democracies, but in the meantime there is no end in sight to them. Endemic ethnic strife in Pakistan seems to belie Iqbal's aspiration for a unified Islam, and stands as a warning for pan-Islamic ambitions as a whole. In this respect, Pakistan could be seen as a microcosm for the entire Islamic world. From Morocco to Indonesia, ethnic and tribal conflicts rage virtually unchecked by Islam. I do not mean to suggest that the Islamic Umma is irrelevant, since it does indeed unite Muslims in pilgrimage and prayer, but it seldom suffices to prevent Berbers and Arabs, Turks and Kurds, or Punjabis and Bengalis from quarreling with one another. Meanwhile those who long for Muslim unity are tempted to pursue their goal by waging bloody wars against the ethnic diversity and international state system that constrain them. The Umma's glory is now declared most ardently by organizations such as al-Qaeda and ISIS. Bin Laden's pronouncements invoke the Umma so incessantly that his translators have chosen to leave the term in Arabic (Bin Laden, 290, 4–19, passim); not surprisingly, most of these references to the Umma call for Muslim unity against a common crusader enemy. ISIS's declaration of the restored Caliphate, meant to serve as the legitimate government of the entire Umma, contains the following exclamation:

> Yes, honor is for this ummah. It is from the honor of Allah (the Exalted)—honor that mixes with the faith residing in the believer's heart. Thus, if faith becomes firm in the heart, honor becomes firm along with it. It is honor that does not hunch, soften, or become disgraced regardless of how great the anguish and tribulation become. It is honor befitting the best ummah—the ummah of Muhammad (peace be upon him)—an ummah that does not accept submission to anyone or anything other than Allah.[24]

In the century that has passed since the first modern Muslim thinkers sought to restore the Umma, the harsh verdict of experience is that proclaiming its unity and glory brings neither prosperity nor peace. The hope for a new era of Muslim unity has yet to materialize.

As I suggested at the end of the Introduction, it is in this atmosphere of tumult that Alfarabi, who has only begun to emerge from centuries of neglect, may warrant a second look. His older understanding of the Muslim Umma, inspired by both his own observations and classical Greek thought, was eminently sober. He did not demonize the Umma, but neither did he sanctify it. The emergence of this Umma onto the world scene was an amazing event that relegated the pagan cities and their local gods to the past. It has complicated the equilibrium among the Ummas, but without fundamentally altering it. Whatever the Umma's internal claims to universality might be, they will never be believed, at least not in the same fashion, by all humankind. Besides, the pursuit of pleasure, money, honor, and domination so characteristic of the pre-Islamic *jāhiliyya* period has in no way subsided, leading to disagreements among Ummas and constant war between competing empires. The Umma will therefore remain a particular Umma that has to coexist, on a more or less equal footing, with the other great Ummas of humankind. Rather than impose itself upon these Ummas as the witness over them, it needs to adapt to their ways, by means of the continual use of prudence. The local gods of antiquity may be dead, but the need to accommodate local feelings endures.

Alfarabi describes the situation of the Umma in his time, but doesn't he also describe its situation today? If anything, the tensions between the and ethnic Umma have only grown stronger. The aspirations of the former have been strengthened by the rise of political Islam, while the aspirations of the latter have been strengthened by nationalism and the development of states. The caution, compromise, and respect for human diversity that characterize Alfarabi's teaching about the Umma may help both Muslim leaders and the foreign powers that continue to intervene in the Islamic world emerge relatively unscathed from this cauldron of ethnic and religious conflict. Studying Alfarabi will not provide any ready-made solution to any of these conflicts, but as I suggested toward the end of Chapter 6, Alfarabi did not believe in ready-made political solutions. At the very least, Alfarabi could encourage a more careful, place-by-place approach to political affairs, in a part of the world where grand political ideals, Eastern, Western, religious, and secular, have in recent times built only graveyards.

Conclusion. The Intermediate Association

I have attempted to interpret and explain Alfarabi's teaching about the
Umma, with all its nuances, as it unfolds across a number of important works.
Rather than simply repeat or summarize my arguments, I conclude by en-
capsulating a number of general points that could be derived from them.

A clever piece of Arabic wordplay neatly expresses the gist of Alfarabi's
treatment of the Umma. The Qur'ānic phrase *umma wasaṭān* could be translated as "central Umma." The Umma is central because of its mission as "witness over all humankind" (Qur'ān 2.143). This memorable verse continues to
affect Muslim notions of their Umma and its role down to the present day.
Alfarabi employs the same expression, but gives it an entirely different meaning (PR 60.64, Ar. 69.19–20; VC 228.11).[1] The context proclaims the status
of the Umma as the political association intermediate in size between the
city and the multinational empire. But when viewed in the light of the rest
of Alfarabi's writings, this statement could imply that the Umma is intermediate in other ways as well. It always falls somewhere in between language,
literature, art, philosophy, religion, politics, and war. This unusually fluid
status of the Umma in Alfarabi, standing in contrast to the fixed, elevated
status that the Umma eventually acquired in the Qur'ān and Muslim tradition, renders it a particularly fruitful subject for inquiry. Our deceptively narrow focus on the Umma has nevertheless allowed us to explore Alfarabi's
views on many other important subjects as well.

Alfarabi had to reckon with two types of Umma that were often in tension with one another. He indicated to present and future generations of
Muslims how these tensions could be reduced. Even though Alfarabi, unlike Locke or Spinoza, did not develop any general theory of religious toleration, his teaching about the need for prudence in dealing with the unique
cultural environment of each and every Umma usually points in the same
direction. In a few rare cases, prudence might involve destroying or enslav-
ing a people, but Alfarabi seldom dwells on such possibilities. The large,

multiethnic empires that covered the map of the Islamic world up until the twentieth century could not flourish without displaying a high degree of flexibility and benevolence toward their diverse subjects.

Alfarabi attacks, indirectly but persistently, two of the biggest obstacles to such flexibility. First, he rejects the notion that a pure Islamic Umma of uncontested piety, which is said to have existed at the time of the prophet, should serve as a model for Muslims of all subsequent ages. Alfarabi's remarkable critique in the *Book of Religion* of the possibility of any return to the small, cohesive community of primordial Islam thus forms an important part of his political project. Since the Islamic Umma has long outgrown its roots as a tiny nucleus of believers led by a living prophet in Medina, it needs to acquire a flexibility befitting its ampler proportions. In the aftermath of the French Revolution, Benjamin Constant warned his fellow Europeans that the bloody outcome of that event had proven the futility of trying to govern a large, modern state in the strict manner of a small, ancient republic (Constant, 493 ff.). This sensible counsel, if heeded, might well have averted the worst of the still bloodier catastrophes that followed. The advice that Alfarabi gives to his fellow Muslims is in a certain sense comparable. Attempting to impose the religious uniformity of a small, close-knit community on an imperial creed that encompasses many ethnic Ummas is sure to provoke only strife. A religion as large and successful as Islam can ill afford to overlook the diversity of the Ummas within it. But this means accepting a vast degree of religious variation.

Second, in both the *Book of Religion* and the *Attainment of Happiness*, Alfarabi indicates that no empire or religion, led by either philosophers or more conventional leaders, could possibly unite an indefinite number of Ummas. Living at the twilight of the Abbasid Caliphate, Alfarabi understood that the sprawling Islamic community had been permanently fractured, and would never be united, culturally or politically, again. Hopes for the conversion of the entire world to Islam, or even a single caliphate governing all Muslims, would have to be shelved, and a number of competing dynasties and Ummas allowed to coexist without too much bloodshed.

Beyond his general argument for ethnic, religious, and political accommodation, Alfarabi seems to have harbored few illusions about political reform, but can anyone blame him for it? In the millennium following his death, his region remained under the thumb of a long series of sultans and shahs, culminating in the multi-ethnic empire of the Ottoman Turks. The European imperialists who acquired the remnants of that empire in the aftermath of the First World War were hardly departing from precedent when they divided up the conquered peoples according to no particular ethnic rule. In the age of postcolonial nationalism, such "artificial" boundaries have frequently resulted in disastrous instability. Yet is there a clear alternative? Arab nationalism, if understood as seeking to unite all Arabic speakers from Morocco to Yemen under a single government, seems no more feasible that its Islamist counterpart. But unlike French, Italian, and the other dialects descended from Latin, many of which became major languages and civilizations in their own right, none of the dialects of Arabic have matured into vernaculars that could form the cultural basis of distinct Ummas and states of their own. Some modern Arab countries, such as Egypt and Tunisia, have nonetheless developed a fairly distinctive national culture: these are the states whose borders tend to be the most stable. But in general it is easier to complain about the arbitrary borders of the Middle East than to fix them in any satisfactory manner. Alfarabi's observation that political boundaries rarely follow ethnic boundaries still holds true of his region today. This fact makes it doubly unfortunate that his arguments for the accommodation of ethnic diversity and local variety within large multi-ethnic political units often appear to have fallen on deaf ears.

The growth of the nationalist Umma, while not anticipated by Alfarabi, does not discredit his understanding of the Umma. Like the ethnic and religious Ummas before it, the nationalist Umma grows up around the memory of certain fateful events and requires political accommodation. In cases where the nationalist Umma has come to prevail, politically at least, over all other kinds of Umma, it would be hard to imagine Alfarabi strongly resisting the establishment of nation-states. The principle of accommodation would surely require that nationalist or secessionist ethnic movements be granted some autonomy, if not outright independence, insofar as the densely intermingled religious and ethnic map of the Middle East permits it.

The relevance of Alfarabi's teaching about the Umma extends well beyond his particular region and religion. The same logic could undoubtedly be applied to various multi-ethnic states and secessionist Ummas elsewhere in the world. So could Alfarabi's understanding of the formation of Ummas. In the aftermath of a large number of national legends, claims to revelation, and political revolutions, many peoples today have been shaped by all three kinds of Umma. Americans provide an excellent illustration of the mixed origins of the vast majority of modern humans. Let us abstract for the moment from the presence of various ethnic and religious minorities, whose integration into the majority culture is bound to vary. Most Americans are the product of the religious Christian Umma, whose basis is the Bible and the traditions spawned by it. The majority of Americans who are not themselves of English descent have forgotten much of their ancestral language and culture to become members of a linguistic English Umma, whose towering genius is Shakespeare. Finally and most characteristically, Americans are heirs to the nationalist[2] Umma that declared its independence in 1776. The great homegrown American statesman Abraham Lincoln drew inspiration from all three Ummas. The aforementioned Young Men's Lyceum address compares the enduring quality of the stories surrounding the American founding to the eternal importance of the Bible. Lincoln's admiration of Shakespeare, and in particular the play *Macbeth*, is attested in his letters (Lincoln, 718–19). An examination of the greatest figures in American literature, such as Twain, Whitman, and Faulkner, would surely reveal inspiration from all three Ummas as well. Such authors become themselves part of the American, English, and even, on some occasions, the Christian Umma: as I argued at the end of Chapter 5, all kinds of Umma can flourish only by growing in response to changing circumstances.

Alfarabi was interested in practical politics, religion, art, and literature, but his deepest concerns lay elsewhere. He was, above all, a philosopher. He maintained the superiority of philosophy to all other human activities, and was interested, above all, in its preservation. The attitude of philosophy to all three kinds of Umma, ethnic, religious, and nationalist, is fundamentally similar. The stories of the Umma, whatever they may be, establish what would later come to be called a *Weltanschauung*. They provide the moral and religious framework, based on common opinion, under which human societies can thrive. They create the rich cultural environment in which civilization, in all its literary and artistic splendor, can bloom. Alfarabi does not, to repeat, seek to undermine any kind of Umma. The Umma is needed to foster cultural continuity and stability, as well as human creativity and excellence. Yet Alfarabi is well aware of the overwhelming power and authority of the Umma's stories, which risk snuffing out the independence of thought that philosophy requires. He therefore takes special care to provide alternate, ambiguous versions of the story surrounding the emergence of both the ethnic and the religious Umma, so that the potential philosophers of his civilization would not be too quick to embrace the dominant views. Yet he develops these narratives subtly and inconspicuously, so as not to undermine the faith of the people, or encourage any of his readers to do so. If faced with the new, nationalist Umma, Alfarabi would have responded in a similar fashion. He would have questioned its foundational story, in a delicate but penetrating way, without causing any kind of public scandal. He might have embraced the view that America needs to foster, among the mass of its citizens, a general belief in the virtues of the founding and its gradual westward march, while nevertheless allowing the publication of novels and films that are critical of it, as well as unfettered historical research in its universities. The tension between the need to protect the popular opinion of the Umma on the one hand, and the desire to pursue critical, philosophical inquiry on the other, will always be with us.

As for the civilization of the Umma, it seems to fall somewhere in between. The value of poetry and the other arts of the Umma lies both in their facility in communicating with the people, and their ability to stimulate the elite. As Alfarabi emphasizes in the *Book of Letters*, the arts of the Umma must appeal to popular opinion. Yet in the *Epistle on the Canons of Poetry*, Alfarabi shows that genuine artistic creativity ought not to be beholden to such opinion. The American version of this ambiguity is admirably expressed by John Ford's finest films, such as *The Searchers* or *The Man Who Shot Liberty Valence*, in which John Wayne is never quite the unflappable hero, nor civilization quite the pacifying force, that they initially appear to be. The questioning character of the best artistic images, and their ambiguous relationship to the things they portray, underlie Alfarabi's view that the cultural vibrancy of the Umma and the fate of philosophy are closely intertwined. In the struggle against religious extremism, the Islamic Umma today could benefit not only from the intellectual guidance of Alfarabi, but also from the artistic inspiration of Naguib Mahfuz, Orhan Pamuk, and Youssef Chahine.

I conclude by reiterating that Alfarabi was not a partisan, or detractor, of any particular Umma. Alfarabi's basic advice to each and every Umma remains the same: political prudence, artistic creativity, and philosophical inquiry must be cultivated by the Umma in the manner most appropriate to its character and traditions. The discovery of this manner is the task of statesmen, artists, and philosophers in each Umma. Alfarabi has laid a solid foundation, but only people of local knowledge can build the edifice.

Notes

INTRODUCTION. ALFARABI AND THE QUESTION OF THE UMMA (NATION)

1. Muhsin Mahdi and Richard Walzer, two leading scholars of the last generation known for taking opposite viewpoints with regard to Alfarabi, agree about the obscurity of his biography (Mahdi 2001, 1; Walzer 1965, 778). The most detailed and up-to-date biography is by Dimitri Gutas in the *Encyclopaedia Iranica* (Gutas 2012). Gutas's exceedingly cautious account, in which most of the sources are dismissed as legendary, confirms just how little reliable information we have. Ulrich Rudolph follows Gutas in debunking the "legends" concocted by eleventh- and twelfth-century biographers (Rudolph, 370–71)

2. For a complete list of Alfarabi's works, see Vallat, 378–87, and Rudolph, 377–403. Rudolph also explains the difficulties involved in merely identifying the lost works (Rudolph, 403).

3. For a list of all the recent scholarship on Alfarabi, as well as medieval Islamic thought more generally, see Thérèse-Anne Druart's excellent website, http://philosophy.cua.edu /faculty/druart/bibliographical-guide.cfm.

4. For ease of reference, I have used abbreviations to cite works by Alfarabi. These are listed in "A Note on Citations and Abbreviations" and are listed at the beginning of the book.

5. I heartily agree with Paul Heck's conclusion that "[Alfarabi's] philosophical *oeuvre* is best understood not simply as part of a Hellenic legacy, now in Arabic, but more as a response to the intellectual concerns of his own day" (Heck, 212). Alfarabi's milieu included Christians, Jews, and Zoroastrians as well as Muslims, but he foresaw that it would continue to be dominated by Muslims. The orientation of his work toward Islam will be demonstrated in many places throughout the book.

6. Joshua Parens deserves credit for examining this aspect of Alfarabi's thought in his book (2006a).

7. Naṣṣār states plainly that "there does not exist in Greek thought anything parallel to the Umma in the Arabic language" (1978, 39).

CHAPTER 1. THE NATION IN PLATO AND ARISTOTLE:
A STUMBLING BLOCK TO VIRTUOUS RULE

1. Muhsin Mahdi and Joshua Parens argue forcefully but intuitively that Alfarabi must have had access to something resembling our text of Plato, especially with regard to the *Laws* (Mahdi 1961, 1–10; Parens, 1995, xxviii–xxxiv). Dimitri Gutas attempts to demolish their claim

(Gutas 1998a). Gutas appears very convinced that the source of Alfarabi's *Summary of Plato's "Laws"* is a summary by Galen, or something "very closely related to it" (Gutas 1997, 117–18), even though the name Galen does not appear in Alfarabi's commentary, and the text of Galen's summary remains lost. Most recently, Steven Harvey undertook a thorough examination of the entire scholarly debate (Harvey 2003b, 51–68). Harvey does not accept many elements of Gutas's analysis but does tend toward his conclusion that Alfarabi may indeed only have had access to the *Laws* through Galen's commentary (Harvey 2003b, 61–66). Thérèse-Anne Druart, editor of the best critical edition of Alfarabi's *Summary of Plato's "Laws"*, was at first inclined to think that Alfarabi did have access to the full text of the dialogue, but then apparently changed her mind (SL, ed. Druart, 112–13; Harvey 2003b, 61 n. 34). Charles Butterworth gives an excellent, up-to-date account of these debates in the preface to his new translation of the *Summary* (*Alfarabi: The Political Writings*, 2: 101–7). While Leo Strauss did not engage in any original historical research on the matter, his incisive interpretation of the *Summary* offers some compelling philosophical reasons why Alfarabi might have wished to deviate so considerably from the Platonic original (Strauss 1959, 140–42, 154).

2. Cf. Mahdi 1961, 5–6. Even Rosenthal is not oblivious to this possibility, conceding that perhaps "al-Fārābī knew a few smatterings of the Greek language as spoken in that period" (F. Rosenthal 1940, 410 n. 7).

3. Mahdi suspects that Alfarabi did study in Byzantium, and might even have learned philosophy in Greek or Syriac before he mastered Arabic (Mahdi 1971, 523). If this is the case, then he definitely would have known Greek. Gutas dismisses this claim as part of the legend of the "polyglot" Alfarabi, transmitted by certain unreliable medieval sources and exploited by Mahdi in his attempt to link Alfarabi to certain versions of Greek philosophy. However, Gutas does seem to accept the widely reported claim that Alfarabi had a Christian teacher, Yūḥannā b. Ḥaylān (Gutas 2012). One imagines that association with Christians, even in Baghdad itself, would have given Alfarabi some opportunity to learn Greek.

4. As Stephen Menn puts it, "[Alfarabi] does not trust Greek philosophy as it is presented to him by the Arabic translation-literature" (Menn, 67). The account of philosophical translation in the *Book of Letters* will be discussed in Chapter 3.

5. Mahdi has helpfully inserted the Arabic page and line numbers into his translation, so the same reference may apply to both the Arabic and English text.

6. For the various meanings of *ethnos* and *genos*, see Hall 1997, 34–36.

7. Some commentators are more skeptical about this passage than others. See Isaac, 69–70; Hall 2002, 212; Sassi, 112–14; Kamtekar, 6; Benardete, 92. Rosen thinks that Socrates is referring not only to Attica in particular, but to moderate climates more generally (Rosen, 151). Averroes seems to agree. He first says that Plato ascribed wisdom only to the Greeks, an opinion that risks disqualifying Averroes as philosopher and commentator, but qualifies this statement with "it seems." Averroes then adds that "we," a pronoun that may or may not include Plato, restate and dilute Plato's view, so that it finally refers to all the peoples in the moderate fourth and fifth climate zones. Under Averroes's guidance, Plato's teaching becomes indistinguishable from the view stated by Alfarabi in the *Great Book of Music*, according to which all the peoples conquered first by Alexander the Great and later by the Arabs enjoyed a moderate climate and therefore a capacity for civilization (Averroes 1974, 27.1–14; BM 108–10).

8. Paul Ludwig shows how Socrates's proposals for unifying the city allude to certain Greek precedents, while ultimately proceeding far beyond them (Ludwig, 210–17).

9. There is much scholarly debate about this point. Gregory Vlastos has argued that the city does possess slaves, and cites this passage as evidence, but he ignores the possibility that Glaucon may simply have misunderstood Socrates: "Glaucon gives every appearance of being of one mind with Socrates throughout this discussion" (Vlastos, 293–94). Other scholars, such as Brian Calvert, remain skeptical (Calvert, 267–72). In my reading, slavery is clearly and explicitly introduced only after the fall of the best regime (*Republic* 547c).

10. Craig's argument for the "natural differences" between Greeks and barbarians must hinge partly on this passage. Yet it is difficult to see how the later references to barbarians in 499c–d and 533d, as well as Socrates's abandonment of the distinction between Greeks and barbarians after 470c5, sustain this view. The same applies to Carl Schmitt's interpretation of this passage (Craig, 12–13; cf. Schmitt, 28–29).

11. It is hard to believe, with Kamtekar, that in promoting Greek unity "Plato may be recognizing a political actuality rather than asserting a scientific necessity" (Kamtekar, 3). The dialogue must have occurred sometime during the Peloponnesian War, when internecine strife, interrupted only by periodic truces, was the norm among the Greeks. Even if the self-righteous Athenian complaints of the *Menexenus* are exaggerated (*Menexenus* 244c1–2, 245b3–e1), many Greeks did indeed ally with barbarians against rival Greek cities. Rosen's gloss about the relationship between Socrates's speech and the political reality is more plausible: "Socrates sounds very much here as if he is lecturing his contemporaries on actual politics, in particular, on the stupidity of Greek fighting Greek" (Rosen, 196).

12. Averroes's commentary reproduces the direction of the argument. He has Plato begin by denouncing Greek crimes against Greeks, but conclude by saying that no class of people, be they Greek or non-Greek, ought to commit such crimes (Averroes 1974, 59.20–60.4).

13. On Glaucon's impatience, see Benardete, 120.

14. The policy recommended in this passage is also blatantly unjust, at least from the point of view of the other cities (cf. Kochin, 57; Rosen, 135), and would probably be ineffective, once the other cities have caught wind of its stratagems (Rosen, 134). It is badly in need of the reconsideration provided by the discussion of Greek unity.

15. Ferrari observes that the introduction of Greek kinship casts all previous definitions of friends and enemies, or inside and outside, into doubt (Ferrari 2007, 186). Kochin's perspective on the difference between the accounts resembles in some crucial respects my own (Kochin, 55–57, 68–72). We both agree that Socrates strives to temper war and realpolitik by substituting some form of education.

16. When speaking of gentleness earlier in the dialogue, Socrates employed the word *praos* (376c1). Here, Socrates prefers the word *hēmeros*, which also has the connotations of "tame" or "civilized." The implication is that the high level of culture and the arts that prevails in Greece should deter war, contrary to Glaucon's inclinations.

17. Benardete sees potential for hypocrisy in this policy, as it would permit the guardians to "punish the rulers of any city which opposes them as war criminals" (Benardete, 122). Kochin presents its educational goals more favorably (Kochin, 68–72). This disagreement might be less important if the city's efforts to educate its fellow Greeks are bound to be ineffectual, as I attempt to show.

18. For an interesting speculation about the possible role of "the common language of the Greeks" in the *Republic*, see Kochin, 70.

19. Rosen suggests that Greek identity as declared here depends on blood ties (Rosen, 196–97). This is philologically plausible, according to the meaning of the words *genos* and

suggenes, but not clearly elaborated in the argument of the dialogue. A common earth and mother are attributed to the city, but not necessarily to the Greek *genos* (470d7–8). Since Rosen perceives the non-Greek origin and implications of the city's official genealogical myth (Rosen, 126), one wonders how, in his view, this myth could be reconciled with the new statement of the "Greek blood" of the city.

20. For the standard diplomatic meaning of these terms, see Hall 2002, 213–14.

21. "The entire discussion on this point is playful, another attribute of noble puppies" (Rosen, 86). Dogs are playfully mocked in 469d7–e2. "The philosopher dogs are now wholly useless" (Benardete, 122).

22. "Love of city, love of Greeks, and love of wisdom." The frequent use of words beginning with the prefix *phil-* is a feature of Greek that Plato loves to exploit.

23. "To be truly philosophic would be to be open to everything one does not know and hostile to everything one takes for granted" (Benardete, 57).

24. Some of the ideas in this section have already been expressed, in an eloquent but rather cursory form, by Allan Bloom in the interpretive essay that accompanies his translation (Plato, trans. Bloom, 388–89).

25. Commentators often seem to skip over *Republic* 497 and all its puzzling implications. Cf. Rosen, 242; Benardete, 150–53; Ferrari 2005, 108–9.

26. "If the city is made, they do not have to start at the beginning with, for example, a man or woman, a country, or a people with a past. Making in speech cuts out place and time, both of which are indispensable for becoming" (Benardete, 47).

27. There seem to be some exceptions in outlying areas of Greece. From *Laws* 680c it appears that Cretans were not familiar with Homer.

28. Bloom asserts that the poets are simply dependent on the legislator (*Republic*, trans. Bloom, 431–32). But the relationship between the two is surely reciprocal, and the poet is often prior in time. Homer sang for a world that would be shaped by Solon and Lycurgus, but Solon and Lycurgus legislated for a people who was already influenced by the poems of Homer. To disentangle the relative influence of poetry and legislation on any given people is not an easy task. While the former helps to create nations, the latter helps to create cities. I will discuss these issues further when I turn to Alfarabi.

29. For a thorough, incisive interpretation of this treatise, see Strauss 1945. I cannot possibly give due credit to this pathbreaking article in the notes. Its influence is evident throughout this section.

30. The broken Arabic plural is *umam*. In order not to confuse readers who do not know Arabic, I prefer to represent this form with the 'Anglicized' plural "Ummas."

31. This point will be analyzed in great detail in the next chapter.

32. Strauss has already observed that the city and Umma are each presented differently throughout the work. "One has to consider #7, where only 'nation' and not 'city,' is mentioned: the nation is kept together by common language. The bond of the city, on the other hand, is the law" (Strauss 1945, 379 n. 2). I attempt to build on Strauss's observation here.

33. The Arabic term translated as "statesman" is *madanī*," derived from the term *madīna*, meaning city. But Alfarabi in these passages suggests that this link may be only accidental, since he omits the term *madīna* from them as consistently as he omits the term Umma.

34. Mahdi translates *malik* as "prince," but "king" is much more literal.

35. "In other words, the required supplement to philosophy is, not just the royal art, but the actual exercise of the royal art by philosophers within a definite political community" (Strauss 1945, 379).

36. Strauss draws our attention to this difficulty as well: "Fārābī speaks also of the 'other nation' in particular and of nations in general, but he prefers to speak of the 'other city' and of cities" (Strauss 1945, 379 n. 52).

37. This list of dialogues includes the *Laws*, which appears to deal only with the virtuous ways of life of the inhabitants of the city (PP 21.1–2). In keeping with this brief statement, Alfarabi's *Summary of Plato's "Laws"* stands out as his only extant political work that never mentions the Umma.

38. I have seen no evidence that what are known to us as Plato's *Letters* would have been available to Alfarabi. In any event, those letters concern reform in Sicily rather than in Athens, so they hardly accord with Alfarabi's account. It seems more likely that Alfarabi is not referring to actual letters, but rather inferring how Plato would have acted in general on the basis of his political philosophy. If public calls for reform turn out to be imprudent, then private letters written to prominent individuals might emerge as a more promising course of action.

39. Moritz Steinschneider compiled a list of all the medieval Arabic translations of Greek works known in the late nineteenth century, and this included most of the works of Aristotle. See Steinschneider, 35–74.

40. The conclusion of this treatise speaks somewhat vaguely of politics and political philosophy, without mentioning any specific work of that name (PA 130–32).

41. All the translations from the *Virtuous City* are my own. The reader is welcome to compare them with Walzer's, which are not always reliable.

42. Naṣṣār also emphasizes the importance of cooperation, without resolving this problem (Naṣṣār 1978, 37–38).

43. In the *Selected Aphorisms*, Alfarabi describes wisdom as identifying "true happiness," while prudence helps us to attain mere "happiness" (SA 53, #35, Ar. 62.10–11). While the expressions "happiness" and "true happiness" are identical to those employed in the *Virtuous City*, I fail to see how one discussion sheds light on the other.

44. I owe this insight to Julie Ward's account of the meaning of *ethnos* and *barbaros* in Aristotle's *Politics* (Ward, 17–19).

45. See Aquinas, *ST* I-II, Q. 105 (p. 94); Marsilius, "Defender of the Peace," in Parens and Macfarland 2012, 391–92.

46. Among the great Muslim medieval political philosophers, Ibn Khaldūn is most forthright in discussing only monarchic and imperial forms of government. Alfarabi does appear to treat democracy, a regime that he would have inherited from Plato and Aristotle, but his version of it is actually a form of monarchy, as I show in Chapter 6.

CHAPTER 2. FROM SPEECHLESSNESS TO CIVILIZATION: THE EVOLUTION OF THE UMMA

1. I cite from Butterworth's excellent new translation, as well as Najjar's Arabic text. However, I consistently leave as "Umma" the term Butterworth translates as "nation." I follow the same policy with regard to Mahdi's translation of the *Attainment of Happiness*. Whenever the translation seems inadequate for the purposes of my argument, I explain it in the notes.

2. The term that Butterworth translates as "tongue" is *lisān*, while the term he translates as "language" is *lugha*. I suggest translating the former as "language" and the latter as "dialect," as I will explain in greater detail in Chapter 6.

3. There is an English translation of the second chapter of the *Book of Letters* by Muhammad Ali Khalidi. Since I cite frequently from the first and third chapters as well, I prefer to cite from the Arabic edition, page and line, while providing my own translations. Wishing to enable readers who do not know Arabic to look up some of the passages, I have cited the paragraph numbers that appear in Khalidi's translation after the number sign.

4. In the *Great Book of Music*, Alfarabi places a similar emphasis on the physical constituents of musical sounds (BM 52 ff.).

5. All translations from the Qur'ān are my own.

6. Druart perceives clearly the difference between Alfarabi and traditional religious views, arguing that for Alfarabi "God has absolutely no role in the origin of language" (Druart 2012, 54–55). Some commentators on verse 2.31, whose opinions were collected by the fifteenth-century scholar al-Suyūṭī, interpreted it as meaning that God gave humans the capacity to invent languages (Roman, 135). But Alfarabi's ubiquitous silence about any connection between God and language implies a rejection of this view as well.

7. Sweeney claims that "The nation is more natural than the city, and hence more perfect" (Sweeney, 563). While Sweeney is right to emphasize the natural origins of the Umma, he underestimates the importance of custom in its subsequent march toward perfection. Alfarabi never identifies human perfection with mere nature.

8. The Arabic root has strong connotations of both agreement and chance.

9. The word translated as "conventional" in the *Political Regime* (*waḍ'ī*) shares the same root as the term translated as "language giver" in the *Book of Letters* (*wāḍi' al-lisān*).

10. For a good summary of the chain of causality that leads to the development of language, see Naṣṣār 1978, 46.

11. The other four, which will be discussed in due course, are rhetoric, poetry, the memorization of sayings, and writing.

12. Naṣṣār suggests along similar lines that one could combine these two meanings, and render Umma as "a group agreeing on a way of life" (1978, 21).

13. Mahdi suggests in his introduction that the absence of direct references to the political works in the *Book of Letters* means that it may have been written prior to them (BL, ed. Mahdi, 43). This suggestion is plausible but somewhat speculative, since Alfarabi does not normally cross-reference his works, and chooses not to refer to specific themes or ideas whenever it suits him. For example, the absence of any references to logic in the *Political Regime* and *Virtuous City* does not necessarily mean that they were composed before the logical works.

14. I define the discussion of the Umma proper as the section between 134.16 and 148.30 (#114 to #138). The passages preceding and following this section do discuss politics and religion, but their explicit theme is not the Umma. Their significance will be considered in Chapters 3 through 7. Vadja has already noted the absence of the term "city" (*madīna*) from the *Book of Letters*, which in his view distinguishes it from Alfarabi's "truly 'political' works" (Vajda, 250).

15. The simple equation of these terms also goes against Qur'ānic usage: while Umma occurs dozens of times in a wide variety of contexts, *sha'b* and *qabīla* each appear only once (cf. Qur'ān 49.13).

16. The proclivity of medieval Muslims for inventing noble genealogies for themselves is widely known: a famous early study of it was done by Ignaz Goldziher (Goldziher 1967, 1: 164–90). More recent research confirms that the creation of genealogies had developed into a sophisticated literary genre by the ninth century (F. Rosenthal 1992, 967). Ibn Khaldūn

also criticizes the notion that the character of an Umma could be traced to its ancestor (Ibn Khaldūn, 1: 172–73, Ar. 1: 136–37).

17. The verb *ẓann*, which Alfarabi employs several times in this passage, usually signifies a questionable assumption (BL 98.16, 99.1–2, 99.22).

18. I propose this as the answer to the question raised by Naṣṣār: how does Alfarabi distinguish between an Umma and a tribe (Naṣṣār 1978, 35–36, 48)?

19. The Islamic term *kalām* is often translated as "dialectical theology." It does indeed refer to a group of intellectuals who understood their main goal to be a defense and promotion of their view of Islam. However, this rendering can be quite misleading, since the Arabic original, which simply means "speech," contains no reference whatsoever to either dialectic or theology. I prefer not to translate this well-known technical term.

20. In modern Arabic these words have come to mean "progress" and "regress" in the Enlightenment sense. The clearest indication of their meaning of "ordered progression" in Alfarabi may be found near the end of the first chapter of the *Book of Letters*. Having spoken of how "the foundation is for the sake of the wall . . . the tool is for the sake of that which is sought in its use . . . the action is for the sake of the end to which it leads," Alfarabi explains that "In all of these cases it follows necessarily that that the purpose of the thing is posterior in time (*ta'ākhar*) to the thing itself, while the thing itself is prior in time (*taqaddam*)" (BL 129.7–14).

21. Alfarabi means those who speak Syriac, a language that once played an important role in the transmission of Greek thought into Arabic.

22. The broader significance of the Arabic term *akhbār* will become clearer in the discussion of the religious Umma in Chapter 4.

23. As far as I know, this work has never been translated into any European language.

24. This issue will be discussed further in Chapter 5, in the context of Alfarabi's treatment of religion.

25. Rousseau makes some interesting remarks on this topic in the sixteenth chapter of his *Essay on the Origin of Languages*, titled "False Analogy Between Colors and Sounds," in which he distinguishes sharply between painting and music with regard to their character and effects (Rousseau 1993, 114–17).

26. Further consideration of this question might require the study of Alfarabi's extremely technical *Great Book of Music*. At present I do not have the technical or historical knowledge of Arabic music to perform such a task. I have studied and cited the introduction, but not the body of the work.

27. The Daylamis were an Iranian people who lived near the Caspian Sea.

28. I discussed this term briefly in the previous section, and will do so again in my treatment of the Qur'ān in Chapter 4. It is hardly surprising that this verse has sustained a lively debate among commentators. Roy P. Mottahedeh gives an excellent account of these discussions and their relevance to the Shu'ūbiyya (Mottahedeh, 163 ff.).

29. The first, and still classic study of the Shu'ūbiyya was done by Ignaz Goldziher (Goldziher 1967, 1: 137 ff.). However, H. A. R. Gibb suggests that Goldziher overestimated the role of political considerations in general and the Abbasid court in particular. Gibb regards the Shu'ūbiyya rather as a movement intended to assert the importance of the Persian cultural tradition against the Arab (Gibb, 69 ff.). H. T. Norris gives a clear, up-to-date summary of the historical background and major themes of the movement (Norris, 31–45).

30. Goldziher 1967, 1: 154 ff.; Mottahedeh, 162.

31. For a description of the main themes, see Norris, 38–45.

32. Ibn Qutayba, a leading opponent of the movement, alleges that it is driven by Persian envy against Arabs (Lecomte, 344).

33. For some direct attacks by al-Jāḥiẓ on the Shuʿūbiyya, see Norris, 43–45.

34. The roots *f-ṭ-r* and *ṭ-b-ʿ*, which signify nature in Alfarabi, also appear in al-Jāḥiẓ, but as the free creations of God (al-Jāḥiẓ 1903, 18–19).

35. The tradition that God taught Ismāʿīl Arabic is cited by al-Jāḥiẓ on several occasions, helpfully collected by Saleh Said Agha (Agha, 82–89). Agha makes the interesting point that al-Jāḥiẓ does not present God as the creator of the Arabs, who predated Ismāʿīl, but rather as the converter of Ismāʿīl to Arabhood at the age of fourteen (81–82). In the century before Alfarabi, thoughtful Muslims were already wrestling with the question of the limits of divine power.

36. Here al-Jāḥiẓ employs the word Umma, although he does not do so consistently (cf. al-Jāḥiẓ 1903, 20, 43).

37. The most important Qurʾānic verses in this context are the aforementioned 49.13 and the yet-to-be-discussed 30.22. These verses will be considered in greater detail in the section on the Qurʾānic Umma in Chapter 4.

38. There are several other descriptions of the talents of various peoples by al-Jāḥiẓ. One passage in *Kitāb al-Bayān waʾal-Tabyīn* credits the Greeks with logic and philosophy, but extols the Arabs for their eloquence. The Indians and Persians are presented as erudite and clever but a little too dependent on books and traditions for their wisdom (al-Jāḥiẓ 1947, 3: 24–26). Another surviving excerpt, which may or may not be by al-Jāḥiẓ, praises the Arabs, Indians, Byzantines, and Persians alike for various worldly accomplishments, but criticizes their superstitious religious beliefs. It has been translated into French by Charles Pellat and accompanied by an informative introduction (Pellat, 65–90).

39. Kraemer's conclusion is ambivalent: "That Abū Ḥayyān al-Tawḥīdī . . . was a literary forger is disconcerting. . . . But there is no cause for doubting his reports concerning the circumstances of [his teacher] Sijistāni's life or his descriptions of the circle" (Kraemer 1986, 44). The discussions that concern us all took place in this circle. For more on al-Tawḥīdī, see Kraemer 1986, 140–64; 1992, 212–22.

40. Unlike al-Jāḥiẓ, al-Tawḥīdī employs the term Umma quite consistently.

41. Passages of al-Tawḥīdī have been summarized in English, but never the discussion as a whole, so all translations are my own.

42. A possible exception occurs in the *Political Regime*, where both Arabs and Turks are said to have qualities unsuitable for virtuous governance (PR 89.118, Ar. 103.6, cf. 84.109, Ar. 97.10). Yet Alfarabi does not use the word Umma in these passages, and seems to be referring to certain groups and tribes rather than the entire people. I will return to this passage in Chapter 7.

43. Goldziher's remark about the philosophers' relation to the Shuʿūbiyya, which is meant to pertain to al-Kindi and the Brothers of Purity (Ikhwān al-Safāʾ), could be applied with equal justice to Alfarabi: "The philosophers were little suited to side with one or another party; they weighed the virtues and faults of nations coolly and rationally, and found that they counterpoised each other in each people" (Goldziher 1967, 1: 162). The relevant passage in the *Rasāʾil Ikhwān al-Safāʾ* permits representatives of six peoples to praise God and his beneficence each in their own way in front of a king, but then inserts a brief list of criticisms of each. The Indians, the Hebrews, the Syrian Christians, the Greeks, the Qurayshi Arab Muslims, and finally the Khorasani Persians are all given their turn (Ikhwān al-Safāʾ, 2: 236–44).

44. As López-Farjeat puts it, "an exhaustive study of linguistic practices" in the manner recommended by Alfarabi "would make us realize that a perfect language is not possible" (López-Farjeat, 200).

45. The Arabic phrase is ʻala al-majra at-ṭabīʻa, which might be literally translated as "following the natural course."

46. I have been unable to figure out the precise, modern geographic equivalent of these medieval lines of latitude.

47. David Hume again takes a position rather similar to Alfarabi's. In rejecting the notion, recently propagated by Montesquieu, that "air or climate" (Hume, 204 ff.) has any real influence on national character, he nonetheless acknowledges that "the poverty and misery of the northern inhabitants of the globe, and the indolence of the southern, from their few necessities" (206) are often insuperable obstacles to the highest intellectual attainments. However, since "the characters of people are very promiscuous in the temperate climes" (206), they never admit of such generalizations.

48. However common such theories might be in the history of philosophy, one could question their applicability in modern times. In premodern times, technology was not yet able to palliate extreme climates. A heated office in contemporary Montreal might enjoy the same temperature as an air-conditioned office in Dubai, but the original inhabitants of those regions would have had little respite from the effects of their ferocious climates.

CHAPTER 3. PHILOSOPHY AND THE UMMA: AN UNEASY COEXISTENCE

1. This question will be taken up again in Chapter 6, when I discuss the *Attainment of Happiness*.

2. For an excellent English language summary of this debate, see Mahdi 1970. Mahdi is careful to preserve the irony and ambiguity of the original account.

3. Langhade suggests the contrary: "The driving force behind this research, which keeps pushing humans forward, is the desire to know and then to know better. This desire has already given birth to arts and sciences such as rhetoric, poetry, the historical sciences, the linguistic sciences, and writing" (Langhade, 271). Although I agree that a certain form of the desire for knowledge drives human cultural development forward, Langhade misses the point I make here: that the desire for knowledge assumes many different forms, and its mature, philosophical, variety crystallizes only after the full development of the Umma.

4. Alfarabi also uses different forms of the verb in the two passages. The fifth form (*tashawwaq*) applies to linguistic science, while the eighth form (*ishtāq*) applies to philosophy. If there is any difference between these terms, it is extremely subtle. Both signify a powerful yearning, and are presented as almost synonymous in most dictionaries.

5. The numbers in Mahdi's English translation follow those of the Arabic text.

6. Deborah Black helped draw my attention to the significance of this passage of Aristotle's *Metaphysics* for Alfarabi (Black, 70).

7. I follow Mahdi's translation here, as it is usually both elegant and accurate, although I fear that the term "insinuate" might have sinister connotations that are absent in the original Arabic verb *hajas* (PA 60.3–4).

8. The term *akhbār* also occurs in the description of the stories of the Umma in BL 143.2 (#139).

9. The term "myth" has acquired a negative connotation in contemporary English. Since it is not immediately clear whether Alfarabi means to debunk these stories, I have preferred the term "legends," which possesses both positive and negative connotations.

10. The term *wāḍi' an-nāmūs* will be consistently rendered as "legislator," while the term *wāḍi' ash-sharī'a* will be consistently rendered as "lawgiver." The well-known term *sharī'a* signifies Islamic law, while the term *nāmūs* comes from the Greek *nomos*. In the *Book of Letters*, Alfarabi usually employs the term *nāmūs*, while in the *Book of Religion* he invariably speaks of *sharī'a*. This issue will be discussed further in Chapter 4.

11. Since this section concerns religion and the Umma, it will be treated extensively in Chapter 4.

12. For a more thorough interpretation of Alfarabi's concept of *jawhar*, as well as some English translations of key passages, see Shukri Abed's useful discussion (Abed, 68–73).

13. Alfarabi himself prefers to use the root *w-j-d*, meaning "to find," in his logical works (Abed, 139–40). Abed's excellent account of Alfarabi's understanding of the copula (126–41) deals with issues that I have not been able to explore, such as the difference between Alfarabi's teaching about language and that of more conventional Arab grammarians, as well as the relevance of certain other Alfarabian treatments of the subject, most particularly his *Commentary on Aristotle's "De interpretatione."*

14. As Norbert Campagna puts it, "One must distinguish between the linguistic category of words, and logical category of concepts. Words expresses concepts, and different languages express one and the same concept with different words" (Campagna, 93).

15. Some French translations of these passages, along with an interesting discussion of them, can be found in an article by Rémi Brague (Brague 1996, 93–95).

16. Alfarabi's approach to the challenge of restating Greek philosophy for Muslims could be studied further by examining his *Summary of Plato's "Laws."* I limit myself to three straightforward observations from the first chapter. First, when Alfarabi uses the name Zeus, which would have been virtually incomprehensible to most Arabs, he defines him as "the father of humankind" rather than a god (SL 131, 1.1, Ar. 125). Second, Alfarabi speaks of Zeus's law first as a *nāmūs*, but then as a *sharī'a* (134, 1.9, Ar. 127), as if it might have been a divine law given by a human lawgiver. Finally, he speaks of poems and examples that were familiar (*mashhūr*) among the Greeks without specifying their content, safely assuming that such details would be unfamiliar to his readers (131, 1.2, Ar. 125). These examples display Alfarabi's awareness of the difference between the Greek examples used by Plato and those more suitable to his own audience.

17. This meaning of the statement will be discussed more extensively in Chapter 5.

18. It may be objected that the Europeans, unlike the medieval Muslims, did indeed absorb Homer and the other great classical poets into their civilization, proving that poetry can be transferred from one people to another. In other words, Alfarabi's assumptions reflect not universal truth but rather peculiarly Muslim cultural experience. This vast and intriguing question calls for far more reflection than I can devote to it here. Homer's influence on European literature is undeniable, but did the Europeans really make Homer their own in the same way that the Italians lay claim to Dante, or the English to Shakespeare? Alternatively, one could argue that in absorbing classical poetry Europeans were simply recovering their own tradition, which had been disrupted but not obliterated during the Dark Ages. Arab poetry, in contrast, seems to have flourished without any interruption from the pre-Islamic period onward, thus eliminating the need for inspiration from any

foreign sources. (This last idea was suggested to me in a personal communication by Michael Sells.)

CHAPTER 4. ANOTHER KIND OF UMMA: THE ORIGIN OF THE ISLAMIC UMMA

1. Islamist groups disagree on many things, but all claim to act for the sake of the greater good and glory of the Umma, as will be discussed further in Chapter 7.

2. Norbert Campagna is aware of the theoretical universality of the Muslim Umma, and therefore identifies Alfarabi's multinational society as a philosophical approximation of it (Campagna, 131). He then describes the particularity of the various nations, owing to both climate and language (132). Although Campagna does not develop these observations, he nonetheless comes closer to bringing out the fundamental tension between the two Ummas than many other scholars.

3. Abu al-ʿAmaythal al-Aʿrābī, a contemporary of Alfarabi who died in the mid-tenth century, lists no fewer than eight traditional Arabic meanings of Umma, five of which are supported by Qur'ānic quotations and three by other traditions (Sayyid, 43–44). Naṣṣār has compiled no fewer than seven definitions of Umma in the Qur'ān, and discussed the relationship between them (Naṣṣār 1978, 15–20). These accounts add some additional meanings, but their general gist does not differ significantly from al-Ṭabarī's.

4. Arabic readers should also consult Ridwān al-Sayyid's and Nāṣīf Naṣṣār's excellent discussions of the problem, which I have cited frequently.

5. Denny gives a comprehensive chart of the various occurrences and meanings of Umma (Denny 1975, 46–47), and later discusses the occurrences of Umma that date from the Medinan period and reflect the new, Muslim understanding of the term (68–70). Elias Giannakis's classification is also worth considering (Giannakis, 106 ff.). It is striking that even Muslim scholars tend to accept the idea of a gradual development in Muhammad's thought, which is already found in traditional Muslim sources (Ahmed, 27 ff.; Akram, 383–84).

6. For a summary of this history, taken from traditional Muslim sources such as Ibn Hishām's life of Muhammad, see Ahmed, 29–37.

7. The term *qawm* had long been used in the pre-Islamic period to designate a kinship group (Watt, 240). "Some of the earliest instances of *Umma* in the Qur'ān are synonymous with *qawm*" (Denny 1977, 42). We owe to Muhammad Iqbal an especially lucid and cogent account of the distinction between Umma (or *milla*) and *qawm*; see Iqbal 2015, 300–313, esp. 308–9.

8. Denny 1975, 46–47; Lichtenstadter, 262–63; Giannakis, 109; Watt, 240–41. It is important to emphasize that the chronology of the revelation of the Qur'ān has little correlation to the actual order of the books, which are arranged more or less according to their length.

9. Here and on the second line, I have translated the Arabic word *muslim* twice, first as "Muslim" and then as "submissive."

10. As Ahmed puts it, "The universal character of the Umma in fact distinguishes it from other kinds of communities" (Ahmed, 29, cf. 36). It must be conceded that in Alfarabi's time there was clearly still some disagreement concerning the composition of this commanding Umma: al-Ṭabarī cites sources that limit it to Muhammad and his nearest associates, as well as those that propose a broader interpretation (al-Ṭabarī, 7: 100–104). Yet the phrase "for humankind (*in-nās*)" proclaims the universality of their mission.

11. The Arabic words translated as "tribe" (*sha'b*) and "clan" (*qabīla*) do not appear anywhere else in the Qur'ān. Their highly uncertain meaning has generated much discussion among commentators (al-Ṭabarī, 26: 178–81; cf. Mottahadeh, 164 ff.).

12. Al-Ṭabarī believes that *qawm* in this context is effectively synonymous with Umma (al-Ṭabarī, 13: 181). This may be the case, but can one simply ignore the fact that the term Umma is never used in any of the Qur'ānic allusions to human linguistic or ethnic diversity?

13. A rare exception occurred under the Almohad dynasty in Spain, whose founder Ibn Tumart ordered the translation of the Qur'ān, and even the call to prayer, into Berber. However, these reforms did not stick for more than a couple of generations (Iqbal 2012, 127–28, 202 n 29).

14. Consider the following quotations from Naṣṣār: "The other concept of Umma, which is grasped by considering a society whose individual members are united by a bond that is neither religion nor ancestry, is absent from the Qur'ānic formulation and the minds of its traditional interpreters" (Naṣṣār 1978, 22–23). "Indeed, the method on which a substantial number of books by Arabs continue to rely, in their use of the term Umma, is the method of the Qur'ān, or an imitation of that method. It is clear that this does not help to advance the scientific analysis and interpretation of society" (28). Naṣṣār understands the problem surrounding the Qur'ānic Umma with admirable clarity, but does not go far enough in interpreting its use in Alfarabi. I cannot agree with Naṣṣār's assertion that Alfarabi "dissolves the duality" of the term Umma by using the term only in its "sociological and historical meaning" (29). On the contrary, the critical or historical interpretation of the Islamic Umma begins with Alfarabi, as I hope to prove in the remainder of the chapter.

15. Sayyid cites the famous *ḥadīth* "The Umma of the prophet will not agree on an error" (Sayyid, 52). This hope of unanimity, even if restricted to the most important tenets of belief, may become harder to realize as the Umma expands into ever more distant realms and incorporates ever more diverse peoples.

16. The turn to the Umma at the end of the *Selected Aphorisms* will be discussed in Chapter 6.

17. I have deliberately left the ambiguous meaning of "first" undetermined at this stage. I refer the reader to Butterworth's useful note: "A first ruler (*ra'īs awwal*) may or may not be first in time, but he is always first in rank" (BR 93, n. 1).

18. The Arabic term is *jam'*, a general word for "community" that appears rather rarely in Alfarabi (BR Ar. 43.1). It is etymologically related to the much more common Alfarabian term *ijtimā'*, or "association," which will be discussed at greater length in Chapters 6 and 7.

19. Butterworth's edition does not contain line numbers. I have counted the lines myself, in the hope that precise references will make it easier for the reader to follow, and assess, my interpretations.

20. The name Medina means quite literally "city" (*madīna*) in Arabic.

21. When Alfarabi wishes to speak of the entire inhabited world, he does so easily by employing the term *ma'mūra* (VC 228.9, PR 76.92, Ar. 87.13, AH 17.13–7, Ar. 68.24–25). This term, which will be revisited in Chapter 6, is altogether absent from the *Book of Religion*.

22. Butterworth's translation of "conquest" is not inaccurate, but it has a rather neutral tone. The word used by Alfarabi, from the Arabic root *gh-l-b* (BR Ar. 43.12), connotes illegitimate domination rather than the legitimate conquests (Arabic root *f-t-ḥ*) of Muhammad and his successors.

23. A similar distinction between true legislators and impostors occurs in Alfarabi's *Summary of Plato's "Laws."* True legislators seek God and the other life, while impostors seek

various wicked, earthly ends (SL 133.7, Ar. 126.7; Strauss 1959, 150–51). In both passages, Alfarabi's terse division of legislators neither establishes nor refutes the truth and virtue of Islam.

24. As Mahdi suggests, deceptive rulerships are likely to become more common in Islamic times, when the prevalence of religion means that even the most worldly rulers must pretend to be religious in some way (Mahdi 2001, 102).

25. Mahdi assumes that the ignorant, errant, and deceptive rulers do produce religion of some sort (Mahdi 2001, 101). While this interpretation abstracts from the omission of ignorant religion in this particular passage, it is encouraged by Alfarabi's other statements on the matter.

26. Mahdi suggests that this theoretical science is the psychology of revelation, as expounded in the *Political Regime* and *Virtuous City* (Mahdi 2001, 104–5, PR 69, 79–80, Ar. 79.3–80.4, VC 210.3–226.6). This assertion is plausible but hardly certain, especially since this mixture of psychology and metaphysics is not, as far as I know, described as a separate science anywhere in Alfarabi's extant work.

27. This well-known Islamic term can mean equally "war," "exertion," or "struggle." Since it possesses all these senses in Alfarabi, it might be misleading to translate it.

28. As I noted in an earlier discussion, it remains unclear whether Alfarabi composed the *Book of Letters* in the order in which we currently possess it. Alfarabi's apparent failure to follow up his remarks at 129.20–130.1 could be taken as yet another sign that the work has been improperly put together. I prefer to think of it as a deliberate incongruity on Alfarabi's part, intended to contrast the divine view of religion with the human view. In the current form of the work, a scant ten lines separate the reference to divine religion in 130.1 from the introduction of human religion in 131.6.

29. Every expression that Mahdi translates as "law" or "legislator" contains *nāmūs* but not *sharīʿa* (AH 22.2 Ar. 70.2; 42.12, Ar. 92.58).

30. Khalidi observes this change in his translation, to which he appends two helpful footnotes (BL, trans. Khalidi, 19 n. 32, 23 n. 38).

31. This observation is corroborated by Alfarabi's *Summary of Plato's "Laws."* In this work Alfarabi freely employs both *nawāmis* and *sharīʿa* in a wide variety of expressions, as if he means to treat both human and divine law (SL, trans. Butterworth, 111–12). But Alfarabi avoids the question of the relationship between divine law and philosophy by never even mentioning the latter.

32. The distinction between divine and human instruction also occurs in Alfarabi's logical works (Mahdi 2001, 221).

33. 153.13, 15, 18, 154.1 (#147), 155.1 (#149), 19 (#150), 156.3 (#151), 157.5, 7 (#154).

34. For reasons that I do not fully understand, Mahdi chooses not to discuss this scenario (Mahdi 2001, 219–25).

35. Alfarabi is said to have studied with Christians, in particular Yūḥannā Ibn Ḥaylān (Walzer 1965, 778–79, Gutas 2012), but in most of his extant works he repays them with utter silence. I have suggested in Chapter 1 that openly acknowledging his debt to Christian teachers would probably have been imprudent.

36. In the *Summary of Plato's "Laws,"* Alfarabi argues that a new legislator should make use of the work of the legislators who came before him (SL 159.3, Ar. 142.3; 165.11, Ar. 146.11). If this view is correct, then it was only prudent for Muhammad to establish the new law of Islam with due regard for the older religions.

37. López-Farjeat, on the contrary, interprets this paragraph as applying to the historical Islam, which "emerges after philosophy" (López-Farjeat, 201, cf. 203–4). Yet "after

philosophy" does not necessarily mean "on account of it": the penetration of philosophy into the remote Arabian Peninsula in the seventh century was probably quite minimal. López-Farjeat's express purpose is to show how Alfarabi could encourage interreligious dialogue (195, 209–10, 212–14). He does an admirable job of explaining how for Alfarabi no actual religion is exclusively true. Yet he tends to suppress Alfarabi's insinuation that many religions are almost entirely false.

38. As much as Fraenkel would like to interpret Alfarabi's view of Islam in this flattering light, he clearly perceives its ambiguity: "Note, however, that al-Fārābī never explicitly identifies Islam with the philosophic religion resulting from this reinterpretation" (Fraenkel, 163–64).

39. A version of this expression does appear in Maimonides' *Treatise on Logic*, in the list of communities treated by political science. Maimonides uses the adjective *kabīr*, as opposed to Alfarabi's *ʿaẓīm*, but the difference in meaning between those two terms for "great" may be insignificant (Maimonides 1996, 99 n. 217, Ar. 32.15).

40. Leo Strauss makes a similar suggestion, in his chapter on Maimonides in *What Is Political Philosophy?*: "In speaking of the great nation in the singular, he [Maimonides] refers to the universalistic and hence exclusive claim raised by each of the three monotheistic religions: on the premises of each, there can only be one legitimate religious community. In speaking of the nations in the plural, he refers to the national character of the religions of the pagans: that national character explains the coexistence of many equally legitimate religious communities" (Strauss 1959, 162). The emergence of the new kind of Umma in a world already populated by pagan or ethnic Ummas is indeed a major theme of the *Book of Religion*, and it is not impossible that Maimonides was influenced by it.

41. A similar teaching about succession may be found in the *Political Regime*, where Alfarabi goes so far as to say that a competent second ruler alters the *sharīʿa* legislated by the first ruler according to the needs of his time. The number of qualified successors is not specified, but the chain does appear to end at some point, after which the rulers are forced to rely on written law (PR 70.83, Ar. 80.15–81.2). Galston observes that Alfarabi's argument for the supremacy of living wisdom coexists uneasily with the Muslim claim that "Mohammed's prophecy is said to surpass all other prophecies and his teaching is considered final" (Galston 2015, 536).

42. To the best of my knowledge, Muʿāwiyya is the earliest Muslim leader whom Alfarabi ever mentions by name. He does so in the relatively inconspicuous *Epistle on the Intellect*, rather than in any of his discussions of religion. This triumphant general and statesman was nonetheless regarded with suspicion by most pious Muslims, a fact to which Alfarabi clearly alludes (EI, 69).

43. The fact that Alfarabi casts doubt on the predominant Sunni version of the early history does not mean that he adopts the Shīʿa version. The allusion to the four rightly guided caliphs, the first three of whom are rejected by the Shīʿa, puts him firmly within the Sunni frame of reference. Furthermore, Alfarabi shows absolutely no interest in the Shīʿa idea that the caliphate ought to remain within the prophet's family (Madelung, 420–21): hereditary rule is absent from his account of the succession of first rulers. Its possibility is considered later in the *Book of Religion* (BR 108.1–10, Ar. 60.14–20), but the relationship of this passage to the founding of religion is not specified.

44. In 108.2, Butterworth translates the Arabic verb *tawāla* as "succeed one another." This term does not have the same etymological link to the caliphate (*khilāfa*) as *khalaf*.

45. The verb *khalaf* is used in a similar context in the *Political Regime* and *Virtuous City* (PR 70.82, Ar. 81.1, VC 250.7). For Alfarabi, the succession of virtuous rulers on earth never

lasts more than a few generations. Majid Fakhry makes a useful comparison of the qualities of Alfarabi's first ruler in the *Virtuous City* with the requirements for the caliph, as set down by al-Māwardī a century after Alfarabi's death, but does not consider the issue of permanent succession, which distinguishes Alfarabi's position most sharply from the predominant Sunni understanding of the caliphate. Besides, Fakhry cannot help but observe that Alfarabi's description is influenced at least as much by Plato as by the conventional caliphal doctrine (Fakhry, 103–5).

46. Averroes suggests, in commenting on Plato's *Republic*, that the ascension of Muʿāwiyya signified the transition from an imitation of virtuous rulership to the timocratic rulership of honor (Averroes 1974, 89.31–34). This interpretation of Muslim history may already be implied by Alfarabi.

47. Sāliḥ Muṣbāḥ observes that Alfarabi's presentation of the jurists does not conform to any conventional Islamic view of the subject. Muṣbāḥ attributes this discrepancy to the fact that Alfarabi read Plato's *Laws* (Muṣbāḥ, 192). The difficulty with this assumption is that jurisprudence, unlike *kalām*, is never discussed in Alfarabi's *Summary of Plato's "Laws."* Alfarabi may have had his own reasons for rethinking the questions surrounding the origin of the Muslim Umma and the jurists' role in it.

48. This difference between *lisān*, or "language," and *lugha*, or "dialect," will be discussed at greater length in Chapter 6.

49. Many religious authors, not surprisingly, were eager to claim that the Quraysh spoke the purest Arabic, but Alfarabi resists this tendency (Langhade, 253–55). The Ḥijāz lies west of the geographic center of the Arabic homeland, and the Quraysh were known to be engaged in trade. Both of these facts would in Alfarabi's view have increased the influence of foreign languages, thus rendering their Arabic somewhat less than "pure" (BL 145.8 ff., #133).

50. For an excellent discussion of the development of *ḥadīth*, see Goldziher 1981, 37–44. Note e on p. 38 cites some more recent discussions of the subject.

51. Since Alfarabi describes Aristotle's philosophy as true, the words he ascribes to Aristotle may be taken as more or less his own teaching (AH 46.12–47.9, Ar. 96.64–98.66). If Alfarabi had considered a certain aspect of Aristotle's teaching irrelevant or false, he would not have presented it to his readers.

52. Or "legends": cf. Chapter 3, n. 9.

53. There is a measure of truth to Sweeney's claim that "The cause of the nation and the cause of religion are the same. . . . Religion and nation tend to coincide because they both reflect the striving of the imagination for the intellectual object that imagination alone can imitate" (Sweeney, 564). Nevertheless, one should not overlook the distinction between mere tradition and divine revelation, as well as numerous instances where different religious and national traditions not only fail to coincide, but clash. These issues figure prominently throughout the rest of the work.

54. Thérèse-Anne Druart observes, somewhat critically, that Alfarabi's "presentation of the origin of language and idioms does not rest on demonstrative assertions. It is fairly coherent and clever, but makes many assertions, while sadly neglecting to offer evidence or arguments in its defense" (Druart 2012, 55). Along the same lines, André Roman offers a critique of Alfarabi's account of the origin of language from the point of view of modern linguistic theory (Roman, 139, 143, 153). Neither of these articles is unintelligent, and I cannot claim to match Roman's knowledge of linguistics and grammar, but I would reply that Alfarabi did not intend to offer demonstrative or scientific arguments concerning a remote, speechless epoch that has left so few historical traces.

55. Two words meaning "clear" occur in the relevant passage of the *Book of Letters*. The word *bayyan* appears in BL 134.17, #114 and 142.6, #129, while the word *ẓāhir* appears in 136.5, #117 and 136.14, #118. Following these indicators, the only clear aspects of the early development of the Umma are the omnipresence of the multitude, the composition of human speech organs, and the precedence of rhetoric to the other syllogistic arts.

56. The one exception, namely, the unresolved discussion of the role of theoretical science in revelation, proves the rule, since Alfarabi insists that this issue was "already made clear" somewhere else (BR 94.17–20, Ar. 44.11–13).

57. The field of early Islamic history or Qur'ānic studies is enormous, and only a few scholars can claim to have mastered it. The full picture of Alfarabi's understanding of early Islam may be revealed only when a genuine expert in the field also begins to study the relevant passages of Alfarabi. (Patricia Crone, who began her career by studying the history of early Islam, has written some good articles on Alfarabi, but never specifically examined this particular issue.) I will limit myself to a preliminary suggestion. According to Fred Donner's classification of approaches to early Islamic source material (Donner, 1–31), Alfarabi would not be a full-blown "skeptic," in the school of Wansbrough and Crone, but rather closer to Goldziher's "tradition–critical approach" (Donner, 13 ff.). He does seem to suppose a "kernel of truth" in the tradition. The abundant historical allusions in the accounts of the origin of religion presented in the *Book of Religion* and the *Book of Letters* would be unintelligible without the assumption that there was indeed an Arab prophet who introduced a new religion to Mecca and Medina, and whose successors followed up his astonishing accomplishments with massive conquests of their own, engulfing all the surrounding territories and peoples. Even some of these assumptions have been denied by the most ardent skeptics (Crone and Cook, 3 ff.). It is also worth repeating that while Alfarabi refuses to trust the veracity of the jurists who established the tradition, he doesn't dismiss them as pure fabricators: while they may have embellished and purified the reports they received, they did not simply invent them.

CHAPTER 5. THE MISSION OF THE VIRTUOUS UMMA: ETHNIC ACCOMMODATION WITHIN ISLAM

1. Amor Cherni seeks to simplify Mahdi's text by relying on the Taymura manuscript, which omitted certain terms, such as *kul wāḥid* (each and every) and *umam* (nations), from the work. Cherni argues that the Taymura is probably closest to the original text, and that the readings omitted by it are redundant in any case (*La religion*, trans. Cherni, 20, 111 n. 195, 115 nn. 199–200). While not sufficiently versed in philology to contest Cherni's assessment of the manuscripts, as an interpreter I hope to have shown that the omitted words are not redundant at all, but crucial for understanding Alfarabi's implied criticism of the assumption that a unified cosmos demands a unified human religion and government.

2. Alfarabi makes a similer point in the *Selected Aphorisms*, in claiming that revelation unaccompanied by theoretical science is able to determine particular actions only "of cities or of a city" (SA 63, #94, Ar. 98.19).

3. In the *Political Regime*, Alfarabi suggests that revelation as such involves the active intellect and therefore knowledge of theoretical things (PR 69.80, Ar. 79.12–80.4). The *Book of Religion*, in contrast, consistently omits the active intellect (BR 111.24–112.1–2, Ar. 64.11.16, 113.12–26, Ar. 66.8–10). The result is that theoretical science and revelation emerge as two entirely distinct phenomena.

4. Butterworth asks precisely this question: "But what is to be done when there is more than one religion in a community" (Butterworth 2007, 61)?

5. I follow Mahdi in reading the word *ḥarbī* (military) instead of *juz'ī* (partial) in the Arabic text (see the *Philosophy of Plato* and Aristotle, trans. Mahdi, 154 n. 32). Because of the strong link between war and compulsion, it makes much more sense in the context of a passage discussing the compulsory education of the Ummas. Furthermore, the word *ḥarb* already occurs in the previous paragraph.

6. I owe this suggestion to Nathan Tarcov and Ralph Lerner, who taught a course on Alfarabi at the University of Chicago, Winter 2011.

7. Butterworth translates "realms," but *'awālim* is simply the plural form of *'ālam*, which he translates as "world," as in the expression "governor of the world." Butterworth renders the same form as "worlds" in SA 47, #74, to which he appends a helpful footnote (n. 44). A literal translation of the cryptic expression *aṣnāf al-'awālim* (BR Ar. 66.3) would be "kinds of worlds" or "ranks of worlds."

8. Arabic has both dual and plural forms. The Qur'ān employs the dual *'ālamān*, while Alfarabi in this passage uses only the plural *'awālim*.

9. Alfarabi's statement in the *Philosophy of Aristotle*, that "we do not possess metaphysical science" (PA 133.1–3), implies this same nagging uncertainty concerning the celestial sphere. As Butterworth puts it, "thorough knowledge of theoretical philosophy" is lacking (Butterworth 2007, 61).

10. See in particular Parens's conclusion: "Differences of place and time, climate, national character, and language justify Alfarabi's championing of religious multiplicity" (2006a, 101). Much of this section aims at a more detailed elaboration of the consequences of this statement.

11. Among the many occurrences of this image, see Qur'ān 9.89, 10.9.

12. In lieu of Alfarabi's claim that religion might differ from Umma to Umma, Naṣṣār modifies his earlier suggestion that Umma and *milla* have absolutely nothing to do with one another (Naṣṣār 1978, 52–53, cf. 50–51).

13. Most interpretations of this passage perceive its provocative character. Fraenkel argues very plausibly that Alfarabi means to defend the legitimacy of various non-Islamic religions (Fraenkel, 164). Cherni perceives that Alfarabi is seeking to establish some "principle of 'tolerance' among the different milal" (the plural of *milla*) (*Cité verteuse*, trans. Cherni, 282, no. 7). Campagna states that "different religions must apply to different nations, and even one religion take the place of another, when the nation has undergone further intellectual development" (Campagna, 96). Naṣṣār acknowledges that this passage is out of touch with prevailing beliefs (Naṣṣār 1978, 53). Rudolph emphasizes that each Umma needs a different religion, "clarifying the differences between individual religions" (Rudolph, 438). All these interpretations point in the right direction, but none adequately confront the question of the unity of Islam and its applicability to all the Ummas that have converted to it.

14. For a helpful discussion of this question, see Galston 1990, 59–68. Alfarabi appears to present a distinct view of happiness in each and every major work.

15. There are numerous accounts of the pleasures of paradise in the Qur'ān. Among the most eloquent are 52.17–24, 56.11–38, and 76.13–22.

16. It is worth noting that much of the growth of major non-Arabic languages within Islam took place after Alfarabi's time. India and Indonesia had yet to be converted, while Persian literature was undergoing a hiatus, which lasted until the composition of the *Shahnama* at the end of the tenth century. Persian then reemerged as a major poetic language, even

as scientific and religious treatises continued to be composed mainly in Arabic (Dabashi, 314). The domination of Arabic within Islam was much greater in Alfarabi's time than it is now. By emphasizing the enduring role of the pre-Islamic Ummas and their languages even after the rise of Islam, Alfarabi seems to have looked beyond the present prevalence of Arabic and foreseen future developments.

17. Cherni perceives the Platonic roots of Alfarabi's statement, but as usual refrains from applying it to Islam (*La politique civile*, trans. Cherni, 180 n. 457).

18. See https://www.youtube.com/watch?v=174xwpnvcKA. I wish to thank Aaron Tugendhaft for drawing my attention to this video. Discussions with him on the question of idolatry have significantly improved this section.

19. Butterworth translates this word as "faithful," but "believers" is a more common translation of the Qur'ānic term.

20. The doctrine of *'iṣma*, or the immunity of the prophets from error, has appeared in various guises and never been universally accepted in Islam, but has gained ground over time (Tyan, 182–83). Qur'ānic criticism in the modern sense remains unacceptable, socially or in some cases legally, in most Islamic countries today.

21. The only direct reference to poetry in the work occurs during the discussion of ignorant governments (PR 87.115, Ar. 101.2).

22. I will say more about the reasons for this omission in Chapter 6.

23. The tale of the pious ascetic at the beginning of the *Summary of Plato's "Laws"* is the only exception known to me (SL 130, Intro. 1, Ar. 124). As far as I know, it is not based on any traditional Muslim story.

24. Averroes likewise restricts himself to providing templates, offering a bold but general criticism of Muslim doctrines about the afterlife, and a proposal for their general reform. Like Alfarabi, Averroes refrains from mentioning any individuals (Averroes 1974, 31.7–25).

25. Arberry's ingenuous comment is revealing of the attitude of scholars of his generation. "This section which follows does not of course occur in Aristotle's *Poetics*, and I am unable to trace its source" (EP 285). It is almost impossible for me to believe, upon reading the charming, eccentric, and brilliant enumeration that follows, that this source could have been anything other than the inimitable mind of Alfarabi himself.

26. Alfarabi might have had some practical influence in this area. The ideas of his disciple and successor Avicenna on the ability of images to mediate between humans and the cosmos clearly influenced a large number of artists (Berlekamp, 28, 32–33).

27. Historians of Islamic art today consider their field subject to so much local and temporal variation that some doubt whether it is correct to speak of a single "Islamic art" at all (Berlekamp, personal communication).

28. Jamal Elias describes this cultural atrocity in harrowing detail (Elias, 4–9).

CHAPTER 6. BETWEEN CITY AND EMPIRE:
THE POLITICAL SIGNIFICANCE OF THE UMMA

1. A similar discussion occurs in my article on the concept of the inhabited world (*ma'mūra*).

2. For a convincing account of the importance of the addressee, see Mahdi 2001, 175 ff. This essay, probably the finest in Mahdi's collection, should not be overlooked by anyone

interested in understanding the *Attainment of Happiness*. I have learned far more from it than I can indicate in the notes, as will be evident to any reader who revisits Mahdi's work.

3. Strangely enough, the word "logic" does not appear in the *Attainment of Happiness*. Nevertheless, the division of the various methods that begins at 3.4 (Ar. 49.2) is readily identifiable with it.

4. The discussion of science in the *Book of Demonstration*, as well as two lists of the sciences elsewhere in the *Book of Letters*, omit linguistic science entirely (BD 65–75; BL 66.18–69.21, 216.19–217.2).

5. Mahdi translates the phrase *al-raʾīs al-awwal* as "supreme ruler." Although Mahdi's rendering is perhaps more cogent, "first ruler" is more literal, and used by Butterworth in translating the *Book of Religion*. It leaves open the question of whether this ruler is first in rank, as "supreme" implies, or in some more accidental quality.

6. "The implication of this material with reference to the addressee seems to be clear. It is up to him to decide whether he wishes to become a prince" (Mahdi 2001, 185).

7. For an excellent account of the vagueness of Alfarabi's presentation of these universals, see Parens 2006a, 78–79. Paul Heck assumes this common nature refers to "theoretical knowledge" (Heck, 199). But theoretical knowledge as such is not accessible to most people, for whom it can be articulated only by means of rhetorical arguments and images (see AH 30.16–17, Ar. 79.46).

8. Unfortunately, this work survives only in Latin. Alfarabi probably used the term "Umma," but it is impossible to know for sure from the extant Latin translation of *gens*.

9. Alfarabi's proposal contains layers upon layers of labyrinthine complexity. The present discussion has treated only the aspects most relevant to its theme. A fuller account of the numerous difficulties inherent in this unwieldy scheme is given by Parens (2006a, 77–80, 85–97). I return to this same passage from a somewhat different point of view toward the end of the present chapter.

10. Colmo's spirited attempt to interpret Alfarabi as breaking with the ancients in subordinating theory to practice analyzes the first half of the *Attainment of Happiness* in great detail but breaks off before the second half, which contains the "practical" proposals of the book. If these proposals turn out to be deliberately impractical, how would it affect Colmo's attempt to present Alfarabi's "Discourse on Method" as a precursor to Machiavelli or Descartes (Colmo, 130–65)? The same question could be asked about Kraemer's attribution of a "*mission civilisatrice*" to Alfarabi (Kraemer 1987, 303).

11. As Rémi Brague and Carlos Fraenkel observe, Alfarabi gives the impression in this passage that philosophy in fact originated in Iraq, and that he is merely completing the circle by restoring it to its rightful home (Brague 1996, 92; Fraenkel, 153–54). I would respond to this interesting suggestion in two ways. First, the use of the expression "it is said" (AH 38.14, Ar. 88.54) implies that Alfarabi may merely be reporting a view about which he himself is unsure, because of the lack of any firm, written evidence for it. Second, one may ask how much either Alfarabi or his readers would have identified the pagan Chaldeans or even their prophet Ibrāhīm with their Muslim successors, just because they happened to inhabit the same geographic area.

12. For reasons I do not fully understand, Mahdi translates *malik* as "prince." I prefer Butterworth's routine translation of the same word as "king."

13. A passage from the *Book of Letters* casts some light on the meaning of this expression: "There is not found in *lughat al-ʿarab*, from when it was first established, any transmitted utterance that could take the place of the Greek *esti*" (BL 112.6). Alfarabi then explains

how Arabic had to subsequently develop the copula so that its speakers could practice logic. The expression *lughat al-'arab* hearkens back to the time when the Arabs knew nothing of philosophy.

14. The *imām* therefore came to signify in Shī'a Islam the true successor of Muhammad and leader of the community. In Sunni authors such as al-Māwardī, *imām* is virtually synonymous with Caliph, with both terms designating the ruler of the entire Muslim community (al-Māwardī, 5 ff.).

15. Parens raises yet another pertinent question surrounding this passage: do we know whether theoretical virtue can be realized (2006a, 107–8)?

16. Alfarabi makes the same argument with regard to the king, but should anyone believe this assertion? Even Alfarabi is not audacious enough to say that it applies to a legislator, and is a king without subjects any more significant than a legislator whose code gathers dust in the archives? A deposed or neglected ruler cuts a far more pitiable figure than a philosopher whose quiet pursuit of wisdom meets with the indifference of the world. Mahdi makes some similar suggestions in the introduction to his translation (*Philosophy of Plato and Aristotle*, trans. Mahdi, xxxv).

17. Alfarabi's freethinking contemporary al-Rāzī was audacious enough to proclaim Socrates an *imām* (F. Rosenthal 1940, 388). But Alfarabi realized that no philosopher could ever become an *imām* in any conventional sense. As Strauss puts it, "the philosophers, as distinguished from the legislators, cannot expect to be deified by the citizens" (Strauss 1959, 154).

18. For yet another use of this versatile term, consider the opening paragraph of the *Attainment of Happiness*, where the phrase *ahl al-mudun* is translated "citizens of cities" (AH 2.2, Ar. 49.1). In view of our analysis here, one might ask whether it refers to all the citizens or only the most skilled.

19. Both terms are employed with some frequency in the *Book of Letters*, and I will discuss them in greater detail later in this chapter. I contest Druart's assumption that the two terms are synonymous (Druart 2012, 51).

20. According to Alfarabi, Plato thought that the philosopher and the king possessed a single faculty (PP 13.7–12). Mahdi glosses the argument of the *Attainment of Happiness* as follows: "If the addressee is to become a true philosopher and not a mere student of theoretical science or a false philosopher, he should learn the language of Plato" (Mahdi 2001, 93).

21. The pronoun "us" is definitely used repeatedly in the concluding paragraph (AH 47.3–9). Whether the addressee is mentioned in the concluding sentence (47.9–11) depends on the manuscript reading: one version has "we," but the reading preferred by Mahdi has "you" (Ar. 97.66, n. 17).

22. Gad Freudenthal gives a good summary of this passage (Freudenthal, 107–11), but exaggerates the importance of climate for Alfarabi, in order to contrast him with Maimonides. Freudenthal supposes that climate plays a role in humans' ability to acquire the intelligibles from the active intellect and receive prophecy (Freudenthal, 111, 114), but I can find no evidence for this interpretation in the *Political Regime*. As I have shown in Chapter 2, the role of climate in determining the capacity of peoples in the temperate zone is in fact very slight. Freudenthal's overestimation of the role of astral influences in shaping the Umma is accompanied by his underestimation of language, which does not figure in his article.

23. The argument of the *Political Regime* "abstracts from man's bodily existence" (Galston 1990, 216). Galston makes many of the observations that have been highlighted here, such as

the absence of the nutritive faculty in the treatment of the soul. She returns to the same theme in her latest article, concluding that in the *Political Regime* "the development of reason . . . appears to entail commitment to cultivating and sustaining a way of life that minimizes the importance of bodily needs to the greatest extent possible" (2015, 530).

24. Galston's claim that the attitude of the *Political Regime* toward imagination is to "systematically underplay its existence and power" (1990, 217) requires minor modification in light of the following discussion. It might be more accurate to say that the treatise systematically underplays the existence and power of language. It is clear Galston has not simply overlooked this passage, which she acknowledges elsewhere in her book (45).

25. Galston's impressive recent interpretation of the *Political Regime* concludes that the work "seems to be pointing out the fragility of the human project understood in terms of cultivating conditions for the life of the mind" (2015, 542 n. 94).

26. "Nevertheless, there is a least a theoretical preference for the city: it is not by chance that Alfarabi called his most substantial political treatise 'the perfect city' and not the 'the perfect nation.' One could say that the perfect city is the ancient nucleus, borrowed from Plato's *Republic*" (Strauss 1936, 12).

27. However, see also AH 16.13, where Alfarabi suggests that an Umma no less than a city might be able to imitate the structure of the cosmos. A cohesive, "virtuous Umma" also appears at the end of the *Book of Religion*; the reasons for this were discussed in Chapter 4.

28. Empedocles and Parmenides are later identified as the source of certain fallacious theoretical opinions (VC 320.9–11). But these natural philosophers are most probably not the source of the political opinions glorifying honor and domination. As for Socrates, Plato, and Aristotle, they are never cited in the *Virtuous City*.

29. I should emphasize that the assertion of the superiority of Muslim politics in the *Virtuous City* does not represent Alfarabi's final view of the matter: in the *Political Regime*, he makes it perfectly clear that ignorant governments are still the norm within the Islamic world as well. I discuss this in greater detail in Chapter 7.

30. The argument of the work involves "gently mixing the teaching of Plato and Aristotle" (Butterworth 2008, 481).

31. This discussion follows up an insight first presented by Charles Butterworth. Perceiving the sudden turn to the Umma, he suggests that "lawgiving is more suited for an association of cities—for a nation. But this is not a lesson to be learned from the ancients. It is one unique to his [Alfarabi's] own setting" (Butterworth 2008, 483–84).

32. As Butterworth observes, "All of the justifiable wars are initiated and conducted by the city" (1990, 85). Butterworth's detailed discussion of this passage is well worth reading (83–89).

33. Butterworth sometime translates this term as "group," and sometimes as "people."

34. Alfarabi qualifies some kinds of war as unjust (*jawr*), but none as just (*'ādil*). In all of Aphorism 67, justice (*'adl*) is mentioned only tangentially, in conjunction with the fifth kind of war (SA 44, #67, Ar. 77.4). See Butterworth 1990, 84.

35. Parens observes that war for the sake of opinion is also excluded from this passage. But he also argues that the principle of war for the sake of someone else's good opens a Pandora's box from which wars for the sake of spreading an opinion will eventually emerge (Parens 2006a, 61–64). Such wars are likely to overflow from the city to the Ummas, as happens in the *Attainment of Happiness*. Yet Alfarabi does no more than hint at this kind of war in the *Selected Aphorisms*.

36. Or, as Butterworth translates, "the virtue of calculation."

37. Butterworth's translation of *tā'ifa* as "sect" amplifies the religious significance of the term. But I am not sure whether this generic word for "group" has any religious meaning in this context.

38. Butterworth capitalizes this sentence for emphasis, but there are no capital letters in Arabic.

39. Butterworth translates "theoretical knowledge." The Arabic word *'ilm* could be rendered as both "knowledge" and "science."

40. Strauss perceives this tendency in Alfarabi: "Alfarabi is forced by theological-political facts of his epoch to enlarge the Platonic framework, and recognize political units larger than the city: the nation and the nations" (Strauss 1936, 12). Or as Butterworth puts it, Alfarabi's "willingness to expand the political horizon beyond the city to the nation and group of nations shows how little he thinks it necessary to restrict himself—at least in this respect—to the teaching of the ancients" (Butterworth 2007, 59).

41. A brief account of the significance of the inhabited world and its relation to deliberation in Alfarabi follows. For a much fuller account of the same question, see my article explicitly devoted to the subject (Orwin 2014, esp. 836–37).

42. This similarity does not come out as clearly in the English translations, since each of the works was translated by a different hand. For example, Butterworth translates as "the virtue of calculation," the same phrase that Mahdi renders "deliberative virtue," and as "shared by nations, a nation, and a city" the same phrase that Mahdi renders "common to many nations, to a whole nation, or to a whole city,"

43. Or, as Mahdi translates, "inhabited part of the earth."

44. I have learned a lot from Parens's treatment of this subject but disagree very slightly with it. Parens speaks repeatedly of Alfarabi proposing, and ultimately opposing, a virtuous regime in "the inhabited world" (Parens 2006a, 5–8, 21, 43, etc.), but does not fully appreciate how rarely the term is actually used. He rightly perceives that the notion of a society encompassing the entire inhabited world is absent from the *Political Regime*, but assumes that it does occur in the *Attainment of Happiness* (cf. Parens 2006a, 89, 145 n. 34); as I have just shown, the term "inhabited world" occurs in that work only before the proposal for a government encompassing many cities and Ummas has begun to take shape. Alfarabi does at first give the impression that his proposed society may eventually cover the entire world, but by speaking only of "many Ummas" in the latter portions of the text he tacitly undermines this assumption. As far as I can tell, Alfarabi raises the possibility of a single government in the entire inhabited world only in the *Virtuous City*. The clarification of this detail does not undermine Parens's main arguments about the illusory character of the entire project of virtuous, multinational rule.

45. The word translated as "elite" and the word translated as "particular" come from the same Arabic root, *kh-ṣ-ṣ*.

46. "This division [between the elite and the vulgar] is the axis that runs through the *Book of Letters* from beginning to end" (Gannagé, 235–36).

47. Modern accounts of the origin of nationalism frequently follow Alfarabi in emphasizing the importance of language. However, they trace the growth of nationalism to a further standardization and unification of the language that could occur only in an industrial society. For Benedict Anderson, this was brought about by the spread of print capitalism (Anderson, 37 ff.), for Ernest Gellner by industrialization and the destruction of the traditional clerisy: "For the first time in human history, explicit and reasonably precise communication becomes generally, pervasively, used and important" (Gellner 2006, 32). Alfarabi

would probably agree that no consciousness of political unity could arise among a given Umma without greater standardization of language than was possible in his day.

48. *Mutakallimūn* is the medieval name for practitioners of *kalām*.

49. The useful metaphor of the ladder is used not by Alfarabi but by Emma Gannagé (236, 240, 250).

50. The term *sharīʿa* occurs in the plural in both these passages (PR Ar. 81.2, VC 250.9). Walzer's translation of "philosopher" in connection with the second ruler is misleading: the Arabic *ḥakīm* means simply "wise man" or "judge" (VC 250.9).

51. Alfarabi employs the term *dīn* rather than the more usual term *milla*, a change captured by Butterworth's translation "creed" rather than "religion." The identity of its transmitters remains somewhat murky: since jurists and *mutakallimūn* are not explicitly mentioned in the work, they cannot simply be equated with them. But the "transmitters of the creed" must have something to do with the *sunna* and *sharīʿa* emphasized in the following aphorism (SA 38, #58, Ar. 66.2–67.12).

52. I say "religious" because it excludes a third, more mysterious kind of *kalām*, which is elaborated in the *Summary of Plato's "Laws."* Alfarabi describes this summary, as well as Plato's *Laws*, as a work of *kalām* (SL 171.1, Ar. 150.1, Strauss 1959, 139–40, Parens 1995, 39–40). In Alfarabi's other works *kalām* is associated with the defense of a specific religion, but in the *Summary*, where the very word "religion" (*milla*) never occurs, *kalām* is associated with the defense of laws (*nawāmis*) as such. The uses of this novel form of *kalām* would have to be studied further. It is certainly possible that the *Book of Religion*, which avoids speaking of the traditional form of *kalām*, engages in the more truly philosophic kind in its concluding section. For our purposes it suffices to observe that in a world composed of multiple, competing religious communities, the more traditional form of *kalām* remains indispensable.

53. Muṣbāḥ suggests this type of *kalām* ought to be strictly subordinate to jurisprudence. However, he does not account for the second, more creative kind of *kalām* (Muṣbāḥ, 193, 198).

CHAPTER 7. THE UMMA AMONG THE IGNORANT ASSOCIATIONS:
NATIONALISM AND THE THREAT OF WAR

1. As Cherni puts it, "One might consider the fundamental principle of this association to be a precursor of nationalism, just as one might consider the three causes cited above as the parameters that define a nation" (*Cité vertueuse*, trans. Cherni, 298 n. 5).

2. These groups are all "too small or too unstable to indulge in any consistent political action" (VC, trans. Walzer, 488).

3. Cherni is mostly correct in saying that with the ignorant community of the city, we "observe for the first time the absence of any element of hatred or violence" (*Cité vertueuse*, trans. Cherni, 298 n. 8). We must clarify, however, that the association of the Umma appears to sustain hatred but not violence.

4. In the description of the ignorant associations in the *Political Regime*, kings are first mentioned in connection with the association of honor (PR 79.99, Ar. 91.11).

5. I employ this term with some reluctance, due to Butterworth's trenchant observation that the standard term for "war," *ḥarb*, does not occur in the ignorant opinions of the *Virtuous City* or anywhere in the *Political Regime* (Butterworth 1990, 93, 100 n. 47). However, I still think that "war" is the best way to render, in ordinary English, the kinds of phenomena

Alfarabi is talking about. By avoiding the term *ḥarb*, which was in frequent juridical use, Alfarabi may be implying that the ignorant rulers of his day attacked whomever they pleased without paying any attention to the debates of the jurists. Wars motivated by honor, greed for power, or vengeance, which are presented as a fact of life among the ignorant associations in the *Political Regime* and *Virtuous City,* are deemed unjust in the *Selected Aphorisms* (SA 44, #67, Ar. 77.9–78.2).

6. For a fuller treatment of democracy in Alfarabi, see my article devoted entirely to the subject (Orwin 2015).

7. In the case of the tyrannical city, one of the manuscripts reads "in the tyrannical cities" and the others "in the tyrannical city" (PR Ar. 88.2–3). According to the interpretation proposed here, the former reading makes more contextual sense.

8. There is some ambiguity about the association of necessity as well, since it is initially not attributed to cities at all. Alfarabi may be alluding to the fact that many subsistence peoples are herdsmen, hunters, and bandits who have yet to be organized into cities (see PR 77.94, Ar. 88.6).

9. Alfarabi anticipates here a famous remark of Machiavelli: "As for the prince who goes out with his armies, who feeds on booty, pillage, and ransom and manages on what belongs to someone else, liberality is necessary, otherwise he would not be followed by his soldiers" (Machiavelli 1998, 64).

10. Patricia Crone is a notable exception. She laments that in the Islamic world only Averroes and Ibn Khaldūn followed up on Alfarabi's incipient efforts to scientifically analyze actual human societies (Crone 2004a, 222–24). Ibn Khaldūn, whom Dimitri Gutas considers to be the true founder of Islamic political philosophy (Gutas 2004, 260), developed a theory of the growth and decline of governments that clearly owes a lot to Alfarabi's account of the gradual corruption of the souls of conquerors by loot and pleasure (Ibn Khaldūn, 1: 351–55, Ar. 1: 294–98, PR 89.119, Ar. 102.12–103.13, cf. Crone 2004a, 206).

11. Mahdi observes that the peace-loving regimes are portrayed as harmless innocents: they "are not considered sufficiently important; and their view, though mistaken, is evidently not dangerous" (Mahdi 2001, 141). Nevertheless, the mere existence of cities of peace means that Alfarabi's assessment of international relations is less uniformly "realist" than that of Hobbes, who maintains that all sovereigns live in a state of near war with their neighbors (*Leviathan,* chap. XIII, para. 12).

12. Crone is justifiably impressed by the number of contemporary allusions in this passage. "Alfarabi clearly detested the Turks and the bedouin who infested his world as upstart rulers, soldiers, warlords, robbers, and brigands" (Crone 2004a, 206, cf. 217–218). Yet the entire passage is written with Alfarabi's usual philosophic calm and detachment: he reveals the unfortunate political consequences of the pursuit of ignorant goods without displaying any hatred toward their pursuers.

13. Butterworth explains this point in n. 46 to his translation (PR 76.93, Ar. 88.3). For other aspects of the meaning of this root, see Najjar 1980, 110.

14. Butterworth translates the verb *ijtamaʿ* as "brought together" in 51.113 and "come together" in 52.115.

15. Najjar's initial claim that Alfarabi discusses democracy "in abstraction" fails to make this connection. And yet Najjar proceeds to note Alfarabi's talent for "authentic contemporary description" (Najjar 1980, 117–18). Does or does not Najjar perceive that Alfarabi is alluding to Baghdad?

16. Modern scholars have estimated that Baghdad may have had as many as 1.5 million inhabitants at its height (Duri, 898–99).

17. It is worth emphasizing that tenth-century Baghdad was not a "democracy" in the modern sense: it was ruled by sultans, caliphs, and armies, without elections, assemblies, or constitutions of any sort. Alfarabi's democracy might in modern parlance be called a monarchy, but one in which the monarch is too weak to impose strong controls on his subjects. I discuss this question at greater length in a separate article devoted to democracy in Alfarabi (Orwin 2015, 174–79).

18. As Mahdi puts it, "The democratic regime is the only regime that provides ample opportunity for their [the arts] development and allows the philosopher to pursue his desire in relative freedom" (Mahdi 2001, 146).

19. Averroes also doubts the longevity of democracy, citing concrete historical evidence. "Unless strengthened by virtue or honor, it perishes rapidly, as in this case with democratic cities existing in this time of ours and that which preceded [it]" (Averroes 1974, 93.18–20).

20. On this point my interpretation resembles Fakhry's. He notes that much of the section is written in an anonymous third-person plural, but concludes that "it is probable that he [Alfarabi] favored the last mentioned pacifist view" (Fakhry, 117).

21. The *Essay on the Origin of Languages* begins with the statement, "Speech distinguishes humans from the other animals: language distinguishes one nation from another" (Rousseau 1993, 57).

22. Anne Cohler emphasizes the importance of the pre-political nation in Rousseau, pointing to a passage in the *Discours sur l'inégalité* that describes its development (Cohler, 119–25). She proceeds to suggest that this primitive nation constitutes Rousseau's political standard (134 ff.). However, all existing nations will have to be radically transformed in order even to begin to approximate this standard (34, 174–75). Marc Plattner and Pierre Hassner both argue that Cohler overemphasizes the importance of the pre-political nation while underemphasizing the novelty of Rousseau's proposals for nation building (Plattner, 191 n. 25, Hassner, 209–10). For reasons that will be indicated shortly, I am inclined to agree with Plattner and Hassner.

23. For a summary of Afghānī's life and thought, see Hourani, 123–29.

24. ISIS, https://ia902505.us.archive.org/28/items/poa_25984/EN.pdf, Arabic, https://thabat111.wordpress.com/2014/06/29/كلمة-تفريغ-وعد-هذا-وعد-الله-إعلان-قيام-ال/.

CONCLUSION. THE INTERMEDIATE ASSOCIATION

1. Alfarabi alludes to the more conventional Islamic meaning of *wasaṭ* in the *Summary of Plato's "Laws."* He calls an account of religion and law that resembles Islam a "middle course" (*ṭarīq wasaṭ*) between excessive hope for future legal reform and excessive aversion to it (SL 166.13, Ar. 147.13).

2. I am aware that the American founding is rarely described as nationalist, in large part because it proclaimed universal principles rather than blood ties, but the word is appropriate if understood according to the terms of our analysis of Alfarabi. From Alfarabi's point of view, the same obstacles that have made it impossible to Islam to realize its universal mission would stand in the way of the American global project as well. The particular nature of both universal claims has been rendered all-too-obvious by the intermittent conflict between them.

Works Cited

PRIMARY SOURCES

'Abduh, Muhammad. 2006. *Al-A'māl al-Kāmila*. Ed. Muhammad 'Amāra. Vol. 1–5. Cairo: Dār al-Sharūq.

al-Afghānī, Jamāl al-Dīn. 1981. *Al-A'māl al-Kāmila*. Ed. Muhammad 'Amāra. Vol. 2. Beirut: Al-Mu'assasa al-'Arabiyya lid-Darāsa wa-an-Nashr.

———. 1968. *An Islamic Response to Imperialism*. Trans. Nikki R. Keddie. Berkeley: University of California Press.

Alfarabi, Abu Nasr. 2001. *Alfarabi: The Political Writings*. Trans. Charles Butterworth. Ithaca, N.Y.: Cornell University Press. [Contains the *Book of Religion*, the *Selected Aphorisms*, chapter 5 of the *Enumeration of the Sciences*, and the *Harmonization of the Two Opinions of the Divine Sages*; cited as BR, SA, ES, HS.]

In Arabic:

a) *Kitāb al-Milla wa Nuṣūṣ Ukhra*. 1968. Ed. Muhsin Mahdi. Beirut: Dār al-Mashriq.

b) *Fusūl al-Muntaza'a*. 1986. Ed. Fawzi M. Najjar. Beirut: Dār al-Mashriq.

c) *Kitāb al-Jam' bayn Rāyy al-Ḥakīmayn*. 2001. Beirut: Dār al-Mashriq.

The *Book of Religion* has also been translated into French: see *al-Milla = a religion*, trans. Amor Cherni. Beyrouth: al-Bouraq 2012.

———. *Alfarabi: The Political Writings*: Vol. II. 2015. Trans. Charles Butterworth. [Contains the *Political Regime* and the *Summary of Plato's "Laws"*; cited as PR and SL.]

In Arabic:

Kitāb as-Siyāsa al-Madaniyya. 1993. Beirut: Dār Al-Mashriq.

"Sommaire du livre des 'Lois' de Platon." 1998. Ed. T.-A. Druart. *Bulletin d'Études Orientales* 50: 110–55.

The *Political Regime* has also been translated in a dual Arabic-French edition, with notes:

———. *La politique civile ou les principes des existants*. 2011a. Trans. Amor Cherni. Paris: Dar al-Bouraq.

———. *Alfarabi on Logic (al-Mantiq 'inda al-Fārābi)*. 1985. Vol. 1. Ed. Rafīq al-'Ajam. Beirut: Dār al-Mashriq. [In Arabic only. Contains several short works, of which only *Alfarabi on Logic*, the first, is cited as FL.]

———. *Alfarabi on Logic*. 1986. Vol. 2. Ed. Rafīq al-'Ajam. Beirut: Dār al-Mashriq. [Contains, among other works, *Short Book on the Syllogism*, cited as SS.]

———. *Alfarabi on Logic*. 1986. Vol. 3. Ed. Rafīq al-'Ajam. Beirut: Dār al-Mashriq. [Contains *Kitāb al-Jadal*, or *Book of Dialectic*, cited as BDi.]

———. *Alfarabi on Logic*. 1987. Vol. 4. Ed. Mājid Fakhry. Beirut: Dār al-Mashriq. [In Arabic only; contains *Kitāb al-Burhān*, or *Book of Demonstration*, cited as BD.]

———. *Alfarabi on the Perfect State (Kitāb Mabādi' Arā' Ahl al-Madīna al-Fāḍila)*. 1985. Trans. Richard Walzer. Oxford: Oxford University Press. [English and Arabic; cited as VC for the text of Alfarabi, and as VC, trans. Walzer, for Walzer's commentary.]The *Virtuous City* has also been translated in a dual Arabic-French edition, with notes: *Opinions des habitants de la cité vertueuse*. 2011. Trans. Amor Cherni. Paris: Dar Albouraq.

———. *Alfarabi's Commentary and Short Treatise on Aristotle's "De interpretatione."* 1981. Trans. F. W. Zimmerman. London: Oxford University Press. [Cited as CA.]

In Arabic:

Alfarabi's Commentary on Aristotle's "Peri hermeneias" (Sharḥ al-Fārābī li-kitāb Āristūtālis fi al-'Ibāra). 1960. Ed. Wilhelm Kutsch and Stanley Morrow. Beirut: Imprimerie Catholique.

———. *Book of Letters (Kitāb al-Ḥurūf)*. 2004. Ed. Muhsin Mahdi. Beirut: Dār Al-Mashriq. [In Arabic only, cited as BL. An incomplete English translation is available in *Medieval Islamic Philosophical Writings*, ed. Muhammad Ali Khalidi, 1–26. Cambridge: Cambridge University Press, 2005. Both editions are cited where possible.]

———. *Book of Rhetoric (Kitāb al-Khitāba)*. 1971. In *Deux ouvrages inédits sur la réthorique*, ed. J. Langhade and M. Grignaschi, 31–121. Beirut: Dār al-Mashriq. [Dual French-Arabic editions, cited as BRh.]

———. *Didascalia in Rethoricam Aristotelis ex glosa Alpharabi*. 1971. In *Deux ouvrages inédits sur la réthorique*, ed. J. Langhade and M. Grignaschi, 149–252. Beirut: Dār al-Mashriq. [In Latin only. The original Arabic does not survive, and the medieval Latin translation has never been rendered into any modern tongue. Cited as DA.]

———. *Enumeration of the Sciences (Iḥṣā' al-'Ulūm)*. 1968. Ed. 'Uthmān Amīn. Cairo: Maktabat al-Anjlu al-Misriyya. [Cited as ES.The whole of the *Enumeration of the Sciences* is not available in English, but it has been translated in a dual Arabic-French edition, with notes. I cite this edition so that readers who know French but not Arabic can check my references: al-Fārābī, *Le recensement des sciences*, trans. Amor Cherni. Paris: Dar al-Bouraq, 2012.]

———. *Epistle Indicating the Way to Happiness (Risālat al-Tanbīh 'ala Sabīl as-Sa'āda)*. 1987. 'Ammān: al-Jāmi'a al-Urduniyya. [In Arabic only, cited as EH.]

———. *Epistle on the Canons of Poetry (Risāla fī Qawānīn Ṣinā'at al-Shi'r)*. 1938. Trans. A. J. Arberry. *Rivista degli Studi Orientali* 17: 267–78. [In English and Arabic, cited as EP.]

———. *Epistle on the Intellect*. 2007. In *Classical Arabic Philosophy: An Anthology of Sources*, trans. Jon McGinnis and David C. Reisman, 68–78. Indianapolis: Hackett. [Cited as EI.]

In Arabic:

———. *Risāla f'il-'Aql*. 1983. Ed. Maurice Bouyges. Beirut: Dār al-Mashriq.

———. *The Great Book of Music (Kitāb al-Mūsīqa al-Kabīr)*. 1967. Cairo: Dār al-Kātib al-'Arabi lil-Ṭabā'a wa-al-Nashr. [In Arabic only, cited as BM.]

———. *On One and Unity (Kitāb al-Wāḥid wa-al-Wiḥda)*. 1989. Ed. Muhsin Mahdi. Casablanca: Editions Toubkal. [In Arabic only, cited as BO.]

———. *Philosophy of Plato and Aristotle*. 1962. Trans. Muhsin Mahdi. Ithaca, N.Y.: Cornell University Press. [Three parts. The first is cited as AH, the second as PP, the third as PA.]

In Arabic each of the three parts is available separately:

a) *Taḥṣīl as-Sa'āda*. 1981. Ed. Ja'afir al-Yāsīn. Beirut: Dār al-Andalūs.

b) *Philosophy of Plato (Falsafat Aflāṭūn)*. 1943. Ed. F. Rosenthal and R. Walzer. London: Warburg Institute.

c) *Philosophy of Aristotle (Falsafat Āristūtālīs)*. 1961. Beirut: Dār Majallat ash-Shi'r.

———. *Short Commentary on the "Poetics."* 1971. In *Averroes, Talkhīṣ Kitāb Ārisṭūtālīs f'ish-Shi'r*, ed. Muhammad Sālim Salīm, 171–75. Cairo: Lajnat Aḥyā' al-Turāth al-Islāmī. [In Arabic only, cited as SP.]

Aquinas, Thomas. 2002. *On Law, Morality, and Politics.* Trans. Richard Regan. Indianapolis: Hackett.

Arabian Nights II. 1998. Trans. Husain Haddawy. New York: Knopf.

Aristotle. 2003. *Metaphysics.* Loeb Classical Library 17–18. Cambridge, Mass.: Harvard University Press, 2003.

———. 1998. *Politics.* Loeb Classical Library 22. Cambridge, Mass.: Harvard University Press.

Averroes. 2008. *Decisive Treatise and Epistle Dedicatory.* Trans. Charles E. Butterworth. Provo, Utah: Brigham Young University Press. [Arabic and English]

———. 1974. *Averroes on Plato's "Republic."* Trans. Ralph Lerner. Ithaca, N.Y.: Cornell University Press. Bin Laden, Osama. *Messages to the World: The Statements of Osama bin Laden.* Trans. James Howarth, ed. Bruce Lawrence. New York: Verso, 2005.

Constant, Benjamin. 1980. *De la liberté chez les modernes: Écrits politiques.* Ed. Marcel Gauchet. Paris: Hachette.

Hobbes, Thomas. 1994. *Leviathan.* Ed. Edwin Curley. Indianapolis: Hackett.

Homer. 1996. *The Odyssey.* Trans. Robert Fagles. New York: Penguin Putnam.

Hume, David. 1985. "Of National Characters." In *Essays, Moral, Political, and Literary*, 197–216. Indianapolis: Liberty Classics.

Ibn Khaldūn. 1958. *The Muqaddimah.* Trans. Franz Rosenthal. Princeton, N.J.: Princeton University Press. [In Arabic: *al-Muqaddima.* 2005. Al-Dār al-Bayḍā': Khizānat Ibn Khaldūn, Bayt al-Funūn wa-al'Ulūm wa-al-Ādāb.]

Ikhwān al-Safā'. 1928. *Rasā'il Ikhwān al-Safā'.* Vol. 2. Cairo: Al-Ṭaba'a al-Arabiyya.

Iqbal, Muhammad. 2015. *Speeches, Writings, and Statements of Iqbal.* Ed. Latif Ahmed Sherwani. New Delhi: Adam Publishers & Distributors.

———. 2012. *The Reconstruction of Religious Thought in Islam.* Stanford, Calif.: Stanford University Press.

al-Jāḥiz, 'Amr Ibn Baḥr. 1988. *Nine Essays of al-Jahiz.* Trans. William M. Hutchins. New York: Peter Lang.

———. 1947. *Al-Bayān wa'al-Tabyīn.* Vols. 1–3. Cairo: Maṭba'at al-Istiqāma. [In Arabic only.]

———. 1903. *Tria opuscula.* Leiden: E.J. Brill. [In Arabic only.]

ISIS. "The umma is the Promise of Allah." https://ia902505.us.archive.org/28/items/poa_25984/EN.pdf. In Arabic: https://thabat111.wordpress.com/2014/06/29 /ال‐قيام‐إعلان‐الله‐وعد‐هذا‐وتفريغ‐كلمة/

Lincoln, Abraham. 1946. *Abraham Lincoln: His Speeches and Writings.* Ed. Roy P. Basler. New York: Da Capo Press.

Machiavelli, Niccolo. 1998. *The Prince.* Trans. Harvey Mansfield. Chicago: University of Chicago Press.

Maimonides. 1987. *'Igrot ha-Rambam.* Ed. Yitzhaq Shailat. Jerusalem: Ma'aliyot. [In Hebrew only.]

———. 1996. *Traité de logique.* Trans. Rémi Brague. Paris: Desclée de Brouwer. [Judeo-Arabic text with French translation; I cite the original as well as the translation.]

al-Māwardī, 'Alī Ibn Muḥammad. 1983. *Al-Aḥkām as-Sulṭāniyya wa-al-Wilāyāt ad-Dīniyya.* Cairo: Dār al-Fikr. [In Arabic only.]

Nietzsche, Friedrich. 1988. *Jenseits von Gut und Böse: Zur Genealogie der Moral*. Berlin: Deutscher Taschenbuch Verlag.

Parens, Joshua, and Joseph C. Macfarland, eds. 2012. *Medieval Political Philosophy: A Sourcebook*. Ithaca, N.Y.: Cornell University Press.

Plato. *Menexenus*. 1999. Loeb Classical Library 9: 332–81. Cambridge, Mass.: Harvard University Press.

———. *Republic*. 1991. Trans. Allan Bloom. New York: Basic Books. [Cited as *Republic*, trans. Bloom for Bloom's interpretive essay.]

In Greek:

Platonis Rempublicam. 2003. Ed. S. R. Slings. Oxford: Oxford University Press.

———. 1980. *The Laws of Plato*. Trans. Thomas L. Pangle. Chicago: University of Chicago Press.

———. 1950. *Platonis Opera*. Ed. John Burnet. Oxford: Oxford University Press.

The Qur'ān. 1998. Trans. Yusuf Ali. Kansas City: Manat International. [English and Arabic; the translation is quite serviceable, but I prefer to use my own translations.]

al-Rāzī, Abu Ḥātim Aḥmad ibn Ḥamdān. 1957. *Book of the Embellishment of Arabic and Islamic Words (Kitāb az-Zīna fī al-Kalimāt al-Islāmiyya al-'Arabiyya)*. Vol. 1. Cairo: Dār al-Kātib al-'Arabī. [In Arabic only.]

Renan, Ernest. *Qu'est ce qu'une nation, et autres écrits politiques*. Ed. Raoul Girardet. Paris: Imprimerie Nationale, 1996.

Rousseau, Jean-Jacques. 1993. *Essai sur l'origine des langues*. Paris: Flammarion.

———. 1990. *Sur l'économie politique: Considérations sur le gouvernment de Pologne; Projet pour la Corse*. 1990. Paris: Flammarion.

Al-Ṭabarī, Abu Ja'far Muḥammad ibn Jarīr. 1955. *Tafsīr al-Ṭabarī*. Cairo: Dār al-Ma'ārif.

Al-Tawḥīdī, Ābi Hayyan. 2004. *Kitāb al-Imta' wa al-Mu'ānasa*. Vols. 1–3. Beirut: Dār al-Maktaba bi-al-Hayyāh. [In Arabic only. However, Muhsin Mahdi provides an excellent English interpretation and summary of the debate between Sīrāfī and Mattā in his article "Language and Logic in Classical Islam," in *Logic in Classical Islamic Culture*, ed. G. E. von Grunebaum, 51–83. Wiesbaden: O. Harrassowitz, 1970.]

Zamakhsharī, Maḥmūd ibn 'Umar. 1947. *Al-Kashshāf 'an Ḥaqā'iq Ghawāmiḍ at-Tanzīl wa-'Uyūn al-Aqāwīl fī Wujūh at-Ta'wīl/wa-huwa Tafsīr al-Qur'ān al-Karīm*. Beirut: Dār al-Kitāb al-Arabī.

SECONDARY SOURCES

'Abbās, Iḥsān. 1977. *Malāmiḥ Yūnāniyya f'il Ādāb al-'Arabī*. Beirut: Al-Mu'assasa al-'Arabiyya lid-Darāsāt wa-al-Nashr.

Abed, Shukri B. 1991. *Aristotelian Logic and the Arabic Language in Alfārābī*. Albany: State University of New York Press.

Agha, Saleh Said. 2009. "Language as a Component of Arab Identity in al-Jāḥiẓ: The Case of Ismā'īl's Conversion to Arabhood." In *Al-Jāḥiẓ: A Muslim Humanist for Our Time*, ed. Arnim Heinemann, John L. Meloy, Tarif Khalidi, and Manfred Kropp, 67–89. Beirut: Ergon Verlag Würzburg.

Ahmed, Manzooruddin. 1975. "Umma: The Idea of a Universal Community." *Islamic Studies* 14, no. 1: 27–54.

Akram, Ejaz. 2007. "Muslim Umma and Its Link with Translational Muslim Politics." *Islamic Studies* 46, no. 3: 381–415.

Alon, Ilai. 2002. *Al-Fārābī's Philosophical Lexicon*. Wiltshire: Aris & Phillips.

Anderson, Benedict. 2006. *Imagined Communities: Reflections on the Origin and Spread of Nationalism*. New York: Verso.

Benardete, Seth. 1989. *Socrates' Second Sailing: On Plato's "Republic."* Chicago: University of Chicago Press.

Berlekamp, Persis. 2012. *Wonder, Image, and Cosmos in Medieval Islam*. New Haven, Conn.: Yale University Press.

Black, Deborah. 1990. *Logic and Aristotle's "Rhetoric" and "Poetics" in Medieval Arabic Philosophy*. Leiden: E.J. Brill.

Bobzin, Hartmut. 2006. "Translations of the Qur'ān." In *Encyclopaedia of the Qur'ān*, 5: 340–58. Leiden: E.J. Brill.

Brague, Rémi. 1996. "Eorum Praeclara Ingenia: Conscience de la nouveauté et pretention à la continuité chez Fārābī et Maimonide." *Bulletin d'Études Orientales* 48: 87–102.

———. 1993. "Note sur la traduction arabe de la 'Politique,' derechef, qu'elle n'existe pas." In *Aristote politique*, ed. Pierre Aubenque, 423–33. Paris: Presses Universitaires de France.

Butterworth, Charles. 2008. "What Might We Learn from al-Fārābī About Plato and Aristotle with Respect to Lawgiving?" *Mélanges de l'Université Saint-Joseph* 61: 471–91.

———. 2007. "Alfarabi's Plato: A Tale of Two Cities." In *The Political Identity of the West: Platonism in the Dialogue of Cultures*, ed. Marcel van Ackeren and Orrin Finn Summerell, 55–76. Berlin: Peter Lang.

———. 1990. "Al-Fārābī's Statecraft: War and the Well-Ordered Regime." In *Cross, Crescent, and Sword: The Justification and Limitation of War in Western and Islamic Tradition*, ed. James Turner Johnson and John Kelsay, 79–100. New York: Greenwood.

Calvert, Brian. 1987. "Slavery in Plato's *Republic*." *Classical Quarterly* 37, no. 2: 367–72.

Campagna, Norbert. 2010. *Alfarabi, Denker zwischen Orient und Okzident: Eine Einführung in seine politische Philosophie*. Berlin: Parodos.

Cherni, Amor. See Alfarabi, many of whose works Cherni has edited and translated into French.

Cohler, Anne M. 1970. *Rousseau and Nationalism*. New York: Basic.

Colmo, Christopher. 2005. *Breaking with Athens: Alfarabi as Founder*. Lanham, Md.: Lexington Books.

Craig, Leon. 1994. *The War Lover: A Study of Plato's "Republic."* Toronto: University of Toronto Press.

Crone, Patricia. 2004a. "Alfarabi's Imperfect Constitutions." *Mélanges de l'Université Saint-Joseph* 57: 191–228.

———. 2004b. *Meccan Trade and the Rise of Islam*. Piscataway, N.J.: Gorgias Press.

Crone, Patricia, and Michael Cook. 1977. *Hagarism: The Making of the Islamic World*. Cambridge: Cambridge University Press.

Dabashi, Hamid. 1995. "Persian Literature." In *The Oxford Encyclopedia of the Modern Islamic World*, 3: 312–24. Oxford: Oxford University Press.

Dallal, Ahmad S. 1995. "Ummah." In *The Oxford Encyclopedia of the Modern Islamic World*, 4: 267–70. Oxford: Oxford University Press.

Denny, Frederick Mathewson. 1977. "Umma in the Constitution of Medina." *Journal of Near Eastern Studies* 36, no. 1: 39–47.

————. 1975. "The Meaning of 'Umma' in the Qur'ān." *History of Religions* 15, no. 1: 34–70.

Donner, Fred M. 1998. *Narratives of Islamic Origins.* Princeton, N.J.: Darwin Press.

Druart, Thérèse-Anne. 2012. "Islam and Christianity: One Divine and Human Language or Many Human Languages." In *The Judeo-Christian-Islamic Heritage: Philosophical and Theological Perspectives,* ed. Richard C. Taylor and Irfan A. Omar, 39–57. Milwaukee: Marquette University Press.

————. 1998–2011. "Brief Bibliographical Guides in Medieval Islamic Philosophy and Theology." http://philosophy.cua.edu/faculty/druart/bibliographical-guide.cfm.

Druart is also the editor of the most recent edition of the *Summary of Plato's "Laws",* listed among Alfarabi's works above.

Duggan, T. M. P. 2009. "Diplomatic Shock and Awe: Moving, Sometimes Speaking, Islamic Sculptures." In *Al-Masāq: Islam and the Medieval Mediterranean,* 229–67. London: Routledge.

Duri, A. A. 1960. "Baghdad." in *Encyclopaedia of Islam,* 1: 898–99. Leiden: E.J. Brill.

Elias, Jamal J. 2012. *Aisha's Cushion: Religious Art, Perception, and Practice in Islam.* Cambridge, Mass.: Harvard University Press.

Enderwitz, Susan. 1996. "al-Shuʿūbiyya." In *Encyclopaedia of Islam,* 9: 513–16. New ed. Leiden: E.J. Brill.

Fakhry, Majid. 2002. *Al-Farābi, Founder of Islamic Neoplatonism: His Life, Works, and Influence.* Oxford: Oneworld.

Ferrari, G. R. F. 2007. "The Three-Part Soul." In *The Cambridge Companion to Plato's "Republic",* 165–201. Cambridge: Cambridge University Press.

————. 2005. *City and Soul in Plato's "Republic."* Chicago: University of Chicago Press.

Fraenkel, Carlos. 2012. *Philosophical Religions from Plato to Spinoza: Reason, Religion, and Autonomy.* Cambridge: Cambridge University Press.

Freudenthal, Gad. 2004. "La détermination partielle, biologique et climatologique, de la félicité humaine: Maimonide versus Al-Fārābī à propos des influences célestes." In *Maimonide: Philosophe et savant,* ed. Tony Levy and Roshdi Rashed, 79–129. Leuven: Peeters.

Galston, Miriam. 2015. "The Puzzle of Alfarabi's Parallel Works." *Review of Politics* 77: 519–43.

————. 1990. *Politics and Excellence: The Political Philosophy of Alfarabi.* Princeton, N.J.: Princeton University Press.

Gannagé, Emma. 2004. "Y-a-t-il une pensée politique dans le Kitāb al-Ḥurūf d'al-Fārābī?" *Mélanges d'Université Saint-Joseph* 57: 229–57.

Gellner, Ernest. 2006. *Nations and Nationalism.* Oxford: Blackwell.

————. 1997. *Nationalism.* New York: New York University Press.

————. 1994. *Encounters with Nationalism.* Oxford: Blackwell.

Giannakis, Elias. 1983. "The Concept of Umma." *Graeco-Arabia* 2: 99–111.

Gibb, H. A. R. 1962. *Studies on the Civilization of Islam.* Princeton, N.J.: Princeton University Press.

Goldziher, Ignaz. 1981. *Introduction to Islamic Theology and Law.* Trans. Andras Hamori and Ruth Hamori. Princeton, N.J.: Princeton University Press.

————. 1967. *Muslim Studies.* Trans. C. R. Barber and S. M. Stern. 2 vols. London: Allen and Unwin.

Grabar, Oleg. 1991. "Masdjid." In *Encyclopaedia of Islam,* 6: 644–708. Leiden: E.J. Brill.

Gutas, Dimitri. 2012. "Fārābī." In *Encyclopaedia Iranica,* http://www.iranicaonline.org/articles /farabi-i.

———. 2004. "The Meaning of Madanī in al-Fārābī's 'Political' Philosophy." *Mélanges de l'Université Saint-Joseph* 57: 259–82.

———. 1998a. "Fārābī's Knowledge of Plato's *Laws*." *Journal of the Classical Tradition* 4, no. 3: 405–11.

———. 1998b. *Greek Thought, Arabic Culture*. New York: Routledge.

———. 1997. "Galen's Synopsis of Plato's *Laws* and Fārābī's Talkhīṣ." In *The Ancient Tradition in Christian and Islamic Hellenism*, ed. Gerhard Endress and Remke Kruk, 101–19. Leiden: Research School CNWS.

———. 1988. *Avicenna and the Aristotelian Tradition*. Leiden: E.J. Brill.

Hall, Jonathan M. 2002. *Hellenicity: Between Ethnicity and Culture*. Chicago: University of Chicago Press.

———. 1997. *Ethnic Identity in Greek Antiquity*. Cambridge: Cambridge University Press.

Harvey, Steven. 2003a. "Can a Tenth-Century Aristotelian Help Us Understand Plato's *Laws*?" In *Plato's "Laws": From Theory to Practice*, ed. Samuel Scolnicov and Luc Brisson, 320–30. Sankt Augustin: Akademia Verlag.

———. 2003b. "Did Alfarabi Read Plato's *Laws*?" *Medioevo Rivista di Storia della Filosofia Medievale* 28: 51–68.

Hassner, Pierre. 1997. "Rousseau and Theory and Practice of International Relations." In *The Legacy of Rousseau*, ed. Clifford Orwin and Nathan Tarcov, 200–219. Chicago: University of Chicago Press.

Heck, Paul L. 2008. "Milla in al-Fārābī and the Brethren of Purity." In *The Age of al-Fārābī: Arabic Philosophy in the Fourth-Tenth Century*, ed. Peter Adamson., 195–213. London: Warburg Institute.

Hourani, Albert. 2007. *Arabic Thought in the Liberal Age: 1798–1939*. Cambridge: Cambridge University Press.

Isaac, Benjamin. 2004. *The Invention of Racism in Classical Antiquity*. Princeton, N.J.: Princeton University Press.

Kamtekar, Rachana. 2002. "Distinction Without a Difference: Plato on 'Genos' vs. 'Race.'" In *Philosophers on Race*, ed. Julie K. Ward and Tommy Lott, 1–13. Oxford: Blackwell.

Kedourie, Elie. 1961. *Nationalism*. London: Hutchinson.

Kochin, Michael S. 2002. *Gender and Rhetoric in Plato's Political Thought*. Cambridge: Cambridge University Press.

Kraemer, Joel. 1992. *Humanism in the Renaissance of Islam: The Cultural Revival During the Buyid Age*. Leiden: E.J. Brill.

———. 1987. "The Jihād of the Falāsifa." In *Jerusalem Studies in Arabic and Islam* 10: 288–325.

———. 1986. *Philosophy in the Renaissance of Islam*. Leiden: E.J. Brill.

Langhade, Jacques. 1994. *Du Coran à la philosophie*. Damascus: Institut Français de Damas.

Lecomte, Gérard. 1965. *Ibn Qutayba: L'homme, son oeuvre, ses idées*. Damascus: Institut Français de Damas.

Lichtenstadter, Ilse. 1949. "From Particularism to Unity: Race, Nationality, and Minorities in Early Islamic Empire." *Islamic Culture* 23, no. 3: 251–80.

López-Farjeat, Luis Xavier. 2012. "Faith, Reason and Religious Diversity in al-Farabi's Book of Letters." In *The Judeo-Christian-Islamic Heritage: Philosophical and Theological Perspectives*, ed. Richard C. Taylor and Irfan A. Omar, 193–215. Milwaukee: Marquette University Press.

Ludwig, Paul. 2007. "Eros in the *Republic*." In *The Cambridge Companion to Plato's "Republic"*, 202–31. Cambridge: Cambridge University Press.

Madelung, W. 1995. "Shīʿa." In *Encyclopaedia of Islam*, 10: 420–24. Leiden: E.J. Brill.

Mahdi, Muhsin. 2001. *Alfarabi and the Foundation of Islamic Political Philosophy.* Chicago: University of Chicago Press.

———. 1990. "Al-Fārābī's Imperfect State." Review of Richard Walzer. *Journal of the American Oriental Society* 100, no. 4: 691–726.

———. 1971. "Al-Fārābī." In *Dictionary of Scientific Biography*, ed. Charles Coulston Gillispie, 4: 523–26. New York: Scribner's.

———. 1970. "Language and Logic in Classical Islam." In *Logic in Classical Islamic Culture*, ed. G. E. von Grunebaum, 51–83. Wiesbaden: O. Harrassowitz.

———. 1961. "The Editio Princeps of Fārābī's Compendium Legum Platonis." *Journal of Near Eastern Studies* 20, no. 1: 1–24.

Menn, Stephen. 2008. "Al-Fārābī's Kitāb al-Ḥurūf and His Analysis of the Senses of Being." *Arabic Sciences and Philosophy* 18: 59–97.

Mottahedeh, Roy P. 1976. "The Shuʿūbiyya Controversy and the Social History of Early Islamic Iran." *International Journal of Middle East Studies* 7, no. 2: 161–82.

Muṣbāḥ, Ṣāliḥ. 1995. "Masālat al-Milla ʿind al-Fārābī." In *Autour de Fārābī*, 185–203. Sfax, Tunisia: Faculté des Lettres et Sciences Humaines, Université de Sfax.

Najjar, Fauzi M. 1980. "Democracy in Islamic Political Philosophy." *Studia Islamica* 51: 107–22.

———. 1954. "The Political Philosophy of Al-Fārābī as a Rationalistic Interpretation of Islam." Dissertation, University of Chicago.

Naṣṣār, Nāṣif. 1986. *Taṣawwurāt al-Umma al-Muʿāṣira: Dirāsa Taḥlīliyya li-Mafāhīm al-Umma fī al-Fikr al-ʿArabī al-Ḥadīth wa-al-Muʿāṣir.* Kuwait City: Muʾassasat al-Kuwayt lil-Taqaddum al-ʿIlmī.

———. 1978. *Mafhūm al-Umma: Baynu ad-Dīn wa-at-Tārīkh.* Beirut: Dār at-Ṭalīʿa.

Norbert, Campagna. 2010. *Alfarabi, Denker zwischen Orient und Okzident: eine Einführung in seine politische Philosophie.* Berlin: Parodos.

Norris, H. T. 1990. "Shuʿūbiyyah in Arabic Literature." In *The Cambridge History of Arabic Literature*, 2: 31–47. Cambridge: Cambridge University Press.

Orwin, Alexander. 2016. In Search of the Vanished Caliphate: From Ibn Khaldūn to Hizb al-Tahrir." *Current Trends in Islamist Ideology.* Washington, D.C.: Hudson Institute.

———. 2015. "Democracy Under the Caliphs: Alfarabi's Unusual Understanding of Popular Rule." *Review of Politics* 77, no. 2: 171–90.

———. 2014. "Can Humankind Deliberate on a Global Scale? Alfarabi and the Politics of the Inhabited World." *American Political Science Review* 108, no. 4: 830–39.

Parens, Joshua. 2006a. *An Islamic Philosophy of Virtuous Religions: Introducing Alfarabi.* Albany: State University of New York Press.

———. 2006b. "Prudence, Imagination, and Determination of Law in Alfarabi and Maimonides." In *Enlightening Revolutions: Essays in Honor of Ralph Lerner*, ed. Svetozar Minkov, 31–55. New York: Lexington.

———. 1995. *Metaphysics as Rhetoric: Alfarabi's Summary of Plato's "Laws."* Albany: State University of New York Press.

Paret, Rudi. 1934. "Umma." In *Encyclopaedia of Islam*, 4: 1015–16. Leiden: E.J. Brill.

Pedersen, J. 1960. "Adam." In *Encyclopaedia of Islam*, 1: 176–78. Leiden: E.J. Brill.

Pellat, Charles. 1976. *Études sur l'histoire socio-culturelle de l'Islam (VIIe–XVe s.).* London: Variorum Reprints.

Pines, Shlomo. 1975. "Aristotle's *Politics* in Arabic Philosophy." *Israel Oriental Studies* 5: 150–60.

Plattner, Marc F. 1997. "Rousseau and the Origins of Nationalism." In *The Legacy of Rousseau*, ed. Clifford Orwin and Nathan Tarcov, 183–99. Chicago: University of Chicago Press.

Reisman, David C. 2004. "Plato's *Republic* in Arabic: A Newly Discovered Passage." *Arabic Sciences and Philosophy* 14: 263–300.

Reynolds, Gabriel Said, ed. 2011. *New Perspectives on the Qur'ān: The Qur'ān in Its Historical Context 2*. New York: Routledge.

———, ed. 2008. *The Qur'ān in Its Historical Context*. New York: Routledge.

Roman, André. 2001. "Aperçus sur la naissance de la langue à partir du 'Kitāb Al-Ḥurūf' d'al-Fārābī." *Studia Islamica* 92: 127–54.

Rosen, Stanley. 2005. *Plato's Republic*. New Haven, Conn.: Yale University Press.

Rosenthal, E. I. J. 1955. "The Place of Politics in the Philosophy of Al-Farabi." *Islamic Culture* 19, no. 3: 157–78.

Rosenthal, Franz. 1992. "Nasab." In *Encyclopaedia of Islam*, 7: 967–68. Leiden: E.J. Brill.

———. 1940. "On the Knowledge of Plato's Philosophy in the Islamic World." *Islamic Culture* 14, no. 4: 387–422.

Rosenthal, Franz, and Richard Walzer. For their edition of *The Philosophy of Plato*, see Alfarabi above.

Rudolph, Ulrich. 2012. "Abū Naṣr al-Fārābī." In *Philosophie in der Islamischen Welt*, vol. 1, *8.–10. Jahrhundert*, ed. Ulrich Rudolph and Renate Würsch, 363–57. Basel: Schwabe Verlag.

Salmon, D. 1939. "The Medieval Latin Translations of Alfarabi's Works." *New Scholasticism* 13: 245–61.

Sassi, Maria Michela. 2001. *The Science of Man in Ancient Greece*. Trans. Paul Tucker. Chicago: University of Chicago Press.

al-Sayyid, Ridwān. 1986. *Umma wa-al-Jamā'a w'al-Sulṭa*. Beirut: Dār Iqrā'.

Schmitt, Carl. 1996. *The Concept of the Political*. Trans. George Schwab. Chicago: University of Chicago Press.

Steinschneider, Moritz. 1960. *Die arabischen Übersetzungen aus dem Griechischen*. Graz: Akademische Druck-U. Verlagsanstalt.

Stern, Samuel Miklos. 1968. *Aristotle on the World-State*. Oxford: Cassirer.

Strauss, Leo. 1975. *The Argument and the Action of Plato's "Laws."* Chicago: University of Chicago Press.

———. 1959. *What Is Political Philosophy?* Chicago: University of Chicago Press.

———. 1945. "Farabi's Plato." In *Louis Ginzberg: Jubilee Volume*, 357–93. New York: American Academy for Jewish Research.

———. 1936. "Quelques remarques sur la science politique de Maimonide et de Fārābī." *Revue des Études Juives* 199–200: 1–37.

Strohmaier, G. 1980. "Homer in Bagdad." *Byzantinoslavica* 41: 196–200.

Sweeney, Michael. 2007. "Philosophy and 'Jihād': Al-Fārābī on Compulsion to Happiness." *Review of Metaphysics* 60, no. 3: 543–72.

Tyan, E. 1978. "'Iṣma." In *Encyclopaedia of Islam*, 4: 182–84. Leiden: E.J. Brill.

Vajda, Georges. 1970. "Langage, philosophie, politique, et religion d'après un traité récemment publié d'Abū Naṣr al-Fārābi." *Journal Asiatique* 268: 247–60.

Vallat, Philippe. 2004. *Farabi et l'école d'Alexandrie*. Paris: J. Vrin.

Vlastos, Gregory. 1968. "Does Slavery Exist in Plato's *Republic*." *Classical Philology* 63, no. 4: 291–95.

Walzer, Richard. 1965. "al-Fārābī." In *Encyclopaedia of Islam*, 2: 778–81. Leiden: E.J. Brill. For Walzer's commentary on the *Virtuous City*, cited as VC, trans. Walzer, see Alfarabi above.

Ward, Julie K. 2002. "Ethnos in the Politics: Aristotle on Race." In *Philosophers on Race: Critical Essays*, ed. Julie K. Ward and Tommy L. Lott, 14–37. Oxford: Blackwell.

Watt, W. Montgomery. 1956. *Muhammad at Medina*. Oxford: Clarendon.

Index of Proper Names

Abed, Shukri, 6, 81–82, 216nn12–13

Abbasid dynasty, 57–58, 61, 64, 79–80, 107, 183, 185, 194–95, 202, 213

'Abduh, Muhammad, 192–93

Abraham. *See* Ibrāhīm

Abu Bakr, 106

al-Afghānī, Jamāl al-Dīn, 5, 94, 114–15, 191–98

Alfarabi: *Alfarabi on Logic*, 67, 78; *Attainment of Happiness*, 68–69, 82, 95, 99, 101, 119–20, 123–24, 131, 136–44, 154, 158–61, 167–70, 202, 225nn3,10, 226nn18,20; *Book of Demonstration*, 82–85, 100, 225n4, 228n44; *Book of Dialectic*, 96, 139; *Book of Letters*, 5–6, 10, 45–55, 63, 66–85, 87, 97, 99–105, 108–12, 123, 132–34, 139–40, 142–43, 146, 155, 161–67, 169, 171, 178, 205, 212n3, 213n20, 219n28, 222n55, 225n13; *Book of One and Unity*, 118, 125; *Book of Religion*, 45, 87, 94–100, 103–22, 125, 131, 137, 144, 151–52, 154–56, 159–60, 169, 175–76, 190, 202, 220nn40,43, 222nn57,3, 229n52; *Book of Rhetoric*, 16, 76; *Commentary and Short Treatise on Aristotle's "De Interpretatione"*, 49, 216n13; *Didascalia in Rethoricam Aristotelis ex glosa Alfarabii*, 16, 139; *Epistle on the Canons of Poetry*, 56, 83–84, 128, 132–33, 205; *Enumeration of the Sciences*, 8–9, 77–78, 108–10, 137, 159, 171; *Epistle Indicating the Way to Happiness*, 78; *Epistle on the Intellect*, 220n42; *Great Book of Music*, 16–17, 63–64, 69, 126–28, 208n7, 212n4, 213n26; *Harmonization of the Two Opinions of the Divine Sages*, 5, 7; *Philosophy of Aristotle*, 10, 37, 71, 74–75, 109, 111, 128, 223n9; *Philosophy of Plato*, 8, 11, 15–17, 31–36, 50, 76, 175; *Political Regime*, 6, 10, 37, 39–40, 45–48, 50–51, 63, 104, 119, 123–30, 144–49, 159–63, 169–70, 175, 178–86, 212n13, 214n32, 220nn41,45, 222n3, 226n23, 229n4; *Selected Aphorisms*, 55, 95, 98, 121, 146–47, 150–51, 153–59, 163, 170, 211n41, 222n2, 230n5; *Short Commentary on the "Poetics"*, 128, 132; *Short Book of the Syllogism*, 82; Summary of Plato's "Laws," 7–9, 40, 95, 119, 150, 180, 208n1, 211n37, 216n16, 218n23, 219nn31,36, 221n47, 224n23, 229n52, 231n1; *Virtuous City*, 11–12, 39–42, 115, 123–25, 131, 133, 145–47, 149–55, 160, 163, 170, 176–84, 186, 201, 218n21, 220n45, 227n28, 229n50

'Alī, 106

Alon, Ilai, 6, 87

America, 190–91, 203–4

Anderson, Benedict, 2–3, 228n47

Aquinas, Thomas, 43

Arabic language, 50–51, 59, 62–63, 78–84, 92–93, 108, 114, 133, 141–43, 148, 164–65, 194–95, 199, 203, 207n4n7, 208nn3,4, 211n39, 214n35, 217n3, 221n49, 223n16, 225n13

Arabs, 3, 17, 50–51, 53, 57–64, 68–69, 84, 92–94, 96, 100, 102–3, 108, 114, 123, 125, 141–42, 165, 179–80, 183, 189, 194, 199, 208n7, 214nn32,35,38, 216n16, 225n13

Aristotle, 4, 7, 12, 15–16, 18, 36–44, 68–69, 74, 82–83, 85, 132, 143–44, 149, 152–55, 159

Athens, 25, 30, 35–36, 153, 209n11, 211n38

Averroes, 4–5, 16–18, 35–38, 40, 64, 125, 131, 208n7, 209n12, 221n46, 224n24, 230n10, 231n19

Avicenna, 4–5, 16, 224n26

Babylon, 42–43, 101

Baghdad, 4, 37, 68, 84, 119, 125, 127, 183–85, 208n3, 230n15, 231nn16, 17

Index of Subjects

Acknowledgments

This book has benefited from the comments of several experienced scholars, who made pitiless efforts to scour errors while remaining unfailingly supportive. Nathan Tarcov sniffed out unfounded philosophical assumptions; Ralph Lerner improved hasty arguments and removed infelicities of style; Jim Robinson fixed a large number of scholarly errors, sloppy transliterations, and ungrounded historical claims; Sari Nusseibeh helped me adjust my approach to the always sensitive subject of Islam. Over the years, Charles Butterworth, Joshua Parens, and Christopher Colmo have all offered helpful insights on Alfarabi. So has my wife Farida, whose acquaintance is owed almost entirely to Alfarabi. Damon Linker has been an exemplary editor, and the book has benefitted considerably from the work of two anonymous reviewers, who fixed many of the problems that remained.

I also wish to thank various people who have provided important intellectual inspiration over the years. These include Thomas Pangle in Toronto, my first and most memorable teacher in political philosophy, Irad Kimhi in Tel Aviv, who introduced me to a more purely philosophical approach to philosophy, and Pierre Manent in Paris, who serves as a constant reminder than scholarship must always be informed by serious reflections on the largest political and religious questions of the era.

Although places neither requite not require gratitude, I should add that the book could not have been written in anything resembling its present form without long visits to a number of cities. In Jerusalem, I encountered the difficulties posed by the contradictory claims of various Ummas, ethnic and religious: it is perhaps no accident that the plan to write a dissertation on this topic was first conceived in that city. In Istanbul, Cairo, and Delhi, I learned about the basic elements of Islamic art and civilization. These experiences provided me with ample material to think about when I returned to the United States, and are reflected in many places in the book.

Finally, I should thank my parents, Donna and Clifford, for contributing in various ways to my education, and daughter, Thanina, for doing much more than merely getting out of the way. She regrets that books by authors such as Plato and Alfarabi do not contain pictures, a defect that may be partially remedied by a lively description of their contents.